Outside MAGAZINE'S

Urban Adventure

New York City

Outside
MAGAZINE'S

Urban Adventure

New York City

David Howard

Outside BOOKS

W. W. Norton & Company New York London

WARNING: MANY OUTDOOR SPORTS CAN BE DANGEROUS AND CAN CAUSE SERIOUS INJURY OR EVEN DEATH

Safety is a vital concern in all the outdoor activities described in this book. Each activity carries a degree of risk, and only you can know your limitations. This book is intended to introduce you to a number of destinations where people pursue outdoor sports and is not a substitute for professional training or sound judgment. Your safety depends on your training and your commonsense judgment as you acquire skills. The author and publisher can take no responsibility for any loss, injury, or inconvenience sustained by any reader as a result of information or advice contained in the guide.

To the memory of my mom, the Rev. Carol C. Howard, to whom life was a joyous adventure

Printed in the United States of America
First Edition

For information about permission to reproduce selections from this book, write to Permissions, W. W. Norton & Company, Inc., 500 Fifth Avenue, New York, NY 10110

The text of this book is composed in Trump Mediaeval with the display set in MetaBlack
Composition by Carole Desnoes
Manufacturing by Haddon Craftsmen, Inc.
Book design by Chris Welch

Library of Congress Cataloging-in-Publication Data
Outside magazine's urban adventure, New York City / David Howard.—1st ed.
p. cm.
ISBN 0-393-32212-2 (pbk.)
1. Outdoor recreation—New York (State)—New York—Guidebooks. 2. New York (N.Y.)—Guidebooks. I. Outside (Chicago, Ill.) II. Title.
GV191. 42.N7 H69 2002
917.47'10444—dc21 2002006900

W. W. Norton & Company, Inc., 500 Fifth Avenue,
New York, N.Y. 10110
www.wwnorton.com

W. W. Norton & Company Ltd., Castle House,
75/76 Wells Street, London W1T 3QT

1 2 3 4 5 6 7 8 9 0

Contents

Acknowledgments

I RECEIVED COMMENTS, suggestions and encouragement from a wide range of people in compiling this book. For their sharing their wisdom, I'd like to thank Maxwell "Mickey" Cohen; John Bianchi and Kara Grobert of the National Audubon Society; Peter Wallace of the East River CREW; Nino DeSimone and Majora Carter of The Point; New York Aquarium curator Paul Sieswerda; Nancy Corona, a ranger at Gateway National Recreation Area; Sue Gilmore, natural resources management specialist at Gateway National Recreation Area; Don Riepe, chief of Resource Management at the Gateway National Recreation Area; Graeme Birchall of the Downtown Boathouse; Robert Sievens of Aquatia; Di Dieter of Atlantic Divers; Randall Henriksen of

the New York Kayak Company; Eric Stiller of the Manhattan Kayak Company; Kathleen Nutt, administrator of the Greenbelt Conservancy in Staten Island; Bob Roistacher of the New York City Community Sailing Association; Mike Davis of Floating the Apple; Dr. John Waldman of the Hudson River Foundation; Katy Weidel, landscape architect, and John Quinn, natural resources specialist, both of the Hackensack Meadowlands Development Commission; Ellen Macnow of the Planning Division of New York City Parks & Recreation; Glenn Hintze of the Manhattan Island Foundation; Bob Boyle; and David DeLucia from the Westchester County Department of Parks, Recreation and Conservation. Michael Frank, Jack Barrett, and Dan White read sections of the book and provided insightful advice.

David Lutz, executive director of the Neighborhood Open Space Coalition/Friends of Gateway, was a font of information as I prepared this book. I'm grateful for his unflagging helpfulness and encyclopedic knowledge of all things green in New York City.

Thanks to Barbara Feller-Roth for her concise editing and to my editor, John Barstow, for his guidance and steadfastness.

And finally, thanks to Ann Quigley, my fiancée, frontline editor, and companion on countless miles of New York–area explorations. Her support, encouragement, and accumulated lifetime of New York know-how were invaluable.

Introduction

PEOPLE COME TO New York for many different reasons: to chase dreams, to become famous or anonymous, to sample high culture, to make and spend fortunes. This book proposes an entirely new reason: to play.

To some, this will be a fairly new concept. People smiled coyly when I told them I was writing this book. They asked whether it would include descriptions of climbing skyscrapers, or chasing drug dealers, or fighting off muggers. Someone suggested competitive car stripping. But then, after the jokes stopped, they'd pause and ask more earnestly: What *is* a New York adventure? What *can* you do here?

The answer: almost anything you'd do at the

Jersey Shore, or in Montauk, or even in the Adirondacks. Paddle a sea kayak on swift water, climb rock faces, ride a horse, wrestle with a prize fish, spot a rare bird, surf a wave (after taking the subway to the beach). And more. In fact, the best answer to the question is this: You can do in New York City almost anything your imagination can conjure. Imagine Gotham as a giant playground. After all, long before NASDAQ and the Dow and Lady Liberty, New York City's sovereign elements were ocean, rivers, trees, and rock.

All a New York City adventure requires (besides reading this book, of course) is seeing the city in a new way, looking at the urban landscape with new eyes. Here's what I mean by that. About seven years ago, a friend and I decided to try paddling kayaks down the Naugatuck River in Waterbury, Connecticut, an old industrial city gone to seed. The Naugatuck was a long-polluted wasteland of a river. Occasionally one of the remaining factories mistakenly dumped something toxic, and fish turned up dead for a mile downstream. Nobody in Waterbury went near the river in those days, but we were curious about what was down there.

We found birds, beavers, fish. With much of the industry gone, the water was improving and the wildlife was returning. We even found rapids—churning, aggressive, fun rapids, especially after a hard rain. People seemed appalled. A cop once stopped as we loaded the boats on the car. "You were in there?" he said, his face twisted up. "You know that stuff is toxic? You're gonna be glowing later." We kept going back. It wasn't pristine, but in its way it was more of a wilderness experience than the scenic country rivers that drew hoards of boaters.

Wilderness can be found in unexpected places—and nowhere is that more true than in New York City. All it takes is noticing. What I liked best about researching this book was constantly encountering people who had already learned to see New York differently, to fit their adventure sport into this tangle of a city. I met a guy pedaling the Central Park loop road on a unicycle. Swimmers doing the crawl stroke around the island of Manhattan. Runners racing up the ultimate urban mountain, the Empire State Building. On the Bronx River, I watched a guy fish with a bunch of line wrapped around a Redi-Whip can; he twirled the baited hook on the end of eight to nine feet of line over his head like a lariat, and tossed it out into the water. A pair of urban explorers took me on a tour of their favorite defunct subway tunnel. Owen Foote took me paddling on the Gowanus Canal while most of the city fixated on how much it used to stink.

If Owen focused on the Gowanus's smelly, sordid history, he never would have thought of it as a fascinating canoe trip. But he saw what it could be. This way of thinking is contagious. It gets people thinking, *What if?* Open a climbing wall right on the sidewalk, up the street from Lincoln Center? Why not?

Eric Stiller of Manhattan Kayak Company dreams of engineering a whitewater kayaking hole in the Hudson River. A fishing group is restoring a native trout stream in Queens. Biking groups see 350 miles of greenway paths eventually encircling the city.

So, what are the limitations? New York *is* a far cry from the Adirondacks. In some ways adventures here are more challenging than in the rural wilds. For example, city officials are not enamored of the idea of using the rivers and harbor recreationally. An organization called Floating the Apple had to overcome repeated obstacles before securing river access for its rowing and sailing programs. Lacking a boathouse, members initially rolled their boats down to the Hudson from a space in midtown. People looked at them as though they were insane. The group persisted, and eventually won the use of a tiny cargo container on the river. The city still hasn't embraced recreational boating, but Floating the Apple grows by the sheer force of will. New Yorkers are famous for this sort of resourcefulness.

In many ways, New York City is now more amenable to adventure sports than ever before. Crime in Central Park is down 80 percent. Boathouses are popping up all over the waterfront. Sailing organizations have stripped away the sport's exclusivity and staked a claim to the harbor. Striped bass are thriving in the Hudson.

A final word: The destinations and activities listed in this book are not comprehensive. They represent our own "best of" list. Although some are obvious choices, other picks are totally subjective. Ultimately, they're designed to get you excited, get you thinking and seeing New York for the playground that it is.

Go forth, then, past the towers of glass and steel to the roiling waters of the harbor, to the beaches, the boulders, the parks. Go out into the city and play.

How to Use This Book

New Yorkers, being New Yorkers, don't need a whole lot of hand-holding. This book is designed simply to send you off in the right direction. Accordingly, you'll find that each chapter provides just enough practical information to get you where you'll need to go and what you'll encounter when you get there. Where applicable, there's also information on getting in touch with an outfitter.

All mileage is approximate—culled from maps, odometers, rangers, and others in the know—which means it should be close, if not always exact. Descriptions of routes are fairly brief and don't include every landmark and twist in the road. They should provide enough information to get you in and out. But it's important to keep in mind that New York City's recreational resources—especially its waterfront and greenways—are constantly evolving. New boathouses and bike paths are opening all the time.

Bring the recommended maps (or pick one up at the trailhead at many mountain biking, hiking, and cross-country skiing destinations). It always helps to also have sound judgment, extra water, and a sense of humor. Follow the suggestions, but by all means experiment with other routes as well. This is not meant to be a comprehensive tome. There simply isn't enough room to cover every trail or river in these pages. For more demanding, information-dense sports—climbing and fly-fishing come to mind, in places such as the Shawangunks and the Catskills—you'll likely want to pick up recommended guidebooks that offer specific, detailed information on routes, creeks, and the like.

Each chapter is divided into three sections: *City Limits, Short Hops,* and *Meccas. City Limits* refers to everything within New York's five boroughs. The other two headings are more subjective. In *Short Hops,* I strove to find the best stuff within one to two hours of midtown Manhattan, with a particular focus on destinations reachable by public transportation. As for *Meccas:* It's sort of a catchall term for the best stuff in the Northeast. These are, for the most part, well-known, established destinations worth the extra travel time.

You'll find a collection of information with each listing, though not all categories appear in every chapter. Here's a rundown of what they mean:

Location: Refers you to the borough, or to the location of the park, beach, or trail in question. For *Short Hops* and *Meccas,* I provide the approximate number of travel miles from midtown Manhattan.

Length: The distance of a trail, route, or network of trails.

Difficulty: Easy, moderate, or difficult. Highly subjective, I know. Keep that in mind. Further description of the entry should further illuminate, for example, whether *difficult* means thigh-burning, lung-scalding difficult or just sort of tough.

Technical difficulty: One to four helmets in Mountain Biking. One essentially means there are easy, flat trails or fire roads involved; four refers to highly technical trails in which the rider should know how to deal with steep ascents and lots of bone-rattling obstacles.

Terrain: This gives a sense of the conditions you'll encounter.

Outfitters/Rentals: Information on who to turn to for instruction or gear.

Heads up: The wild card. This refers to highlights, nearby food, license or permit requirements, or special hazards to be aware of, among other things.

Books and maps: What to consult, and where to find them, whether it's on-line or at the corresponding park or trailhead. The park contacts listed herein can offer other info on issues such as backcountry camping. And we list a few authoritative guides that will help you delve deeper into a particular sport.

Description: This is the meat of each entry. It's designed to give you a strong overall feel for what you're about to attempt.

Route: On-trail, on-road, or on-river directions.

Directions: How to get to the site, by subway, bus, train, or car, as appropriate. *Note:* Any road with a state abbreviation in front of it—as in NY 59—refers to a state road. CR, as in CR 525, refers to a county road. New Jersey also uses secondary roads, designated as SR.

As you go, consider combining information in different

chapters. Many hiking trails pass idyllic campsites. The trails listed in the Mountain Biking chapter may also work for cross-country skiing, and so on. Where it's really obvious, I offer cross-references. Otherwise, it's always worthwhile to look for ways to maximize your experience.

One further note: Many New Yorkers have dogs. In most sports discussed here—diving and sailing, for example—the pets will stay home. But for the few where their presence may be appropriate—hiking and cross-country skiing—the general rule of thumb in metropolitan New York is that dogs are welcome on leashes. Plan to bring a leash, and if you get there and find out dogs are free to run, all the better.

You, on the other hand, are always free to run. Get out there, have fun, and take care of each other.

Outside
MAGAZINE'S

Urban Adventure

Hiking

ADVENTURE IN ITS purest form involves nothing more than your own two feet. With a decent pair of walking shoes and an ample supply of food and water, it's amazing the ground you can cover—and how much you can learn if you keep your eyes, ears, and mind open along the way. A hike can be a ramble down Broadway through kaleidoscopic Times Square or a multiday scramble over scree in the rugged Hudson Highlands. In this chapter we cover both extremes, and a bunch of categories in between. Want an overnighter deep in the woods? A stroll on the beach? A high-speed ascent of the Empire State Building—minus the elevator? It's all here.

New York is, after all, a walking city—especially for those who hope to mine its secrets. Go to a bookstore and check out the number of New York City walk books. Look in *Time Out New York*'s listings for tours of Chinatown, the East Village, the waterfront—all interesting, but only small pieces of the vast mosaic. Despite the enthusiasm for two-legged touring, the city unfortunately continues to allow cars to be an overbearing presence, even in largely pedestrian areas such as Times Square, Columbus Circle, and Central Park. But it's generally safe to walk in the city, and the proliferation of new greenway paths in all five boroughs removes the danger of motorized traffic entirely.

Of course, living in the country's densest city doesn't mean you're confined to the jammed sidewalks. Everyone should escape now and then. Fortunately, there are numerous places nearby—the Appalachian Trail and the Delaware Water Gap among them—where you can step off a train or bus and be far from civilization after 30 minutes of walking.

In addition to the aforementioned necessities of comfortable shoes and sustenance, consider bringing along *The New York Walk Book* or *The New Jersey Walk Book*, remarkably thorough references published by the New York–New Jersey Trail Conference. They're as good as having a guide along for the walk.

City Limits

FORT TRYON, INWOOD HILL, AND RIVERDALE PARKS

Location: Manhattan and the Bronx
Length: About 3 miles

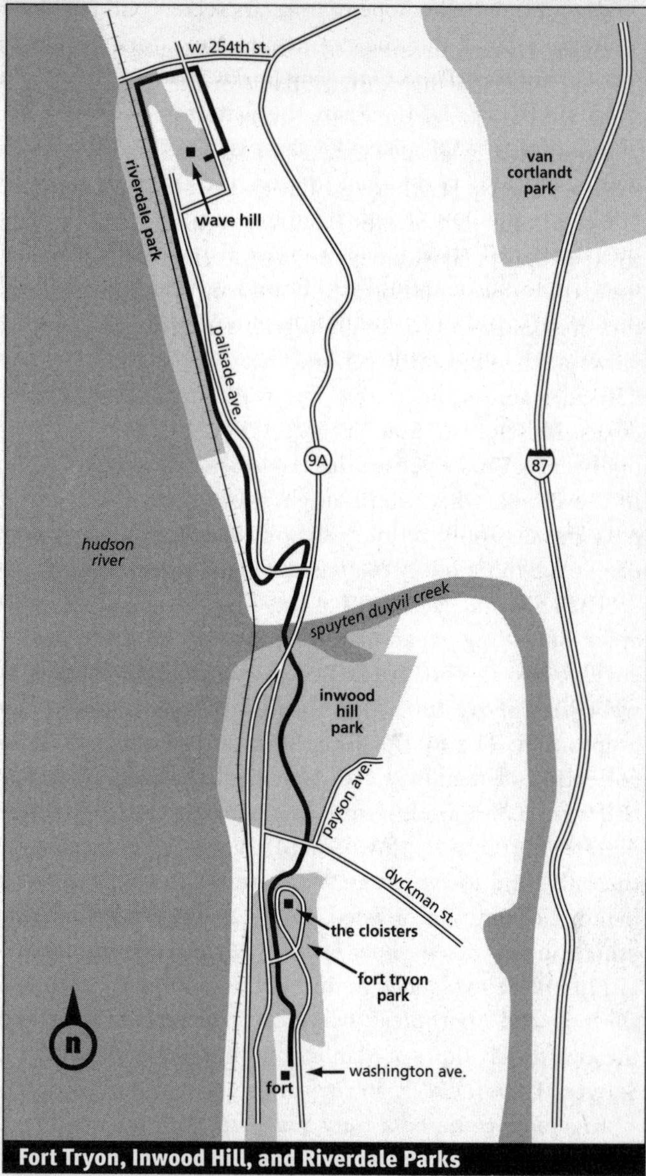

Fort Tryon, Inwood Hill, and Riverdale Parks

Difficulty: Hilly

Maps: Hagstrom maps of Manhattan and the Bronx. Inwood Hill Park maps are available at the Urban Ecology Center, located near the 218th Street entrance.

Description: It always amazes me to ride the A train to the northern tip of otherwise-flat-as-a-pancake Manhattan. Eons ago, this part of the island was squished into a ridge so steep that today you have to take an elevator 165 feet up from the subway platform to the street. The hike follows this crest along its rocky undulations, delivering towering views of the Hudson River and the petrified pillars of the Palisades across the water. The walk is filled with paradoxes. Most of the Manhattan section—which you'd normally expect to be dense with crowds—is devoid of people. In the Bronx, where some might worry about safety, you pass through only refined, swanky neighborhoods where people are more likely to consider *you* a threat.

The appealing weirdness of this hike is evident immediately. Sprawling expanses of daffodil and heather gardens envelop you in Fort Tryon Park; the air is fragrant as you walk high above the river. The Cloisters is a time-travel proposition: The Metropolitan Museum of Art packed its collection of medieval art—windows, statues, tapestries half a millennium old—into a moodily lit castle. At Manhattan's northern tip, Inwood Hill Park's 196 acres include the only wild forest left in Manhattan—a compendium of hickory, cherry, cottonwood, birch, and hackberry, among others, jutting above sheer walls of Manhattan schist. This is a fun place to wander. Squirrels scurry around old Indian shelters and "potholes" carved by glaciers. Swans pick through the shallows of Manhattan's last wetland, a cove off Spuyten Duyvil Creek, in the park's northernmost section.

Riverdale could be a tony San Francisco neighborhood. On slender, rolling Palisade Avenue, mansions with sweeping Hudson overlooks appear at wide intervals. This road offers dazzling views of the river, the Palisades, Spuyten Duyvil Creek, and the George Washington Bridge. Riverdale Park has some of the wildest forest this side of Bear Mountain, including massive 200-year-old red oak trees. Finish up at the café at Wave Hill, where Teddy Roosevelt and Mark Twain took residence before it became a public garden and cultural center.

Route: Turn right from the subway station onto Fort Washington Avenue, which leads to Fort Tryon Park. Follow the Hudson overlook path, passing the Cloisters on your right. Follow the path downhill and exit on Riverside Drive. Cross Riverside and walk north on Payson Avenue.

From Payson, take a left into Inwood Hill Park. Follow the Hudson overlook paths north to the top of Manhattan. To get to the footpath on the west side of the Henry Hudson Bridge, walk under the bridge and up to the toll booth. Cross into Riverdale in the Bronx.

Turn left on Kappock Street, and left on Independence Avenue. Turn right on Palisade Avenue. Enter Riverdale Park on the left near 232nd Street. You can more or less follow the park trail paralleling the river all the way to the train station. At 254th Street, the park ends, and Metro-North's Riverdale Station is to the left. To stop into Wave Hill, less than a half mile away, turn right on 254th Street, then right on Independence Avenue. Wave Hill is on the right.

Directions: By subway, take the A train to 190th Street. Return on Metro-North from the Riverdale station.

BROADWAY

Location: Manhattan

Length: About 14 miles

Difficulty: Mostly flat, but sidewalks are unforgiving, so wear good shoes

White's description: *Note:* Several years ago, Dan White, a California-based journalist, hiked the 2,666-mile Pacific Crest Trail from Mexico to Canada. In addition to a few unwanted bear encounters and some blisters the size of New York City cockroaches, he gained a new appreciation for walking as a means to observe and ponder. One chilly late-autumn day, he undertook Manhattan's own "thru hike"—the entire length of Broadway, the Indian-trail-turned-Great-White-Way. He began where the Broadway Bridge connects Manhattan to the Bronx.

> This heavily Dominican neighborhood isn't Manhattan as tourists know it. I'm surrounded by low-set buildings, humble storefronts, skyscraper-less horizon. But the neighborhood isn't entirely free of gentrification's grasping, manicured fingers. On one corner is a trippy boutique with beaded handbags and neon scarves. The road passes mom-and-pop stores, *carnicerias*, bakeries, crazy discount marts where everything's for sale. Glass doors of steaming restaurants release the smells of suckling pigs on spits and baking empanadas. Stores offer to wire money to El Salvador, Mexico, Venezuela, Peru.
>
> I admire the stylized theater marquee of the Christ Unified Church at West 175th Street, with its message "Come on in or smile as you pass. Jesus is the cornerstone." I try to come on in but the door is locked. Broadway gives way to tenements, brick boxes casting shadows over empty playgrounds. At 162nd, I soak up a riot of Greek mythology in bas-relief: slaves rowing, waves crashing, Neptune and Aphrodite rising above the spume. Broadway is full of hidden treasures like this. Far ahead, the Chrysler Building rises from the mist like a ghost ship's mast. The road drops past snowy cemeteries with tombstones shaped like crosses and shields. The Hudson lies to my right, cold and warship-gray as I cross into

Harlem, which is full of people, comfort-food outlets, discount groceries, fancy emporiums. Men stand in the cold, stomping their feet.

Then black gives way to white in a pigmentation flash. I mount a long hill above Harlem, watching the ethnic diversity fade with every step. I'm near Columbia and Barnard. Students stuff their cheeks with futomaki at a sushi bar. Walking the promenade, I watch ladies in fur scooping poop after sweater-wearing dachshunds. Gentrification does have its upside. The enormous Barnes & Nobles have easily accessible public bathrooms.

When the contrasts of Broadway are too much, I follow garlic and meat smells into Arties, at West 83rd Street, where I enjoy "Hotdog Happy Hour." Then I vacuum down a perfect bagel at H & H, at West 80th. Onward into the wind and cold. Times Square gives me a neon headache the size of a Miss Saigon production. Here, my dad once pointed at billboards for quadruple X movie theaters. "This is the bottom of the barrel—the absolute bottom," he said with delight. These days, families with young children come at all hours.

Crowds force me into the street, where taxis nearly clip my ankles. Dizzy, I look up at electronic tickertape rattling off stories of bombings, kidnappings and new IPOs. Strangely, the midtown part of my journey reminds me the most of nature. I feel like a steelhead trying to make its way up a waterfall with no fish ladder. I break into a run, and don't stop until West 4th Street. The Village. Bondage mannequins in fetishware. Parking garages and jean shops. As I approach the city's oldest section, the cross streets are narrow and short. Up ahead is the Wall Street bull, which looks to be rearing up or falling over, depending on the angle. Across the water, Lady Liberty glows like a green lantern. She's a pretty sight, but not particularly inviting or congratulating. She looks more annoyed.

Legs aching, my mind overloaded with fashion hounds and hot dogs, I limp the last block. In some ways, Broadway was a stand-in for my thru hike. Periods of meditation, enjoyment and beauty interspersed with body aches and disorientation. I saw a bull instead of bears. And there are no bushes, so thank God for Barnes & Noble.

Directions: By subway, take the A to 168th Street and switch to the 1 train; get off at 215th Street. Start from the Broadway Bridge.

Step Right Up

OST PEOPLE CAN'T imagine *walking* up the Empire State Building, much less galloping up the landmark's 1,576 steps. But this is New York, after all. The New York Road Runners Club (212-423-2221, www.nyrrc.org) stages an annual race from the lobby to the 86th floor observatory deck. Since the first race was staged in 1978 with 15 runners, the Empire State Building Run-Up has become an international event. In 2000, Paul Crake of Australia finished the course in a lung-scalding, record-setting 9 minutes, 53 seconds. Participants have included Chico Scimone, an orchestra conductor from Italy, who took part in 10 races. Scimone finished his last race in 33 minutes, 34 seconds—when he was 88 years old.

The event is by invitation only, but you can apply to enter. For an application, write to the club at 9 East 89th Street, New York, NY 10128, and write "Empire State Building Run-Up Application Request" on the envelope.

SHEEPSHEAD BAY TO FLOYD BENNETT FIELD

Location: Brooklyn

Length: About 5 miles

Difficulty: Easy

Heads up: Check out the good Turkish restaurants along Emmons Avenue in Sheepshead Bay.

Description: Floyd Bennett Field is the perfect antidote to city life. In contrast to the closed-in feeling of skyscraper-worshiping Manhattan, the old 1,500-acre airfield has enormous empty spaces—an urban prairie most remarkable for its absence of anything at all except unobstructed horizons. Floyd Bennett Field, named for the pilot who flew Admiral Richard Byrd over the North Pole in 1926, was New York's first public airport and was used by renowned pilots such as Amelia Earhart and Howard Hughes before becoming obsolete. It's now Gateway National Recreation Area property, which includes a new forest, public gardens, and a bioreserve of grasses, sedges, and wildflowers maintained by the New York City Audubon Society's Grassland Restoration and Management Project. Model airplane buffs flock here, their buzzing "gas hawks" joining kestrels and northern harriers in the sky, small-scale reminders of the airport's glory years. Actually, everything looks like a toy: Even cars coming at you in the distance resemble Matchboxes.

You can visit old hangars that are like quiet, crumbling cathedrals, occupied only by rotting signs and flaking bricks. One of them, Hangar B, houses old airplanes under repair, and you can inspect the machines when the crews—many of them military veterans—are in there working. You'll see Raptor Point, a quarter-mile length of beach dotted with white shells and holes dug by horseshoe crabs, which cluster here in late spring and summer to mate and lay eggs. The North Forty Nature Trail features head-high grasses called phragmites and a new forest of aspen, pine,

Sheepshead Bay to Floyd Bennett Field

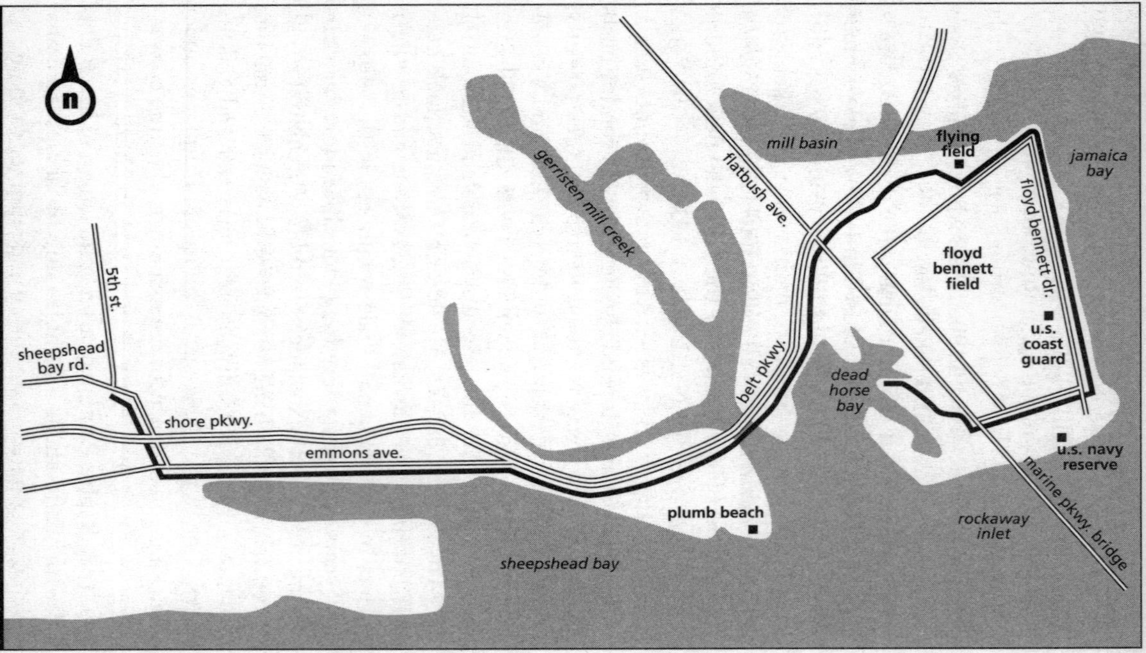

and birch where a transplanted population of eastern box turtles roams. There's a wooden blind overlooking a pond where in summer you might spot snowy and great egrets, glossy ibis, and green herons, among other birds.

The journey to Floyd Bennett from Sheepshead Bay adds to the experience. Most of the walk is on a greenway path or the beach. And Sheepshead Bay is one of my favorite places in the city, a fishing village busy with party boats and maritime ambiance. This hike is ideal for a spring or fall day; avoid it in the heat of summer, because there's little shade.

Route: From the subway station, turn right and walk to Emmons Avenue on the waterfront. Turn left and walk on the sidewalk until Emmons Avenue ends; bear right onto the greenway path. If you want, walk down to the beach; return to the greenway after Plumb Beach. Cross Flatbush Avenue and turn right to enter the North Forty Nature Trail. This small trail network exits into Floyd Bennett Field. Turn left and walk to Raptor Point, at the edge of Jamaica Bay. Turn right and walk along Floyd Bennett Drive past the Coast Guard station. Follow Floyd Bennett Drive when it turns right, and exit the park. Take the bus on Flatbush Avenue, or cross the street for a short detour on the Dead Horse Bay trails.

Directions: By subway, take the Q train to Sheepshead Bay. To return home from Floyd Bennett Field, pick up the Q35 bus on Flatbush Avenue; that delivers you to the 2 train.

New Year's Folly

THE AMERICAN LITTORAL Society has one of the quirkier New Year's Day traditions going. Members walk the beach near Breezy Point in Queens, where every year, at 10 minutes past noon, they try to signal a group of friends on the New Jersey side of the bay. Seven miles away, on Sandy Hook, the Jersey walkers do the same. They've held mirrors to the sun and used flares, rockets, and binoculars. (A cell phone is considered cheating.) The tradition dates back to 1981, and so far the venture has failed every time. After a few moments, with nothing more than a shrug, the Breezy Point walkers pop open champagne bottles and celebrate. There's always next year.

Mining Gotham's Secrets

L. B. DEYO LOOKS down onto the subway tracks, then back at me. "Are you comfortable with going down here?" he asks. I nod, and he leaps off the 5-foot platform, his head disappearing briefly and then bobbing up again. Two of his cohorts follow, and then I jump down, too, looking self-consciously at the people approaching from the other end of the platform. We quickly melt into the darkness and start walking into an abandoned tunnel.

The track is inactive, so there's no apparent danger. Still, my senses are hyperalert. Every time I catch a glimpse of a light, or hear rumbling, I think, *Train*. Deyo and David "Lefty" Leibowitz, editor in chief and publisher, respectively, of *Jinx* magazine, show no signs of anxiety. Their hobby—and their magazine's chief focus—is urban exploration. They're part of a loose global network of people who delve into underground passages, climb bridges, explore abandoned and condemned buildings. They don't vandalize anything; rather, they make some record of their exploration—photographs, video footage, or an article—and post it on the Internet, which is the chief catalyst of the infiltration movement. In the past couple of years, the number of urban infiltration sites has increased notably. New York–based explorer Julia Solis holds dinner parties in tunnels as subway cars clatter past, and sifts through records from defunct insane asylums. She chronicles all of it on Dark Passage (www.darkpassage.com), her Web site. Other sites include Forgotten NY (www.forgotten-ny.com), Infiltration (www.infiltration.org), and the Urban Explorers Network (www.urbanexplorers.net).

Deyo and Leibowitz, both 29, explored tunnels and climbed buildings for kicks in high school. For the magazine, they created a distinct style: They explore in suits and dark glasses, appearing in pictures as coolly detached operatives. (Picture the blandly menacing villains in *The Matrix*.) They've spent time in tunnels, but they prefer aboveground exploits, especially bridges. They've climbed the Brooklyn Bridge, the Manhattan Bridge, and the Broadway Bridge. They climbed the Williamsburg Bridge in daylight and hung the *Jinx* flag from the top. Deyo says his most exciting moment came the first time he reached the roof of Grand Central Station. "It's as grand in scale as the concourse," he says. "There are incredible peaks and valleys, and the detail of the stonework is amazing." He was struck by the enormous size of the rooftop statues of Mercury, Athena, and Poseidon. "Mercury is thirty feet tall," Deyo says. "I climbed him and sat on his head." He's also accessed the roof of the 55-story Hilton Hotel. He and a friend were caught and thrown out of the Waldorf after illegally accessing the roof.

Deyo and Leibowitz aren't in uniform tonight, but they are in the mood to explore new turf. We wander a section of tunnel that is eventually lit by rows of blue and white lightbulbs. Wires dangle from above; there are empty paint cans, piles of rubble. Graffiti abounds; Deyo finds a new entry by a graffiti artist legendary for spray-painted "diary entries" set to rhyme. There's a loud rumble, and a train passes on the next set of tracks. Soon, another train passes on the other side. We're surrounded by live tracks, an eventuality the *Jinx* leaders didn't expect. We backtrack. "That was a little irresponsible," Deyo says, grinning a bit.

The magazine and Web site (www.planetjinx.com) angle hard for street credibility. There are stories about sex, terrorism, and prison among the urban adventure pieces, many told in agitated hip-hop voices. There are lots of pseudonyms. In person, Deyo and Leibowitz are soft-spoken and articulate. The night of our subway visit, Deyo wore black pants and a T-shirt; he has short red hair and a patch of hair under his bottom lip that makes him look like a young Tom Waits. Leibowitz has short brown hair and a light beard. In his glasses, green sweater, and jeans, he looks quite all-American. Their third cohort tonight is Rene, the *Jinx* graphic designer who by day works at the *Wall Street Journal*.

As we walk in the tunnel, Leibowitz explains that their hobby may involve selective trespassing, but the crimes are victimless and the results worthwhile. "In most cases there's no sign, nothing that says, 'Do not enter,'" he explains. "We have a lot of imagined boundaries in our society; you just have to want to know what's beyond those boundaries." He postulates that there is historical and anthropological significance in going to and making records of places nobody else may ever see again.

We visit a small room where someone used to live. The last time they were here, the *Jinx* crew saw television lights flickering through a crack in the door. Someone yelled, "What the hell are you doing here?" There's no one in here tonight; the room is dark, but with flashlights we can make out a TV and some clothes.

> I realize we are no longer on subway tracks. There's only the tunnel, and gravel, and darkness. Occasionally something drips on my head. Eventually we duck through an opening in a plywood wall, climb a few makeshift steps to a platform, and step past a sagging chain fence. Soon, with a strange suddenness, we're on the street again. Leibowitz looks around. "Just like that," he says, "you slip back into the world."

STATEN ISLAND GREENBELT

Location: Staten Island
Length: About 7 miles
Difficulty: Moderately hilly
Description: Given that one of Staten Island's distinctions is being home to the world's tallest landfill, you'd be forgiven for having diminished expectations heading over on the ferry. Maybe that's why the Greenbelt is so surprising. Staten Island has more parkland than any other borough, and the Greenbelt, among other distinctions, boasts the highest point on the Atlantic seaboard south of Maine.

This walk, which covers roughly half of the 13-mile, blue-blazed Greenbelt Circular Trail, will also test your lungs and thighs more than any other walk within city limits. Its summit is 410-foot Todt Hill, which as of this writing is still the highest point on the island (Fresh Kills Landfill may overtake it in 2002). You'll climb to the top through a quiet forest of oak, birch, and sweetgum; there's a birch stand at the summit. On a clear day you can see the ocean from the thick woods. You'll pass through High Rock Park, a 90-acre patch of highlands where there are swamps with bat boxes, one with a family of owls living in it. And look for kettle ponds, created by glacial action. As the Wisconsin ice sheet retreated, huge chunks broke off and melted, creating the ponds.

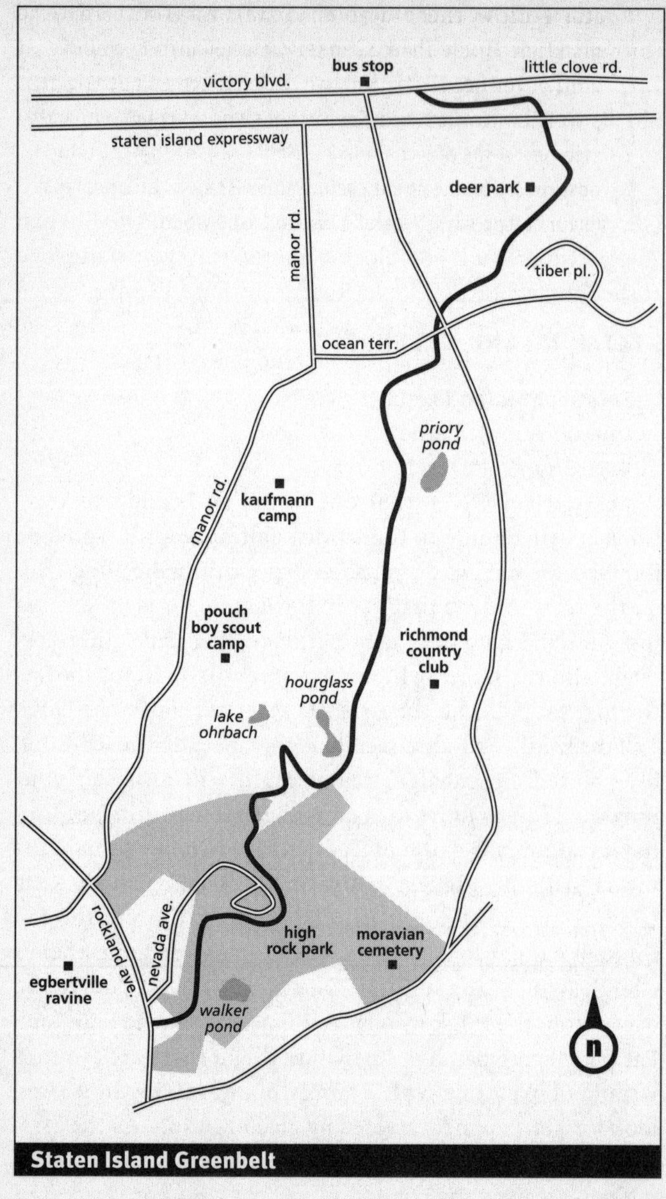
bus stop
victory blvd.
little clove rd.
staten island expressway
deer park
manor rd.
tiber pl.
ocean terr.
priory pond
kaufmann camp
manor rd.
pouch boy scout camp
richmond country club
hourglass pond
lake ohrbach
rockland ave.
nevada ave.
high rock park
moravian cemetery
egbertville ravine
walker pond
n

Staten Island Greenbelt

Route: Follow the blue-blazed trail up Todt Hill and through High Rock Park Conservation Center, ending at Rockland Avenue. Turn left on Rockland and walk two blocks to Richmond Road. Cross the road and take bus S74 to the ferry.

Directions: Take the Staten Island Ferry. From the St. George ferry terminal, take bus S62 or S66 to the Slossen Avenue stop. Walk one block back the way you came, and turn right on Little Clove Road. Cross under the Staten Island Expressway and take your first right. When the road ends, follow the dirt trail to the blue-blazed trail.

Wild Thing

MOST NEW YORKERS look into the tangled thickets of city parks and see weeds. "Wildman" Steve Brill sees lunch. He picks Japanese knotweed and dandelion greens in Central Park and makes a meal out of them. And he'll take you along.

In 1981, Brill, a naturalist with a trademark bushy beard and pith helmet, began running "edible tours" of city parks, showing participants how to forage for vegetables, fruits, nuts, seeds, and herbs. In spring 1986, parks commissioner Henry Stern asked police to arrest Brill for criminal mischief, saying Brill had defied his orders to stop "eating our parks." Two undercover rangers participated in a tour, photographed him, and arrested him as the event broke up. The arrest made national news and kept the tabloids' headline writers busy (the *Daily News* went with "Teeth off the Grass"). Stern eventually backed down, and a month after the arrest, the city hired Brill to run his tours.

Brill leads walks from spring to late fall in numerous city parks and sites in Westchester and on Long Island; for a schedule, check his Web site (www.bigfoot.com/wildmansteve) or write to him at 143-25 84th Drive, Apt. 6C, Jamaica, NY 11435. For reservations, call (718) 291-6825 a day in advance. The suggested donation is $10.

Short Hops

OLD CROTON AQUEDUCT TRAILWAY

Location: Yonkers, New York, 16 miles north of Manhattan

Length: About 8 miles if you stop in Irvington, 10 miles if you detour to Lyndhurst

Difficulty: Fairly easy; no hills

Heads up: You can duck into coffee shops and delis in the villages of Hastings, Dobbs Ferry, and Irvington along the way.

Maps: The Old Croton Trailway State Park (914-693-5259) publishes a map.

Description: The aqueduct offers barely a trickle of water these days, but the trail built over it has the benefits of a river: It links towns that otherwise might share no commonality. And the aqueduct tells a story. Beneath the packed dirt of the trail lies the brick-and-mortar tube laid by immigrant labor in the mid-1800s. The aqueduct was designed to slant downward just enough over 27 miles to let gravity deliver water from the dammed Croton River to reservoirs in Central Park and the present site of the New York Public Library on 42nd Street.

The system was designed to provide the city with water for a century, but it was obsolete in less than half that time. Still, its benefits live on. The trail delivers hikers to the quiet woods, backyards, and historic mansions of Westchester County rather than to its all-too-visible strip malls. In

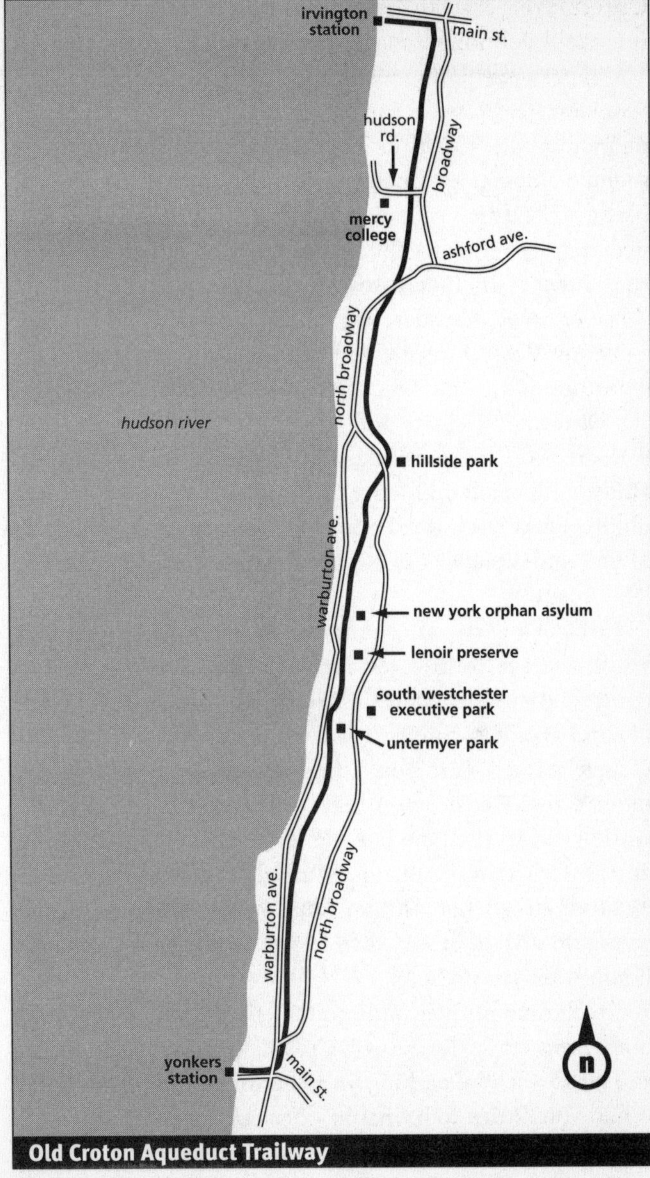
irvington station
main st.
hudson rd.
broadway
mercy college
ashford ave.
north broadway
hudson river
hillside park
warburton ave.
new york orphan asylum
lenoir preserve
south westchester executive park
untermyer park
warburton ave.
north broadway
yonkers station
main st.
n

Old Croton Aqueduct Trailway

Untermeyer Park in Yonkers, remains of an old estate include a columned amphitheater, mosaics, and gardens. You'll pass ventilating towers built at one-mile intervals to relieve water pressure and prevent stagnation. The grounds of Lyndhurst, a Gothic Revival mansion in Tarrytown, include colossal sycamores, Norway spruces, and weeping beeches. The tree canopies shade enough space for a Kennedy family reunion. The grounds, which fall away toward the Hudson, include a rose garden and a greenhouse. A sense of peace pervades, but it's not hard-core wilderness.

Route: Pass Untermeyer Park up a hill on your right. Continue north, passing the ruined caretaker's cottage of the Untermeyer estate and a stone building that served as a waste weir for aqueduct maintenance. In Hastings-on-Hudson, turn left on Main Street for a food pit stop, or diagonally cross the intersection of Farragut Parkway, Main Street, and Broadway to continue on the trail, which parallels Broadway.

In Dobbs Ferry, after crossing Broadway on a diagonal, you'll see the former residence of the Croton Aqueduct overseers on the right. The trail headquarters is just beyond. Walk through a parking lot to Cedar Street in Dobbs Ferry, where you'll find several delis and restaurants. Cross Cedar Street and turn left. Walk on the sidewalk briefly, then take a right on the dirt path going downhill. The trail continues through Ardsley-on-Hudson and Irvington, where the aqueduct spans a steep ravine. On Irvington's Main Street, turn left to go to the train station if you want to end here.

I recommend the 2-mile round-trip detour to the Lyndhurst property in Tarrytown. Cross Irvington's Main Street, and cross a school parking lot to continue on to Lyndhurst. When you return to Irvington, turn right on Main Street to catch the train.

Directions: By train, take Metro-North to Yonkers. Walk

up Main Street and turn left on Riverdale Avenue, which becomes Warburton Avenue as you pass Philipse Manor Hall on your left. About a mile later, turn right on Philipse Road. (The Hudson River Museum is on your left.) Climb a short hill and turn left onto the trail.

HARRIMAN AND BEAR MOUNTAIN STATE PARKS

Location: Suffern and Bear Mountain, New York, 36 and 46 miles north of Manhattan

Length: Hike 1 is about 10 miles; hike 2 is about 11 miles.

Difficulty: Strenuous, with several scrambles. There's lots of loose stuff, so bring hiking boots that protect your ankles.

Heads up: You can pick up supplies in Suffern (for hike 2), but the only concession in the park is the Cub Room, a little restaurant at the Bear Mountain Inn that serves good sandwiches and soup.

Books and maps: You can order two excellent guides: *The New York Walk Book* and *Harriman Trails: A Guide and History*, as well as a two-part map, Harriman Bear Mountain Trails, from the New York–New Jersey Trail Conference Web site (www.nynjtc.org/store/index.html). The maps are also available at the parks' visitors centers.

Description: In terms of day hikes within easy reach of the city, this is simply as good as it gets. Harriman State Park and adjacent Bear Mountain offer a combined 51,000 acres of mountains, lakes, swamps, forests, open fields, and the ruins of mining villages. There are 25 reptile species and nearly 100 bird species, along with a handful of resident beavers, otters, minks, bobcats, and black bears. There are hundreds of miles of blazed trails and scores more of unmarked trails. One you've probably heard of, the Appa-

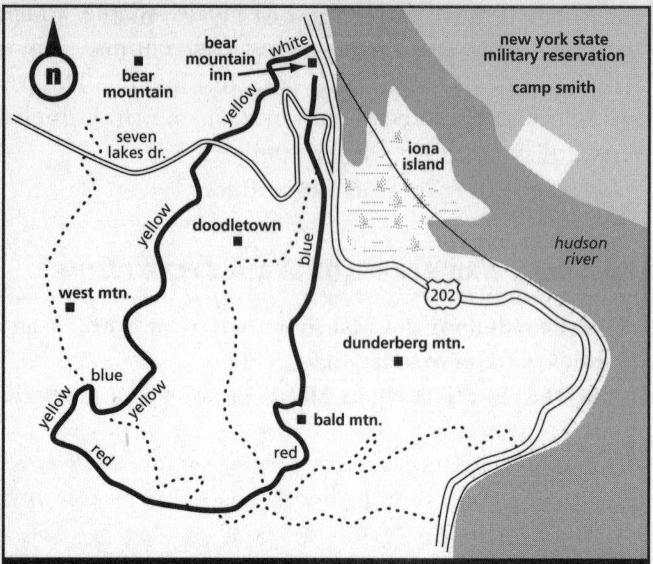

Harriman and Bear Mountain State Parks, option 1

lachian Trail, has a bit of a history here. The AT's first section was constructed on Bear Mountain in the early 1920s. The trail also hits its lowest elevation point here—about 120 feet above sea level, at the Trailside Museum and Zoo.

The hikes here are spectacular and challenging, often leading straight up ridges to the tops of peaks. The place is so special, we'll detail two separate hikes: one in the northeastern part of the park, the other in the southwestern. Each can be done in a day, but keep in mind that they're strenuous, filled with grinding climbs and precipitous descents. Highlights of the first hike include commanding views of the Timp, one of the park's most striking rock visages, and the Hudson River Valley. The second hike, which begins at a train station along the park's western border, has some imaginative elements. You'll climb the rock formation known as Kitchen Stairs and pass giant boulders in the Valley of Dry Bones, followed by two huge boulders called Grandma and Grandpa Rocks. Watch for resident timber rattlesnakes, and bring water and lunch. Backcountry camping is allowed at or near shelters along the trail (see "Camping" page 357, for more information). Consult the trail maps or park staff for locations.

Route: *Hike 1:* By bus, take ShortLine (800-631-8405) from Port Authority to the Bear Mountain Inn. By train, on weekend mornings, two Metro-North trains stop by request at Manitou. From Manitou, walk a mile or so south on NY 9D and across the bridge. Follow signs to the inn.

Pick up the Suffern–Bear Mountain Trail (yellow blazes) at the inn and start climbing. Cross Seven Lakes Drive after a mile. In another mile, cross a wooded path formerly called Doodletown Road. Climb West Mountain and continue to the intersection of the Ramapo-Dunderberg Trail (white blazes with red dots). Turn left on the Ramapo-Dunderberg Trail. Descend Timp Pass, and follow trail around the Timp, which was closed after a washout damaged the trail. Walk through the "saddle" between the Timp and Bald Mountain, then climb Bald Mountain. Just after the summit, turn left on Cornell Mine Trail (blue blazes) and begin the long descent back to Bear Mountain Inn. When the trail spills out onto US 9W, walk about 50 feet and turn left at the signpost for Doodletown. Take the first right onto the 1777 Trail (blue blazes) and return to the inn. The blazes can be elusive on both hikes in this section, so pay close attention.

Hike 2: By train, take the PATH to Hoboken, and New Jersey Transit to Suffern. From the station, turn left on Orange Avenue, which merges with NY 59. The trailhead is on NY 59 about 500 feet beyond the highway overpass; watch carefully for a trail marker on the right. By bus, take ShortLine (800-631-8405) to Suffern.

Follow the Suffern–Bear Mountain Trail (yellow blazes) up the steep hill to the overlook on Nordkop Mountain.

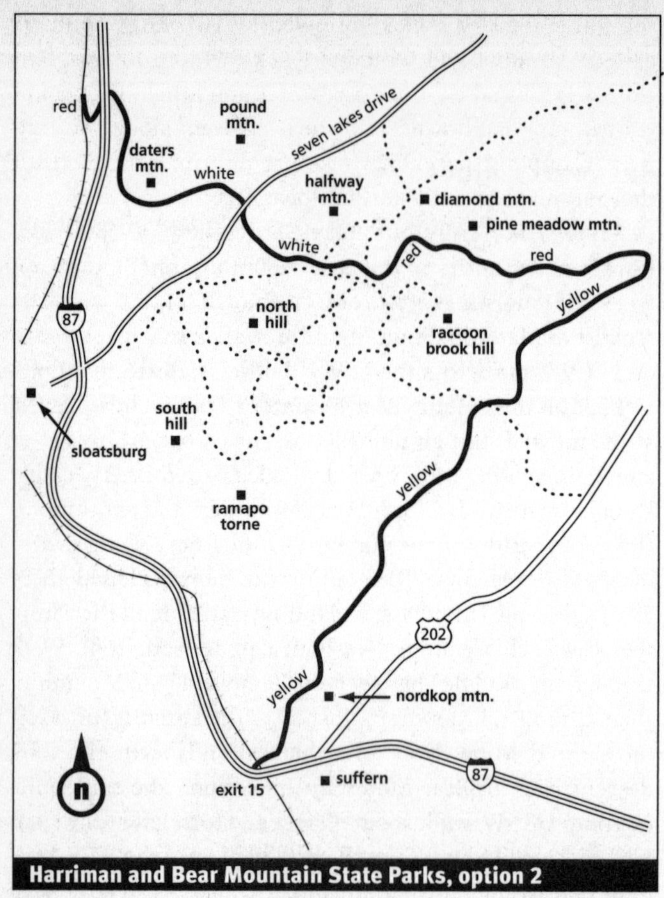

Harriman and Bear Mountain State Parks, option 2

Continue over the mountaintop and hike for several miles. A mile after passing the Stone Memorial Shelter, turn left on the Pine Meadow Trail (red-on-white blazes). Walk past Pine Meadow Lake and cross the footbridge over Pine Meadow Brook, then bear right onto the Kakiat Trail (white blazes) heading west. Follow this trail to the Ramapo-Dunderberg Trail (white blazes with red dots) and turn left.

From here it's less than a half mile to the trail's end and the Tuxedo train station. Return to Hoboken.

BREAKNECK RIDGE

Location: Cold Spring, New York, 54 miles north of Manhattan

Length: 5.5 miles

Difficulty: Strenuous

Heads up: As a posthike reward, get one of the fine hamburgers at the Depot (914-265-5000), located next to the railroad tracks in Cold Spring.

Books and maps: The *New York Walk Book* and *Paths Along the Hudson: A Guide to Walking and Biking,* by Jeffrey Perls.

Description: When you're about 15 minutes into this hike, turn and look back. The immediacy of the payoff—long, panoramic views of the Hudson—always amazes me. Not that anything about Breakneck Ridge is easy. The trail jolts upward 1,000 feet in the first half mile—pure mountain-goat stuff that hints at the inspiration for the peak's ominous name. *The New York Walk Book* calls this the "most strenuous hike in the Hudson Highlands" and suggests avoiding the trail in strong winds.

Clamber up the rocky face, which sits atop a tunnel dug for NY 9D and Metro-North. High over the big river, a freight train headed for Albany—its multicolored cars stretching out for a mile or more—looks like a Lionel. Storm King Mountain's imposing granite dome looms across the way. Turkey vultures float past at eye level.

Finally at the top, you get the whole vista: West Point, Constitution Marsh, a river valley that inspired an entire school of painters. Those who don't suffer from vertigo should peer over the Breakneck precipice, a blackened-granite wall that drops away for several hundred feet. Much of the rest of the hike consists of gradual descents followed by steep climbs to yet more lookout points. There are ways to add distance to this 5.5 mile route, but all the verticals make it feel longer. Loop back around on the Wilkinson Memorial Trail, which lopes over Sugarloaf Mountain. Enjoy that last long hundred-mile gaze—including Bannerman's Castle on Pollepel Island—before tackling the last vertical challenge: descending a set of notches cut into the face of Sugarloaf.

Route: Follow the Breakneck Ridge Trail (white blazes) along as it merges with the Notch Trail (blue blazes). Bear left on the Notch Trail when they split. Turn left on the yellow-blazed Wilkinson Memorial Trail, which leads back to NY 9D.

Directions: By train, take Metro-North to Cold Spring. From the station, cross over the tracks and turn right on Main Street and then left on Fair Street. Bear left at the end of Fair Street onto NY 9D. The trailhead is on the left immediately after the tunnel. You can get closer to the trailhead by taking Metro-North's special early train (212-532-4900) to the Breakneck Ridge stop.

Ice Hikes

THE FROZEN WATERFALLS in Delaware Water Gap National Recreation Area provide a whole new meaning to the old cliché "a walk in the park." The sport of ice hiking requires a bit more exertion and concentration; you have to put those crampons in just the right spot, or you could find yourself in a sudden and uncontrollable body luge. But here, at least, you can't fall too far. Slateford Falls and Buttermilk Falls are among the sites that offer 10 to 50 feet of vertical climbing. Contact the Mohican Outdoor Center (908-362-5670, www.mohicanoutdoorcenter.com) for more information.

LONG ISLAND SEASHORE TRAIL

Location: Watch Hill, Long Island, 59 miles east of Manhattan

Length: Up to 14 miles round-trip

Difficulty: Mostly easy; no hills, but hiking on sand can wear you out

Heads up: The Watch Hill Campground is 0.25 mile from the ferry dock. See "Camping," page 358, for more information.

Maps: Available at the Watch Hill Visitors Center

Description: This trail is more or less a stroll on the beach—albeit one that lasts up to 7 miles—traversing a spectacular strip of remote, roadless land that sits far out in the Atlantic Ocean. The trail, which slices through the federal Otis Pike Fire Island Wilderness, connects Watch Hill and Smith Point. This section of white-sand beach and pine and hardwood forest is protected because of the presence of endangered piping plovers, but the reality is this wilderness is too much of a schlep anyway for the Coppertone-and-cooler crowd. (Bikes are not allowed here, much less cars.) It's lonely among the high dunes, especially just before and after the conventional start of summer; you're far more likely to spot a white-tailed deer than a volleyball net.

Amazingly, you won't just find saltwater on this barrier island. Freshwater ponds tucked between the bay and the open ocean shelter cattails and toads. Migrating waterfowl—among them herons and egrets—stop in. Shellfish flourish in the brackish marshes. The idea is not to hurry. All you have to keep pace with here is the slender island itself. The beach constantly gets slammed by waves and storms, which lift and shift about 500,000 cubic pounds of sand per year. The Fire Island Lighthouse was built in 1858 along the island's western tip, but it's now almost 5 miles east of the new tip. There are bluefish, striped bass, winter flounder, and other saltwater swimmers out here, so bring your pole. And there's a star watch at the Smith Point Visitors Center the first Sunday of every month.

A few final notes: It's a good idea to bring food and a camp stove from the mainland, although the Watch Hill Campground has a snack bar and restaurant, and you can get coffee and a snack at Bellport Beach, halfway between Watch Hill and Smith Point. (There are also showers and phones here.) Be sure to hide your gorp when you turn in for the night. The island's resident red foxes are not above stealing, and they may come begging when you wake up. Also, ticks are a real problem here, especially if you take the inland trail.

Directions: By train, take the Long Island Rail Road to Patchogue. From the station, take a right on Division Street and a left on West Street; the Watch Hill Ferry terminal (631-475-1665) is on the right. Once you arrive at Watch Hill, start heading east toward Smith Point. This hike can work as a 1- or 2-day excursion. Options include doing a loop hike that begins and ends in Watch Hill, or a "thru hike" to Smith Point. No ferry service is available from Smith Point; the William Floyd Parkway connects this section of Fire Island with the mainland. From Smith Point, take a bus (Suffolk County Transit) or a $6 cab ride to the Shirley train station.

Pack It In

GOING ON AN overnight wilderness hike requires some preparation and forethought, especially for New Yorkers used to 24-hour delis on every corner. In fact, even day hikers should head off with enough gear to spend an unplanned night in the woods. To help you pack smartly, we asked Bill O'Brien, past coordinator and longtime board member of the Appalachian Long Distance Hikers Association, for a peek inside his backpack. Here are his essentials. (Italicized items are suggested for day hikers.)

- Tent, sleeping bag, closed-cell foam pad
- Pair of earplugs (a good night's sleep is essential)
- *Baseball cap for sun and rain*
- Waterproof cover for your pack
- Rain gear
- *Synthetic insulating layers; no cotton, even in summer*
- *At least 2 liters of water* and a water filter
- *High-energy food, such as PowerBars or gorp*
- *Map and compass (and the ability to use them)*
- *Butane lighter* and camping stove
- *Lightweight knife*
- *Headlamp or flashlight*
- *Resealable baggie of moleskin (for blisters), jock-itch cream, and bandages; bug repellent; sunblock*
- *Lightweight tarp, if not carrying a tent*
- *Light nylon cord*
- Large, heavy-duty plastic lawn and leaf bags to keep things in your pack dry
- *Hiking stick*

Note: Make sure your hiking shoes are broken in before you start walking. For more suggestions, check out www.aldha.org/advice.htm.

Meccas

APPALACHIAN TRAIL

Location: Georgia to Maine, with access points in Rockland and Putnam Counties, New York

Books: *The Appalachian Trail Data Book* gives mileages

between shelters, springs, roads, and other landmarks, listed both north to south and vice versa. *Walking the Appalachian Trail* vividly portrays the people, places, history, and sociology of the trail.

Description: The AT is the most storied, most traveled, most celebrated of all American trails. The epic path is 2,167 miles long, and 162 of those miles are in New Jersey and New York. You have to go west and north of the city to catch parts of it winding through the Delaware Water Gap National Recreation Area and the Hudson Highlands, but the AT is worth it. It never lacks for grandeur, finding its way up and over almost every peak along the way.

There are numerous possibilities for day trips. The New Jersey highlands section of the trail offers gems such as Sunfish Pond, a glacial lake, and narrow Raccoon Ridge, a dramatic razorback crest that falls away both to the west—with views down to the Delaware River—and the east. The famous white blazes lead through Harriman and Bear Mountain State Parks, where the AT had its origins in 1922. Highlights here—many accessible by bus or train—include Bear Mountain, Anthony's Nose, Cat Rocks, and Pawling Nature Reserve.

If you're willing to go north, nothing tops the sheer drama of the 34-mile Presidential Range in New Hampshire. The White Mountains have famously brutish weather; it's common for the weather station atop 6,288-foot Mount Washington to record snow and hurricane-force winds every month of the year. Midsummer, in fact, is the only reasonable time to summit Washington; the lower peaks—Jackson, Eisenhower, Monroe, Jefferson, Adams, and so on—are more accessible and nearly as spectacular. Fortunately, the Appalachian Mountain Club's chain of eight huts with bunks and hot food allow you to ramble 56 miles from the Franconia range through the Presidentials without a sleeping bag. (The huts are extremely popular, so make reservations early.)

Directions: Metro-North (212-532-4900) makes limited weekend stops near two sections of the AT. Take either the Harlem Line to the Appalachian Trail, or the Hudson Line to Manitou. The ShortLine bus (800-631-8405) runs to the Bear Mountain Inn, where you can pick up the AT.

PINELANDS NATIONAL RESERVE

Location: Ong's Hat, Lebanon State Forest, New Jersey, 109 miles south of Manhattan

Difficulty: Relatively flat, but sometimes the trail is soft and sandy

Books: *The New Jersey Walk Book* has more specifics. For a more literary take, get John McPhee's classic *The Pine Barrens*, which brings the wild region starkly to life.

Description: With its sweet water, sandy soil, and mazes of gnarled lowland forest, the Pinelands are a quirky choice. There are no sweeping mountain vistas; the highest point here is Apple Pie Hill, all 205 feet of it lording over the blueberry patches and cranberry bogs. The tea-colored water has no raging rapids. And the spongy, mushy trails can be murder on your ankles and knees, like a day hike through quicksand.

Yet this million-plus-acre region never ceases to be intriguing and uniquely rewarding. The 50-mile Batona Trail (short for "back to nature") traverses the region, which amazingly covers more than 20 percent of New Jersey. There are campsites along the way, and plentiful cedar-colored creeks with delicious, clean water. Some 17 trillion gallons of this same water lie in an aquifer below the Pinelands, one of the largest and cleanest water supplies in the East. Still, because of the sandy soil, the region can seem exceedingly dry. The Pinelands are the anti-Appalachian Trail, a study in subtlety rather than grandeur. But it *is* wilderness. The woods are home to several species—the Pine Barrens tree frog, northern pine snake, and carpenter frog—that you'd be hard-pressed to find elsewhere, and one species of the flower named bog asphodel that exists nowhere else.

Plan to spend 4 days to hike the entire Batona Trail, which runs from Lebanon State Forest through Batsto and Wharton State Forests to Bass River State Forest. You can shorten it with day hikes at various access points along the pink-blazed trail. Wharton has swamps and lakes and a reconstructed bog-iron and glassmaking center. Some spots, such as Deep Hollow Pond and the Quaker Bridge across the Batsto River, are accessible only by walking.

Directions: By car, take the New Jersey Turnpike to exit 4, and follow NJ 70 east. At Four Mile Circle, follow signs for Magnolia Road/CR 644 toward Pemberton. Drive 0.5 mile to Ong's Hat; parking for the trailhead's northern terminus is in the gravel lot on the right, across from Anapas Diner. Or head south on NJ 72 for another mile to the Lebanon State Forest (609-726-1191) visitors center, where you can get trail maps and a camping permit. The trail ends at Stage Road in Bass River State Forest.

Swamp Tours

THERE'S FAR MORE to the Meadowlands, in northern New Jersey, than landfills and John Gotti's likely grave. Check out the swamps, meadows, birds, and mammals of this most urban of wildernesses with local authority John Quinn, author of *Fields of Sun and Grass: An Artist's Journal of the New Jersey Meadowlands* and 10 other books. The Hackensack Meadowlands Development Commission (201-460-8300, www.hmdc.state.nj.us) sponsors the walks.

Where to Connect

Clubs and Organizations

- New York–New Jersey Trail Conference (201-512-9348, www.nynjtc.org) is a nonprofit federation of 85 hiking clubs and 9,000 individual members working on trail construction and maintenance and conservation issues.
- Shorewalkers (212-330-7686, www.shorewalkers.org) is a walking and environmental group dedicated to promoting and preserving New York City's surrounding shores.
- Appalachian Mountain Club, New York–North Jersey chapter (www.amc-ny.org)
- The Sierra Club New York City Group (www.newyork.sierraclub.org/nyc) runs local and regional outings.
- New York Hiking Club (212-246-9593, www.nynjtc.org/clubpages/nyh.html) organizes hikes and other events in metropolitan New York.

Shops

- Eastern Mountain Sports (20 West 61st Street, Manhattan, 212-397-4860; and 611 Broadway, Manhattan, 212-505-9860) stocks hiking shoes and all manner of camping supplies.
- Paragon Sports (867 Broadway, Manhattan, 212-255-8036) carries hiking and mountaineering gear.

- Tent and Trails (21 Park Place, Manhattan, 212-227-1760), a slender reed of a store, carries all trail essentials.
- Campmor (Saddle River, NJ, 800-226-7667, www.campmor.com)
- REI (New Rochelle, NY, 914-632-9222, www.rei.com)

Events

- The Great Saunter is a 32-mile circuit of Manhattan organized by the Shorewalkers. The annual walk, which includes a dozen parks, begins and ends at South Street Seaport.
- The AIDS Walk New York (www.aidswalk.net/newyork) is a 10K walkathon benefiting Gay Men's Health Crisis.
- The MS Walk (www.msnycwalk.org) for multiple sclerosis includes 2.5-, 7.5-, and 12.5-mile routes.

Books

- Appalachian Long Distance Hikers Association. *The Appalachian Trail Thru-Hikers' Companion*. Harpers Ferry, WV: Appalachian Trail Conference, published annually.
- Buff, Sheila. *Nature Walks In and Around New York City*. Boston, MA: Appalachian Mountain Club Books, 1996.
- Chazin, Daniel D., ed. *The Appalachian Trail Data Book*. Harpers Ferry, WV: Appalachian Trail Conference, published annually.
- Luxenberg, Larry. *Walking the Appalachian Trail*. Mechanicsburg, PA: Stackpole Books, 1994.
- McPhee, John. *The Pine Barrens*. New York, NY: Noonday Press, 1978.

- Mittelbach, Margaret, and Crewdson, Michael. *Wild New York*. New York, NY: Three Rivers Press, 1997.
- Myles, William. *Harriman Trails: A Guide and History*. New York, NY: New York–New Jersey Trail Conference, 1992.
- *The New Jersey Walk Book*. New York, NY: New York–New Jersey Trail Conference, 1998.
- Daniels, Jane, ed. *The New York Walk Book*. New York, NY: New York–New Jersey Trail Conference, 1998.
- Perls, Jeffrey. *Paths Along the Hudson: A Guide to Walking and Biking*. New Brunswick, NJ: Rutgers University Press, 1999.
- Petry, Loren C. *Beachcomber's Botany*. Old Greenwich, CT: Chatham Press, 1992.

Bird-Watching

SOME READERS WILL be surprised to see this in an adventure book. The fact is, birding may not be as physically demanding as some of the other activities, but it's one of the most competitive sports anywhere. Birders are indefatigable in their efforts to add birds to their life list. (It's indicative of their passion that they don't "see" birds, they "have" them, as in, "I have a ruby-crowned kinglet. Did you get that?")

In New York City they have a wealth of fertile birding grounds. Central and Prospect Parks, Staten Island's seaside, the shallows of Jamaica Bay—they are our backyard feeders and birdbaths, and birders watch them avidly. Birds and their admirers congregate in remarkable numbers dur-

ing the spring and fall migrations, though bird-watching is increasingly a year-round pursuit.

What makes New York special? Many believe that birds follow ancient migrating habits that took them along the Atlantic seaboard long before cities were built. This route, which birders call the Atlantic Flyway, includes a densely populated and heavily industrial stretch from Washington to Boston. New York's parks—5,000 acres of forest and wetland—are welcome patches of green on a long ribbon of concrete.

The distinct advantage for New Yorkers is that most of the birds that pass over will stop here, and they alight in fairly confined, manageable areas. There's a wide range of birding to be done in the city. In one day, you can wander huge sections of city parks, covering wetlands and forest environments. Another advantage for city birders: Birds who take up residence here—including peregrine falcons and a famous pair of red-tailed hawks—become acclimated to humans and don't mind people following their every move. As a result, bird-watching in New York has thousands of avid devotees; birders pursue their sport with the same zeal as surfing fanatics or rock hounds. Some birders spend more time at Central Park's Summer Stage concerts gazing at raptors overhead than watching the musicians perform.

There is a lot of ground to cover as you head out, so if you're a beginner, take a tour or use a book such as *New York's 50 Best Places to Go Birding in and Around the Big Apple*.

City Limits

CENTRAL PARK

Location: Manhattan

Heads up: Hawk watches sponsored by the Urban Park Rangers (212-360-2774, www.nycparks.org) are held on Sundays at 9 A.M. during migrations. A birders' journal in Loeb Boathouse chronicles daily sightings and nesting information.

Maps: Central Park maps are available at the Arsenal on 64th Street and Fifth Avenue, second floor, or at the Dairy, located midpark at 65th Street.

Description: Virtually no other place in the world offers Central Park's combination of proximity to birds, diversity of temperate species, and sheer numbers. The 843-acre park has an international reputation and is notoriously addictive. On one fall migration tour, I met an attorney for the city and a magazine editor, both playing hooky from their morning work schedule for Starr Saphir's Central Park birding walk (see *Central Park's Starr-let,* page 60). About 275 species stop here annually, and in spring it's possible to see 100 species in a single day, when clouds of flycatchers, vireos, warblers, and swallows descend on Manhattan's green places for food and rest. The Ramble, an elaborate 37-acre crosshatch of paths, stony creeks, and wooded glens, offers long, lingering looks at not only familiar eastern warblers and sparrows but also rarer birds such as the elusive Bell's vireo.

Hang out with birders and you'll find there's almost always a buzz about some new development: A bald eagle is spotted, or a green heron family settles in an oak tree, or a pair of pied-billed grebes winters in the park. Fans of raptors will find plenty to entertain here as well; a red-tailed hawk named Pale Male mated and raised young above the top-floor window of a Fifth Avenue brownstone where Mary Tyler Moore lives. Someone usually had a scope trained on the nest. During fall migration hawk watches at the Henry Luce Nature Observatory at Belvedere Castle, counts regularly reach 8,000 or more.

Directions: The Ramble is midpark between 74th and 79th Streets. Belvedere Castle is just north of the Ramble.

Central Park's Starr-let

"OH *WOW*, THAT was a flicker," Starr Saphir coos, and a dozen sets of binoculars quickly rise to a dozen sets of eyes. "Ooh, this is such fun when you actually get to see birds arrive. Did everybody get that?"

We are in Central Park, Starr and I and a dozen of her clients, for the autumn warbler migration. It's a clear October morning, and the stars of the show are center stage: the yellow-rumped warblers, eastern phoebes, waxwings, red-bellied woodpeckers, ruby-crowned kinglets . . . and, well, Starr Saphir.

From our meeting point on Central Park West, a knot of people unself-consciously crowds behind this unlikely pied piper. Saphir, 61, is a fey, ponytailed woman in a scarf and faded blue sweater, an old gray satchel dangling from her arm. She often knows which birds are around before she sees them. "I just heard an eastern phoebe chirp," she says, scanning the branches, and again the binoculars snap to attention. She has seen each species hundreds of times, but her enthusiasm is infectious.

Over the past 18 years, Saphir has established herself as *the* Central Park authority on the 37 or so species of warblers that visit annually. Saphir's cachet among the birding community is such that she draws both newcomers and regulars. "She attracts really knowledgeable people because no matter how long you've been doing this, you can always learn more from her," says Maria Carmicino, a magazine editor and Saphir disciple.

Saphir's sunny disposition adds to the fun. Her talks are punctuated with puns, and she lacks the competitive edge of many birders. When someone spots a brown creeper, Saphir bubbles: "Good for you! That's only the second one I've seen this fall. Thank you for that."

Saphir is largely self-taught. She became fascinated with birds when she was six and her grandfather's car broke down on Long Island's Jericho Turnpike. Standing next to the road, she spotted a black-and-white warbler. "I knew what it was, and I got excited," Starr says. "I just started looking for birds." She studied on her own for 25 years, then moved to California, where for 6 years Saphir regularly birded with some noted experts. People started asking her to lead birding walks. Since she moved back to New York in 1982, her one-woman operation, StarrTrips, has run entirely on word-of-mouth business. She also moonlights for New York City Audubon, the American Museum of Natural History, and several universities.

Her clients' reactions keep her excited about birding. A regular, Carl, had been looking unsuccessfully for years for a red-breasted nuthatch. One day in 2000, Saphir's group paused near a marble bench when the prized nuthatch landed in a nearby pine tree. When Saphir pointed it out, Carl was ecstatic. The group cheered. For Starr Saphir, it was another good day at the office.

Heads up: Saphir's tours (212-304-3808) run 4 days a week during the spring and fall migrations, meeting on Central Park West at either 81st or 103rd Street. The American Museum of Natural History (212-769-5100, www.amnh.org/education) offers a series of eight walks in which you'll learn how to use field marks, habitat, behavior, and song as aids in bird identification.

PROSPECT PARK

Location: Brooklyn

Heads up: The Brooklyn Bird Club (www.brooklynbirdclub.org) hosts birding outings.

Maps: The Brooklyn Bird Club has a downloadable map and four detailed walking tours available on its Web site.

Description: Here's one for a bar-stool debate: Which is better for birding, Central Park or Prospect Park? It's like arguing Mays versus DiMaggio; the answer, of course, is they're both great. Like Central Park, Prospect was created to be everything to everybody. It has thick woodland, lakes and ponds, meadows, valleys, and hills packed into its 526 acres, so it attracts a gamut of birds. The warbler numbers in Prospect Park rival those in Manhattan. And if you're a hawk lover, kestrels, peregrines, and harriers are all regulars during migrations because of abundant food supplies. Waterbirds—among them ring-necked ducks, spotted sandpipers, and the occasional common black-headed gull—flock to the 50-acre Prospect Lake, its islands, and a peninsula that pokes in from the west.

Spring peak is late April through late May, especially when the wind is blowing out of the south; Lookout Hill is the first high point that northbound birds come to. The autumn peak for raptors and passerines is mid-August through October. The large oaks in the Quaker Cemetery are a common hangout for red-tailed hawks and other raptors. And Prospect Lake usually draws some interesting winter guests; in 2000, they included Eurasian wigeons, hooded mergansers, and northern shovelers. The park abuts Brooklyn Botanic Garden and Greenwood Cemetery, more than doubling the birding potential.

Directions: By subway, take the 1 or 2 train to the Grand Army Plaza station, then walk three blocks west on Plaza Street to the Grand Army Plaza park entrance. For Lookout

Hill, enter the park at Vanderbilt Playground at the corner of Vanderbilt Avenue and Prospect Park Southwest.

On the Lookout

IF YOU'RE A serious birder, you've undoubtedly got some prize, rare bird you've been looking for your whole life. You probably don't have time to peruse the parks every weekend, hoping for that unlikely sighting. The New York Rare Bird Alert (212-979-3070, www.virtualbirder.com/vbirder/realbirds/rbas/NY.html) has weekly updates of the unlikely species visiting the city, and their location.

PELHAM BAY PARK

Location: Bronx

Books and maps: *Nature Walks in and Around New York City* has a good description of the Kazimiroff Trail. Maps are available at the park visitors center.

Description: I had one of those this-can't-be-Gotham moments here. My girlfriend and I were biking on the greenway from Orchard Beach near dusk when we stopped for a water break next to the lagoon that borders Hunter Island. I had barely stepped off the bike when I looked up at a stunning collection of great blue herons, belted kingfishers, swamp sparrows, and snowy egrets, the latter a brilliant white against the darkening water. It was autumn, so there was no beach traffic and virtually no other noise. When the herons took off, we could hear their wings across the water.

At 2,764 acres (including 660 underwater acres that would engulf all of Prospect Park), Pelham Bay is the biggest park in the city. It covers the entire northeastern shoulder of the Bronx, taking in 13 miles of shoreline, saltwater and freshwater marshes, dense forest, meadows, and Orchard Beach. Try the Kazimiroff Nature Trail, which slices through 189 acres of Hunter Island. There are great horned owls and northern saw-whet owls out in the woods, and the shrubs and vines draw dozens of bird species, from brown thrashers to mockingbirds to orioles and wood thrushes.

Directions: By subway, take the 6 train to Pelham Bay Park station. Take the BM29 bus to City Island, or (in summer only) the 12 bus to Orchard Beach. Or bring a bike and use the greenway path.

By car, cross the Triboro Bridge and go east on I-95 to the Pelham Bay/Orchard Beach exit, then follow signs to the parking areas. The trail starts at the Orchard Beach parking lot.

CLOVE LAKES PARK

Location: Staten Island

Heads up: Staten Island Urban Park Rangers (718-967-3542) run birding walks.

Maps: Available at the park

Description: John Thaxton, in *New York's 50 Best Places to Go Birding in and Around the Big Apple,* calls Clove Lakes "one of the most user-friendly first-rate birding spots." The 200-acre park features a well-marked trail that ascends high into a forest of maple, oak, and yellow poplar. From several points you're looking across the treetops, and in spring they're filled with warblers. Easily the most popular park on Staten Island, Clove Lakes also includes a sprawling meadow and four freshwater lakes connected by several streams that draw all sorts of waterfowl. Martling's

Pond, in particular, is an attraction for the likes of northern waterthrushes and spotted sandpipers. Some of the trees here are more than 100 years old, including one of the city's largest tulip trees, near Forest Avenue.

Directions: By bus, take the S62 from the Staten Island Ferry terminal to Victory Boulevard and Clove Road, then walk down Clove Road to the park.

By car, cross the Verrazano Narrows Bridge and take the Clove Road exit off the Staten Island Expressway. Follow the service road to Clove Road, turn right, and go through three traffic lights. Turn left into the park. Access the hiking trail south of the ice-skating rink, near Marx Street at Victory Boulevard.

Gateway National Recreation Area

Location: Queens and Brooklyn

Description: The national park, formed in 1972, is a jigsaw puzzle of 26,000 acres sweeping from Queens and Brooklyn across to Staten Island and New Jersey. It's a birders' paradise of bays, beaches, wetlands, forests, and dunes. Here are three top spots.

FORT TILDEN

Location: Queens

Heads up: The American Littoral Society (718-634-6467) offers free hawk-watch programs during migration season.

Maps: Get maps at Fort Tilden, Building 1.

Description: Watching a kestrel or peregrine falcon cruise thermals and swoop down on its prey is a stunning experience. The thrill is magnified, though, when you're at eye level with the raptors. That's the beauty of the Fort Tilden viewing platform, built in 1998 atop Battery Harris East, a 1920s-era bunker protected by a massive concrete gun emplacement. On a good day, volunteers see a couple hundred migrating merlins, kestrels, sharp-shinned hawks, falcons, osprey, and the occasional immature bald eagle. Some birds buzz past at close range; I once turned just in time to see a sharp-shinned hawk veer within 20 yards of the platform. The platform also offers some perspective on the surrounding maritime forest of bayberry and Japanese black pine as well as views of Manhattan, Coney Island, and Long Island. Bring a scope to check out the peregrine nesting box atop the Marine Parkway Bridge.

Directions: By subway, take the 2 train (or 5 train at rush hour) to Flatbush Avenue, then pick up the Q35 bus to the park.

By car, take the Belt Parkway to exit 11S, then follow Flatbush Avenue over the Marine Parkway Bridge; the park is on the left. From May 15 to September 15, you need a parking permit for Fort Tilden, available at Building 1 (718-318-4300).

Birdman

SOME OF CHRIS Nadareski's workdays go something like this: 1. Coffee. 2. Report to office. 3. Climb Marine Parkway Bridge to band leg of 3-week-old peregrine chicks. Well, *somebody* has to do it. As the resident expert on urban peregrines for the Department of Environmental Protection, Nadareski scales bridges and skyscrapers to monitor the city's falcon population.

JAMAICA BAY WILDLIFE REFUGE

Location: Queens

Maps: Pick up a map with a free permit at the visitors center (718-318-4340).

Description: The nature trails winding through this 9,155-acre preserve lead past marshes, ponds, seaside goldenrod, and exposed mudflats. Strategically placed benches facing Pumpkin Patch Channel and West Pond are ideal for studying some of the 325-plus species of water-, land, and shorebirds that have visited this rare swatch of urban wetlands over the past quarter century. In May, the peak time for shorebird migration, the mudflats are standing-room-only, with black-bellied plovers, avocets, semipalmated sandpipers, and more.

West Pond draws both a spectacular collection of shore-

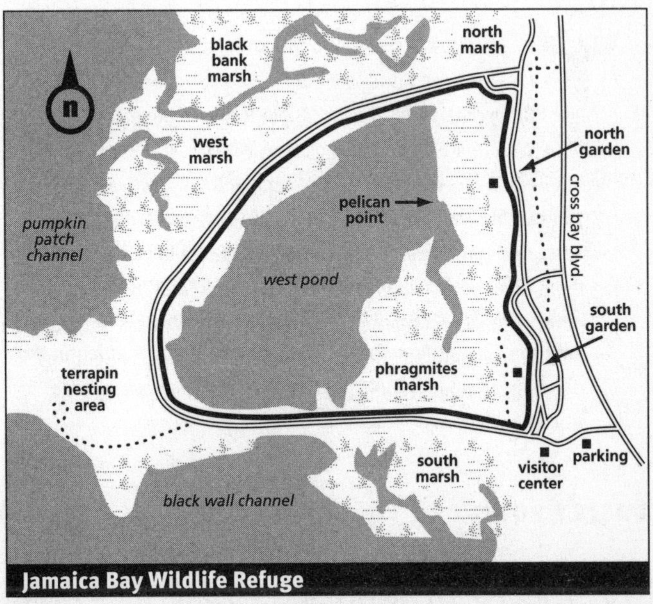

Jamaica Bay Wildlife Refuge

birds and their admirers. On one autumn visit I stopped to watch an excited elderly couple observing a family of brants through a scope. A visit during migration could yield glimpses of stilt sandpipers, night herons, oystercatchers, glossy ibis, and snow geese—all seemingly comfortable despite the roar of planes from nearby JFK International Airport. Boxes for bats, house wrens, tree swallows, barn owls, and kestrels dot the paths.

Directions: By subway, take the A train to Broad Channel, then walk on Noel Road to Cross Bay Boulevard. Turn right and walk about 0.75 mile to the park entrance.

By car, take the Belt Parkway to exit 17; go south on Cross Bay Boulevard across North Channel Bridge. The entrance is about 1 mile past the bridge.

Fisher Kings

THE GROWING OSPREY population in Jamaica Bay makes for some memorable Nature Channel–type moments. Biologists erected nesting platforms at Jamaica Bay Wildlife Refuge for the osprey, which were nearly wiped out by DDT-laced pesticides. Several pairs are active there, so you can hunker down with binoculars and watch mating rituals and adult birds raising their young. Better still, you can watch them dive, talons extended, and haul fish from the water. Park ranger Nancy Corona once found a fish flopping on the ground behind the visitors center. Her theory: An osprey caught the fish, only to have the meal slip from its talons as it flew by.

BREEZY POINT

Location: Brooklyn

Heads up: Go to Fort Tilden's Building 1 (718-318-4300)

for a 1-day birding permit. During the spring and summer, you're prohibited from picnicking, jogging, playing ball or Frisbee, beaching a boat, using motorized vehicles or fireworks, and bringing pets. Visitors are discouraged from walking near restricted areas, because the birds often lay eggs outside the fencing.

Maps: Available at Fort Tilden, Building 1

Description: The sandy fingertip of the Rockaway peninsula has a special function: It serves as a crucial home to piping plovers, tiny shore birds listed as an endangered species in the state for 15 years, and common terns, a threatened species. Visitors are kept at arm's length (see *Breezy Point Drama,* below) from March 15 to August 31, when the plovers fly up from Florida and South America to nest. Rangers will encourage you to stay back near the high-tide line and use binoculars or a scope to see the birds. The rest of the time, the beach is wide open. In autumn, peregrines, kestrels, and merlins swoop along the coast. If you're lucky, you might see a snowy owl in winter, camouflaged in downy white among the dunes. This is also a renowned fishing spot (see "Fishing," page 218).

Directions: By car, take the Belt Parkway to exit 11S, then follow Flatbush Avenue south over the Marine Parkway Bridge. Turn right off the bridge and drive to the 222nd Street parking lot at the end of Breezy Point.

Breezy Point Drama

THERE'S BEEN ALMOST as much drama on Breezy Point Tip recently as on any Broadway stage. The protagonist is a small shorebird called the piping plover, which has spent more than 15 years on the federal government's threatened or endangered species list. Despite the city's dense human population, about a dozen pairs of plovers migrate to Brooklyn annually to lay eggs on the sand.

The villains in this bit of ecological theater are a parade of natural predators and unwitting humans. The notoriously shy birds round up their brood and hide in the dunes when people approach, depriving the young of essential nutrition. In the late 1980s, with the endangered bird's numbers dropping, rangers closed part of the beach. That helped the people problem, but herring gulls continued to pillage the eggs. Rangers responded by firing off noisemaking explosives to discourage gulls from nesting, cutting their numbers from nearly 300 breeding pairs to about 60.

Still, the beach bustles with activity. Biologists now place protective devices over plover eggs, but the population is still on the edge. The "extras" in this drama—nearly 4,000 common terns—screech and dive to protect their young when crows and gulls lurk nearby. Two hundred pairs of skimmers add further excitement. "Most people have no idea what goes on out there," says Sue Gilmore, a natural resources management specialist at nearby Fort Tilden. "It's an amazing sight to see."

The only question that remains: How will the story end?

Short Hops

SANDY HOOK

Location: Gateway National Recreation Area, Highlands, New Jersey, 53 driving miles south of Manhattan

Heads up: Monmouth County Audubon Society (732-872-2473, www.monmouthaudubon.org) offers birding walks.

Books: The visitors center (732-872-5970) sells a pamphlet, *Birds of Sandy Hook*, that lists several hundred species seen at the park and when you're likely to see them.

Description: Sandy Hook is Breezy Point's matching bookend: a windswept spit of sand, lumpy with dunes, that juts into the entrance to New York Harbor. The 1,665-acre peninsula is also important to sensitive bird populations, supporting some of the largest nesting populations of least tern, common tern, black skimmer, and the endangered piping plover in the Northeast. The holly forest, mudflats, and small islands also are home to a small number of roseate terns, an endangered species.

The crowds of beachgoers are enormous in summer, but Sandy Hook is a year-round destination. Loons and cormorants are among the robust waterfowl that stay around in winter. There's a hawk-watch area atop a knoll near the lighthouse where it's common to see hundreds of kestrels, peregrine falcons, turkey vultures, and the occasional bald eagle. Among other distinctions, Sandy Hook boasts the nation's oldest lighthouse.

Directions: By ferry, New York Waterways (800-533-3779) runs ferries to Sandy Hook during the summer. Other times of year, Seastreak (800-262-8743) and the New York Fast Ferry (800-693-6933) serve Highlands, just outside the entrance to Sandy Hook.

By car, take the Garden State Parkway to exit 117; follow NJ 36 east to the park. There is a vehicle entry fee during the summer only.

CONSTITUTION MARSH SANCTUARY

Location: Cold Spring, New York, 54 miles north of Manhattan

Heads up: The sanctuary staff offers canoe rides on the marsh, located between Garrison and Cold Spring on the

Hudson's eastern shore; look for some of the hundreds of resident snapping turtles.

Maps: Available at the preserve (845-265-2601, www.audubon.org/chapter/ny/ny/cms.html)

Description: This 270-acre sanctuary is among the few large marshes left on the 154-mile tidal section of the Hudson River. That means there's significant avian activity year-round. In winter, bald eagles roosting across the river on Iona Island fly in to dine on fish trapped in the marsh's ice. Red-tailed hawks look for the tracks of small mammals in the snow. In spring, ducks come in droves when the ice thaws, followed by herons and kingfishers, which perch on tree limbs over the channels. In fall, up to 100,000 swallows roost in the marsh at night before heading south. Ospreys and loons demonstrate their fishing acumen in summertime.

Directions: By train, take Metro-North to Cold Spring. From there, it's about a 2-mile trip; walk or bike up the hill and turn right on NY 9D. Turn right onto Indian Brook Road. Follow the signs into the preserve, which is on the right.

By car, take the Taconic State Parkway north and exit onto NY 301 west. In Cold Spring, turn left onto NY 9D. From there, see directions above.

CONNETQUOT RIVER STATE PARK PRESERVE

Location: Long Island, 56 miles east of Manhattan

Heads up: Request a free 1-year visitation permit by mail before going (P.O. Box 505, Oakdale, NY 11769), though rangers may give you a 1-day pass if you show up without one.

Maps: Pick up a map at the park (631-581-1005).

Description: This stunning 3,475-acre preserve encompasses a spring-fed freshwater river that slices through some of the most beautiful woodlands on Long Island's South Shore. You'll find lots of water-loving birds: ospreys that cruise the river, eyeballing the swarms of trout; clusters of paddling wood ducks; herons, egrets, and swans standing in the shallows or perched on branches. The woods are dense with pileated woodpeckers, ruffed grouse, eastern screech-owls, and many songbirds, including the beautiful winter wren. Ring-necked pheasants nest here, and if you hike around a bit—an 8.5-mile trail traverses the length of the park—you might encounter wild turkeys nervously tittering and bounding across the paths.

The river begins north of the park, and there are state-run hatcheries of brook, brown, and rainbow trout, so the fishing here is exciting (see "Fishing" page 224). There's also a canoe outfitter nearby.

Directions: By car, take the Belt Parkway to the Southern State Parkway; take exit 44 onto NY 27 (Sunrise Highway). The park is on the north side of the road, so you have to drive a few hundred yards past the park entrance and make a U-turn. There's a vehicle entrance fee year-round.

QUAKER RIDGE HAWK WATCH

Location: Greenwich, Connecticut, 32 miles north of Manhattan

Maps: Maps and site information are available at the park (203-869-5272, www.audubon.org/local/sanctuary/greenwich).

Description: If you visit this Audubon Society of Greenwich property between September and November, you'll notice a person seated on a high expanse of lawn, studying the sky. This is the full-time hawk-watcher, which is good work if you can get it, especially here. The ridge is a "fun-

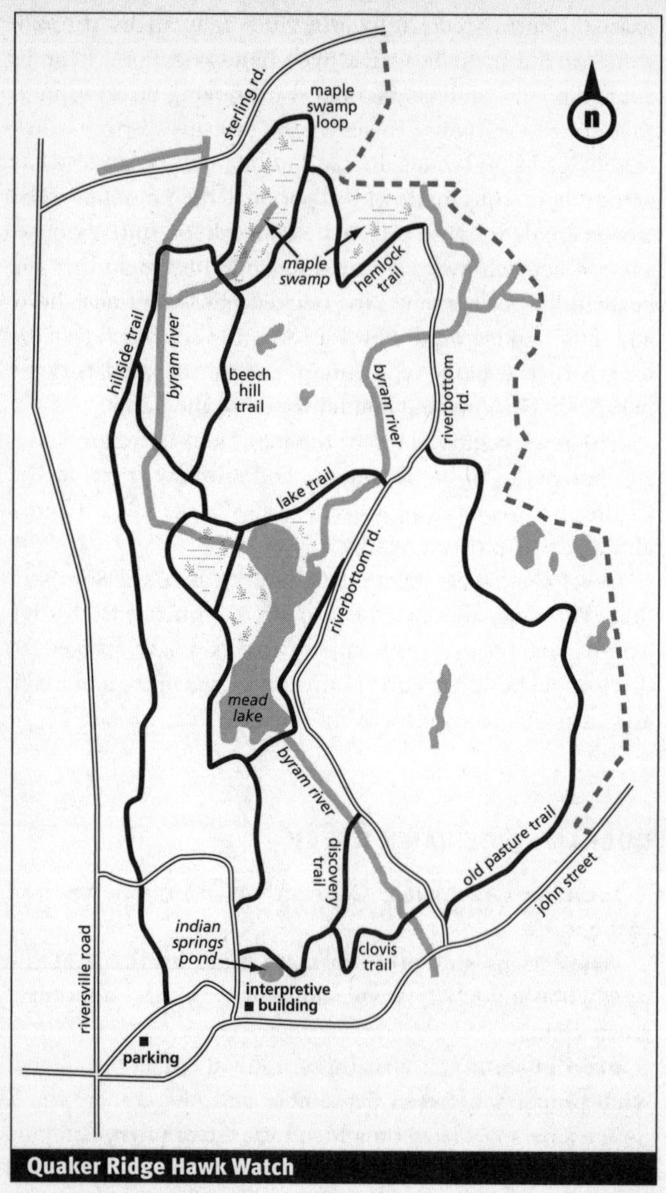

Quaker Ridge Hawk Watch

neling" point, where migrating birds coming from points north and east squeeze around the southernmost corner of New England to avoid flying over the open water of Long Island Sound. Quaker Ridge is a perfect place to see broad-winged hawks, because those raptors stay farther off the coast than most birds to ride the thermals created by inland contours. The hawk watch is set up at a relatively high point where you can get a close look. As many as 15 species —including bald eagles, red-tailed hawks, northern harriers, and Cooper's hawks—fly over by the thousands. In 1995, Quaker Ridge set an Audubon Society record by tallying 30,000 broad-winged hawks in a day. Look for cool, clear days when the wind is blowing from the north. There are also 16 miles of nature trails and boardwalks with bird blinds.

Directions: By car, take the Hutchinson River Parkway, which becomes the Merritt Parkway; take exit 28 and turn left off the ramp onto Round Hill Road. After 1.5 miles, turn left on John Street. The entrance is on the right at the Riversville Road intersection. There is an admission fee.

Mecca

CAPE MAY POINT STATE PARK

Location: Cape May Point, New Jersey, 163 driving miles south of Manhattan

Heads up: The New Jersey Audubon Society (609-884-2376, www.njaudubon.org) runs the Cape May Bird Observatory, a research and education center.

Description: It is axiomatic among birders that a bad day on Cape May is better than a good day almost anywhere else. Universally regarded as one of the best birding sites in the country, Cape May is bordered by Delaware Bay to the west and the Atlantic Ocean to the east. Birds fly to Cape May Point at the end of the peninsula, find water in all directions, and stop to rest and feed before the 40-mile flight across the bay. As a result, birders have seen 400 species here, and Cape May's astounding hawk watch features a Hitchcockian swarm of raptors. A few numbers to throw around: The bird watch counts about 60,000 hawks every fall, and more than a million seabirds migrate within sight of land—all in addition to the prodigious numbers of warblers. This is heady stuff, exciting even for old birding hands. From the platform at Cape May Point, you'll probably see thousands of hawks—sharp-shinned and Cooper's—and falcons—kestrels and peregrines—on a fall afternoon.

In spring, migrating and breeding warblers serenade visitors with a thousand songs. On the trail to the Nature Conservancy's 40-acre property adjacent to Cape May Point State Park, you'll hear and see dozens of species of songbirds flitting around the goldenrod and rushes. It would take pages to list the species of warblers, grosbeaks, and sparrows that flock here.

Directions: By car, follow the Garden State Parkway to its southern terminus; go through the town of Cape May to Sunset Boulevard and turn left at Lighthouse Road.

Where to Connect

Clubs and Organizations

- New York City Audubon Society (212-691-7483, www.nycas.org)
- The American Littoral Society (718-634-6467) leads walks and organizes tours of the marshes and islands

of Jamaica Bay several times a year on the fishing boat *Dorothy B VIII.*

- National Audubon Society of New York State (212-691-7483, www.ny.audubon.org)
- Brooklyn Bird Club (www.brooklynbirdclub.org)

Events

- The Urban Park Rangers' Falconry Extravaganza (212-360-2772, www.nycparks.org) in Central Park offers close-up looks at falcons, eagles, and hawks.
- The Celebration of Birds (845-265-3773), in Cold Spring, includes bird-banding demonstrations, bird identification, walks, a bird of prey program, and nest-box construction.
- The World Series of Birding (609-882-2736, www.njaudubon.org) is an annual event at Cape May Point State Park.
- Cape May Spring Weekend (609-882-2736, www.njaudubon.org)

Books and Maps

- Buff, Sheila. *Nature Walks in and Around New York City*. Boston, MA: Appalachian Mountain Club Books, 1996.
- Connor, Jack. *Season at the Point: The Birds and Birders of Cape May.* New York, NY: Atlantic Monthly Press, 1992.
- Dunne, Pete, David Sibley, and Clay Sutton. *Hawks in Flight.* New York, NY: Houghton Mifflin, 1989.
- Fowle, Marcia T. *New York City Audubon Guide to Finding Birds in the Metropolitan Area.* New York, NY: Audubon, 2001.
- Mittelbach, Margraet, and Michel Crewdson. *Wild New York.* New York, NY: Three Rivers Press, 1997.

- Perls, Jeffrey. *Paths Along the Hudson: A Guide to Hiking and Biking.* New Brunswick, NJ: Rutgers University Press, 1999.
- Stone, Witmer. *Bird Studies at Old Cape May: An Ornithology of Coastal New Jersey.* Mechanicsburg, PA: Stackpole Books, 2000.
- Tanacredi, John T. *A Visitor's Companion.* Mechanicsburg, PA: Stackpole Books, 1995.
- Thaxton, John. *New York's 50 Best Places to Go Birding in and Around the Big Apple.* New York, NY: City & Company, 1998.
- Winn, Marie. *Red Tails in Love: A Wildlife Drama in Central Park.* New York, NY: Pantheon Books, 1998.

Road Biking

MANHATTAN NEVER LOOKS more beautiful than when I'm riding over the Brooklyn Bridge at dusk. The dark expanse of the East River lies below. The bridge soars above. And then you crest the bridge and begin to pick up speed, rolling effortlessly into the vast, glassy sea of lights.

I know lots of people must think it's nuts to ride a bike in the city, and I'll be honest: The first time I rode here, I couldn't stop looking over my shoulder. I felt like fresh chum in a shark tank. The buses, the swerving taxis, the jammed streets, the delivery trucks, the ambulances. It's daunting. At first. But drivers here—contrary to reputation—are not that bad. Drivers in China are bad. In Ireland,

you'd think drivers were carrying a live organ. In Chile, my girlfriend and I once took a ride in a van in which the driver started drag-racing an army truck. Our driver wound up accidentally nudging the soldiers' vehicle into a tumble off the road. On New York streets, thankfully, nobody drives much faster than 30 mph. And there's a pattern to the madness. Cars get bottled up at lights; when the signal changes, eager motorists press hard on the accelerator and everybody surges quickly ahead to . . . the next red light, 100 yards away. And so it goes: Blare horn. Accelerate. Stop. Repeat. On a bike, you'll slide past these lines of traffic like a cigarette boat on a sea of bottled-up barges. The buses and trucks are as slow and predictable as cows, and a bike can usually beat them to any destination in town. Smaller obstructions—double-parkers suddenly pulling into traffic, pedestrians darting through stalled traffic on side streets—are actually more dangerous. My only two biking accidents came when I collided with cab doors that opened in front of me. I only barked my shins both times, barely enough to draw blood.

Aside from efficiency, the best reason to get on a bike here is that there are great places to ride. There are now 60 miles of bike paths and greenways in New York City, with plans on the table for another 290 miles. Some are discussed in this chapter, but new greenways will have been created by the time this book reaches your hands. For updates on bike-path construction, see www.treebranch.com.

Outside of the city, naturally, you'll find things a little more mellow. It's easy to get out of the city with your bike; the excellent commuter train system is bike-friendly and delivers you deep into the quiet countryside.

City Limits

CENTRAL PARK LOOP

Location: Manhattan

Length: 6.1 miles

Difficulty: Easy, with relatively modest hills, except for a 0.25-mile climb in the northern section of Central Park

Books and maps: The New York City Department of Transportation provides a free biking kit with borough maps and safety tips. Call (212) 225-5368, or download maps from www.ci.nyc.ny.us/html/dcp/html/bikenet.html. Each borough map notes bike shop locations.

Description: On warm spring afternoons and summer mornings, this is the New York that Woody Allen gets so dewy-eyed about. The loop road offers romantic views of the Great Lawn, the reservoir, and the skylines to the west and south. People languish on blankets, having a deliciously slothful day. Of course, if you're riding, you can't afford to take much attention away from the front of your handlebars. In good weather, there's a roller-derby atmosphere to the Central Park jaunt; packs of in-line skaters and bikers buzz along like mad hornets, weaving between joggers, baby strollers, hansom cabs, and walkers just trying to cross the road. Recently I kept pace for a while with a guy on a unicycle. I wouldn't call cycling Central Park a meditative experience, but there's a whimsical beauty to this sea of people moving to a million different rhythms. Also, compared to the street—where you contend with messengers, jaywalkers, street vendors, garment racks, double-parked vehicles, and people hailing taxicabs—this is, well, a day in the park. Ride around the loop counterclockwise or you'll risk an accident and the wrath of other cyclists.

Directions: Almost every walkway leads to the loop road.

The easiest entry points are at Columbus Circle, 72nd Street on either side, or 110th and Central Park West.

Pushing for Pedals

THE FIRST THING I notice at the preride Critical Mass gathering is the abundance of long beards, halter tops, and dreadlocks. A woman hands out Ralph Nader leaflets. There's a shopping cart full of free fruit. One rider has daisies pasted on his helmet; another wears a T-shirt that reads "One Less Car."

These charming Gandhi-on-a-Schwinn sensibilities might initially be confused with the trappings of passive protest. But there's nothing timid about these rides, which are designed to raise awareness and push for alternative transportation improvements in New York. Every month, several hundred bikers and in-line skaters parade through Gotham, halting traffic on some of the city's busiest thoroughfares, to promote safer streets and bike lanes, among other initiatives.

Some rides have themes. My favorite is the Musical Mass; people play flutes and kazoos and blow New Year's noisemakers. A bike-drawn cart contains musicians playing trombone and a sort of accordion. From Union Square our throng plows west and then north, pushing up Sixth Avenue in a cacophonic brigade that makes most onlookers smile. Some motorists aren't amused by the inconvenience. There are several moments—especially when we loop around Columbus Circle four times—when drivers blare their horns for minutes at a time. Several bikers stop next to a driver's open window and holler "BEEEEEEEP," holding the word as long as the motorist holds his horn. At each intersection, several of the people in the parade peel away to stand in front of traffic. By the end of the night, I am among the human roadblocks.

The free ride is held the last Friday of every month. Time's Up (212-802-8222, www.times-up.org) stages other events, such as the Cyclone Ride, which combines a bike outing to Coney Island with a fling on the legendary roller coaster.

HUDSON RIVER BIKE PATH

Location: Manhattan

Length: About 11 miles

Difficulty: Easy except for a steep hill near the George Washington Bridge

Books and maps: The New York City Department of Transportation provides a free biking kit (see Central Park Loop, page 81). Also check www.treebranch.com for greenway updates.

Description: If Central Park is New York at play, the Hudson waterfront is where the bills get paid. You'll traverse the city's steely backbone on this Hudson River Greenway ride, from the glassy towers of Wall Street to the working river's gritty waterfront. It includes the Hudson River Esplanade, a wide freeway with established lanes for walkers, bikers, and skaters. The partly finished path in Chelsea and Midtown is a windy and narrow passage that hugs a waterfront of jagged wooden pilings, old brick industrial sites, fenced-off lots, and vacant piers. Helicopters lift off from Liberty Heli-Tours, blasting you with wind and noisy chatter. The Chelsea Sailing School skiffs bob in the water, their masts waving like scolding fingers. Farther north are the shady confines of Riverside Park.

Someday you will be able to pedal along the river more or less from the southernmost tip of Manhattan to the George Washington Bridge on a continuous path. In fact, advocates were edging close to that goal until the September 11 terrorist attacks slowed their progress. A new section of the path south of Chambers Street was destroyed when the World Trade Center collapsed, and the greenway's southern end, in the area of the Financial District, was closed indefinitely as this book went to press.

But in a sense, this is nothing new: the constantly evolving path has always varied wildly in quality and continuity, so old hands have never blinked at detours that send them out onto city streets for a few blocks, or on a service road next to a sewage treatment plant. Better to focus on the substantial recent improvements, such as the new link between Riverside Park and Fort Washington Park. For now, the path is a work in progress. But rest assured: This is a plum route even if it still requires a few oddball detours.

Directions: By subway, take the 1, 2, A, or C train to Chambers Street and ride west to the Hudson.

Rules of the Road

I WAS RIDING A bike on New York City streets for more than two years before I knew I was required to signal my turns and stops—and could be fined $40 for failing to do so. (For a left turn, extend your left hand straight out to the side; for a right turn, extend your left arm and bend your elbow so your fingers point upward. If you're braking, bend your left forearm down.)

Some other rules the cops may or may not enforce:

- Stay off the sidewalk. This one's pretty obvious, but if you opt for a shortcut and get caught, police can seize your wheels. Ticket: $40; or confiscation of your bike.
- Don't carry a passenger. The only exception is children between 1 and 3 years old who are in a child seat. Ticket: $40.
- Stay within the speed limit. That means you, A. J. Foyt. This

is not usually a problem on the streets, where cars are restricted to 30 mph. But did you know you're not supposed to top 15 mph in Central Park? Ticket: $30.

- No headphones. Riding here is tricky enough without sealing off one of your senses. Ticket: $40.
- Use a light. From dusk until dawn, your bike should have a white light in front and a red light on back. Ticket: $30.
- No rodeo riding. That means keep at least one hand on the handlebars and one foot on the pedals at all times. Ticket: $40.

SHORE PARKWAY BIKE PATH

Location: Brooklyn and Queens

Length: About 15 miles

Difficulty: Easy

Heads up: Café Istanbul (1715 Emmons Avenue, Sheepshead Bay, 718-368-3587) is well worth a visit. Coney Island has some of the most popular pizza around at Totonno's, 1524 Neptune Avenue.

Books and maps: The New York City Department of Transportation provides a free biking kit (see Central Park Loop, page 81).

Description: This ride follows a bike path along the immense waterfront of lower New York Harbor, passes beneath the towering Verrazano Narrows Bridge, slices past beaches and wetlands, and wends between grasses high enough to blot out the flow of traffic. The caveat: The bike path, as it traces the wide sweep of the Brooklyn waterfront into Jamaica Bay and Queens, has a missing piece. You have to ride through charmingly seedy Coney Island and Brighton Beach on the street, which is not such a bad thing. Brighton Beach, also known as Little Odessa, has shops brimming with Russian delicacies. Stop for chocolates, or

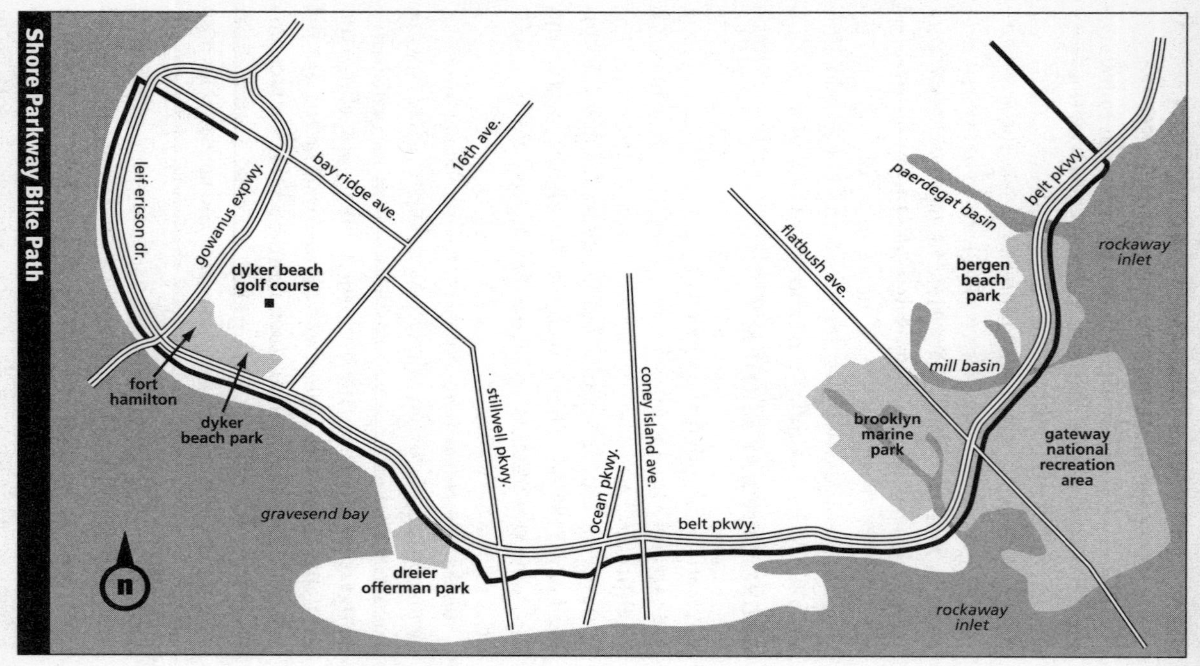
Shore Parkway Bike Path
leif ericson dr.
gowanus expwy.
bay ridge ave.
16th ave.
dyker beach golf course
fort hamilton
dyker beach park
stillwell pkwy.
coney island ave.
ocean pkwy.
flatbush ave.
paerdegat basin
belt pkwy.
belt pkwy.
rockaway inlet
bergen beach park
mill basin
brooklyn marine park
gateway national recreation area
gravesend bay
dreier offerman park
rockaway inlet
n

pickles and brown bread at M&I International (249 Brighton Beach Avenue). Whoop it up on the wooden Cyclone coaster on Coney Island, and check out Sideshows by the Seashore (Surf Avenue and West 12th Street) and the boardwalk. For a real dose of Coney culture, take in the Mermaid Parade, usually held in June.

The first 5-mile section of bike path starting at Owl's Head Park in Bay Ridge, Brooklyn, along lower New York Harbor, is spectacular. You're right next to the water, and you can watch the freighters and other traffic ply the currents. Waterbirds swirl and perch on the fencing, looking for lunch. The 693-foot Verrazano Narrows Bridge, the second longest suspension bridge in the world, is immense and impressive. For lunch, there are some good Turkish restaurants on Emmons Avenue in Sheepshead Bay. The longest section of the path follows an 8-mile run that takes in Plumb Beach, parts of Jamaica Bay, and Canarsie Pier. The path ended in Starrett City, near the Queens border, as this book went to press, but the greenway will eventually run all the way to JFK Airport. Construction on that section is scheduled for completion in autumn 2002.

Route: From the subway station, go west on Bay Ridge Avenue to Owl's Head Park, which borders the harbor. Turn left and head south on the bike path to Bensonhurst Park in Bath Beach. Continue south on the service road for the Belt Parkway; when it ends in Coney Island, follow Beach 52nd Street to Cropsey Avenue. Turn right. Turn left on Neptune Avenue and follow it to Sheepshead Bay, where the street name changes to Emmons Avenue. Pick up the bike path again at the intersection of Knapp Street. The path continues for about 5.5 miles to Canarsie. Turn left on Rockaway Avenue and ride to the L train at Glenwood Road.

Directions: By subway, take the R train to Bay Ridge Avenue.

Crossing Over

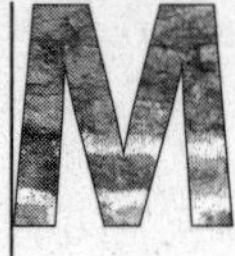

MOST CITY BRIDGES have a dedicated lane for bikers and pedestrians. To get the lowdown on directions, construction, and restrictions, visit Transportation Alternatives' top-notch Web site: www.transalt.org.

BRONX GREENWAYS

Location: The Bronx

Length: About 25 miles

Difficulty: There are few hills, so it's an easy ride. Your biggest challenge will be not missing any of the turns. I recommend tracing the route on a map beforehand.

Heads up: Eat fish and chips on picnic tables at Johnny's Famous Reef Restaurant, at the south end of City Island (718-885-2086).

Books and maps: The New York City Department of Transportation provides a free biking kit (see Central Park Loop, page 81).

Description: A quick game of free association: If someone says "the South Bronx," what images come to mind? Riots? Crime? Ruins? If you were weaned on *Fort Apache, The Bronx*, this easy half-day tour is pure revelation. The trip largely comprises state-of-the-art, off-street greenways that wind through rebuilt, prosperous streets; travel along the fast-improving Bronx River and its greenway; and enter an old-world fishing community and a sprawling park. No, the Bronx is not Dubuque, but this is a good thing. And anyway, the ride is safe, largely traffic-free, and flat.

The route—courtesy of Richard Gans of Transportation Alternatives, creator of the annual Tour de Bronx—begins at the center of the redevelopment effort: Charlotte Street

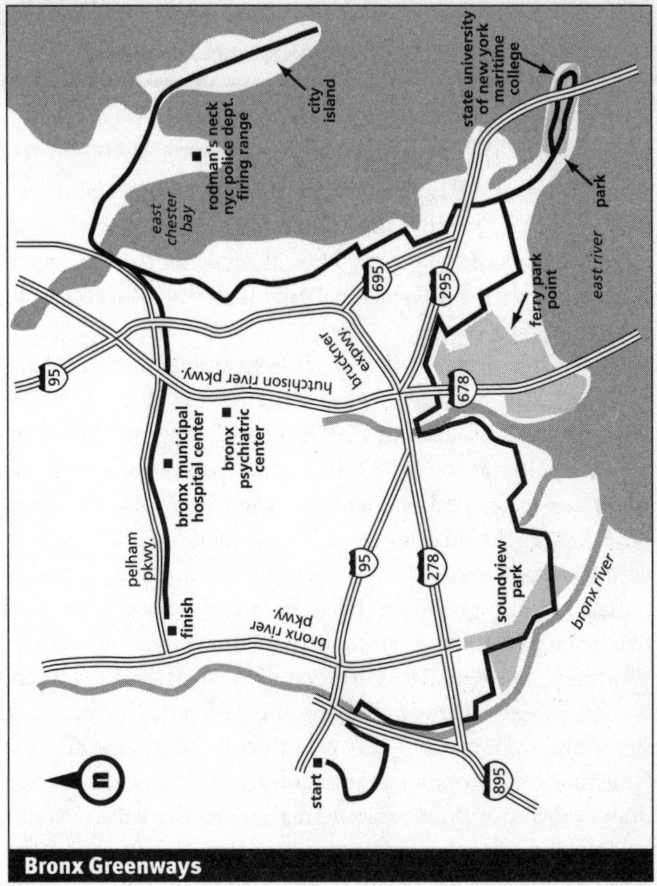

in the Claremont Village neighborhood. Rioting and crime once had this area looking like Pompeii after Mount Vesuvius erupted. But residents, with support from the Carter administration, began turning it around. The results more than two decades later are remarkable. Head east across the Bronx River onto the greenway that bends into Soundview Park. Here the Bronx River spills into the East River, and you can see Riker's Island, La Guardia Airport, the Whitestone Bridge, and parts of the Manhattan skyline.

Other highlights include a loop around SUNY Maritime College, located on a slender peninsula nosing into the East River, below the Throgs Neck Bridge; the leafy bike path through Pelham Bay Park; and the uncontrived quaintness of City Island, another of the remarkable little secrets out on the fringes of the Bronx. The ride ends on the borough's most popular greenway, the Pelham Parkway Greenway, near the Bronx Zoo.

Route: From the subway, go south on Boston Road. (You're going the right way if there's no elevated train above you.) Turn left on Charlotte. Left on Jennings. Left on Boone. Right on East 174th Street. Cross over the Bronx River and take the first right on Bronx River Avenue. Left on Story. Right on Colgate. Left on Lafayette, which borders Soundview Park.

Turn right on the Soundview Park Greenway. When you reach the park exit, go straight on O'Brien Avenue. Left on White Plains Road. Right on Lacombe, which borders Pugsley Creek Park. Continue along the park's border by turning right on Screvin. Left on Norton. Left on Zerega. Continue on Zerega for about 1.5 miles, until you reach the drawbridge over Westchester Creek. Turn right to cross the bridge, and take the first right onto Brush. Left on Lafayette. Right on East 177th Street, which borders St. Raymond's Cemetery. Right on Randall. Left on Balcom. Left on Sampson. Right on Brinsmade. Left on Schurz. Right on Pennyfield to the end.

Loop around the SUNY Maritime College peninsula and come back out to Pennyfield. Bear right onto Prentiss and cross over the Throgs Neck Expressway. Left on Expressway Service Road. Right on Schley. Left on Clarence. Right on Lafayette. Left on Shore Drive, which becomes Stadium Avenue.

Ride to the Pelham Bay Park entrance and continue north on the greenway path. At the first intersection, turn right on the Shore Road bike path. Get on the sidewalk before crossing the drawbridge over the Hutchinson River —traffic moves at highway speed over this bridge—and turn right on the City Island Road bike path. Cross the City Island Bridge. Take City Island Avenue to the end, and return the same way. Re-cross the Hutchinson River and continue straight on the greenway to the Bruckner Expressway entrance ramp. Cross the ramp, turn right after the traffic light, and enter the greenway. Take the left fork on the greenway and continue west for several miles to the Pelham Parkway station for the 2 and 5 trains.

Directions: By subway, take the 2 or 5 train (rush hour only) to 174th Street.

Lock and Key

T WASN'T SO long ago that you could buy a bike for $100. Now it costs that much just to lock it safely in New York City. The thing is, if you're going to ride here, you have no choice. Thousands of bikes are reported stolen here annually, and the crime is probably underreported.

How bad is it? Lock manufacturer Kryptonite's sturdiest unit is a mammoth 3-foot chain that's too thick for any bolt cutter. It's called the "New York Lock" because it's the only lock the company will warranty in Manhattan. A cable the diameter of spaghetti may be fine for the suburbs, but it won't do here. The staff at Bicycle Habitat, a shop that specializes in bike security, offers a few suggestions for avoiding theft.

- Lock your bike to an immovable object such as a parking sign or a lamppost, not scaffolding. Don't lock it to a post that is so short that a thief could lift the bike over it.

- Lock the frame, wheels, and seat with the best locks you can find, including a thick chain and sturdy U-lock.
- New bikes are theft magnets; consider making yours look undesirable with spray paint or duct tape.
- Keep a business card taped on the underside of your seat as a possible way to prove it belongs to you.

STATEN ISLAND'S GREENBELT

Location: Staten Island

Length: About 15 miles

Difficulty: Easy

Heads up: A few stops worth considering along the way: Historic Richmondtown, a village depicting 300 years of Staten Island life, and the Jacques Marchais Center for Tibetan Art, a prominent collection housed in a stone complex that resembles a mountain temple.

Books and maps: The New York City Department of Transportation provides a free biking kit (see Central Park Loop, page 81).

Description: With its winding roads and heavy traffic, Staten Island can be a vexing place to ride. Fortunately, the Greenbelt Conservancy has improved the situation dramatically with a dedicated bike path that was sailing through its final planning phases as this book went to press. The ride takes in sizeable chunks of woods and salt marsh before opening into Great Kills Park, where the cool waters of lower New York Bay beckon on a hot day. There are abundant bird populations for ornithology-minded bikers, and Revolutionary War 101 for history buffs.

The ride gets interesting when it abruptly hooks east, away from the road, after hugging the border of La Tourette Park. You'll find rolling hills and an old stone bridge as you traverse an oak forest. The landscape opens as you reach

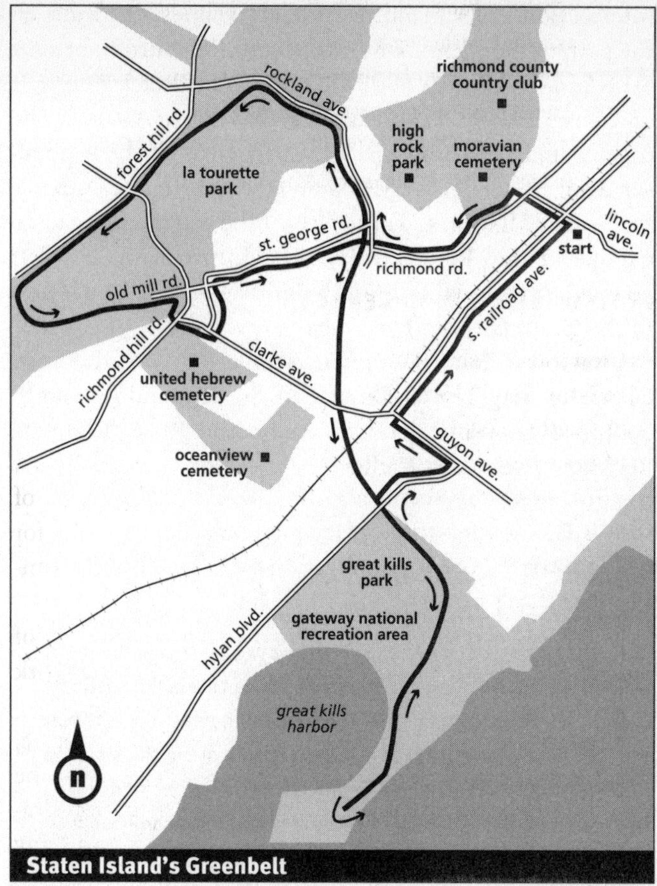

Staten Island's Greenbelt

Richmond Creek, with gorgeous views out over salt marshes. As you near Richmondtown on Old Mill Road—which is no longer open to traffic—you reach a crest used by the British as a lookout point during the war. Nearby St. Andrew's Church was the site of a battle during the war. The final leg before Great Kills Park is the Amundsen Trail, where meadows stretch out on either side of you.

Route: The bike path begins in La Tourette Park at the

intersection of Rockland and Brielle Avenues. Continue on the path to the Richmondtown restoration. Turn right after St. Andrew's Church onto Richmond Hill Road. Turn left on Clarke and left on St. Patrick's. Right on St. George. The path resumes just after McCully; turn right on the Amundsen Trail, which leads to Hylan Boulevard and the entrance to Great Kills Park. Follow the bike path and road to Crooke's Point. Return to Hylan and turn right. Turn left on Guyon. Turn right on South Railroad Avenue and return to the Grant City station.

Directions: Take the Staten Island Ferry to the Staten Island Railway. Exit at Grant City Station, and ride north on Lincoln Avenue. Left on Richmond Road. Right on Rockland Avenue to Brielle.

Green Guardian

CITY PARKS HAVE come a long way since the dust-bowl days of the early 1990s. But Dave Lutz isn't satisfied. An avid bicyclist, Lutz has spent the past 15 years pushing for the creation and expansion of the city's greenway system. He is an eloquent and tireless advocate of open spaces, parks, and gardens, and his merrily acerbic online newsletter, Urban Outdoors, keeps more than 10,000 subscribers posted on park developments and attempts to usurp or restrict public land. "Open space is a basic human need," he once wrote, "and it is not here for one generation to sell and the next to do without." The Web site he manages as executive director of NOSC, the Neighborhood Open Space Coalition/Friends of Gateway (www.treebranch.com), gets about 1,000 hits a week.

Lutz has a bushy mustache and a long, drawn face. He laughs easily and often, but he can be caustic and indignant, especially when it comes to the city's efforts to privatize or limit park access with golf courses and other restricted-use development. "These are bad times for people who think their government has a responsibility to the people," he says. "In the 1600s the Dutch created Bowling Green, which represented more parkland per capita than we've had since. When I first got involved professionally with this, the parks were in shambles. The low point was around the end of the Dinkins administration. Now there are some parks that are gems, but the most important thing is that the people's expectations are rising. People now understand the parks don't have to look awful and unapproachable.

"During the bad times, the government got away with saying, 'Parks are a luxury, and we have to deal with survival.' They're not a luxury, they're a basic necessity. We have twice the population density of other major cities. We absolutely have to provide spaces outside."

Lutz, a native of Bensonhurst, lives as he preaches. He bikes 6 miles to work every day from his home in Brooklyn's Red Hook neighborhood to Manhattan. His helmet and gloves add to the clutter on his desk overlooking Seventh Avenue. He's worked a community garden for 8 years. In summer he launches his canary-yellow sea cycle, a pedal-powered catamaran, from Red Hook and rides over to Staten Island and up to the George Washington Bridge. Lutz has always loved the outdoors, and he volunteered at organizations such as the Sierra Club and the Appalachian Mountain Club, leading walks and bike rides. At Pace University he "majored in extracurricular activities," he says with a laugh. "I barely squeaked through. It took a long time to figure out I could make a living at extracurricular activities."

Despite progress, Lutz points out that the waterfront remains largely inaccessible. Many parks in outer boroughs are dilapidated. But there are the victories. He has helped bring about 60 miles of bicycle greenway paths and has proposed another 290 miles. He mobilized bikers to protest when the city threatened to close Park, Madison, and Fifth Avenues to bikes. He has a little Thoreau in him—"one of the ways of achieving justice in this country," he told me, "is by breaking the unjust laws"—but he has become effective at working within the system. Together with hundreds of community gardeners, Lutz and the NOSC successfully lobbied New York's attorney general to stop the city's efforts to bulldoze public gardens. Clearly, this is what energizes him. "We had to fight like hell for those gardens," Lutz says, "and in that fight, there's joy."

Short Hops

THE LYCRA ROAD

Location: George Washington Bridge to Peekskill

Length: About 42 miles from the George Washington Bridge

Difficulty: Hilly on Henry Hudson Drive; easier on US 9W

Heads up: Runcible Spoon Bakery (37 North Broadway, Nyack, 845-358-9398); Piermont Community Market (485 Main Street, Piermont, 845-359-0369); Kelly's on the Green (300 Railroad Avenue, Peekskill, 914-734-2100)

Books and maps: Hagstrom maps of Bergen, Rockland, and Westchester Counties.

Description: You've heard of the Silk Road? Call US 9W the Lycra Road. Gaudy bike duds are an inevitable part of the landscape, beginning on the dazzling expanse of the George Washington Bridge and continuing along the Hudson River to the town of Nyack. It's not for nothing that this has become the de rigueur route for city bikers. The

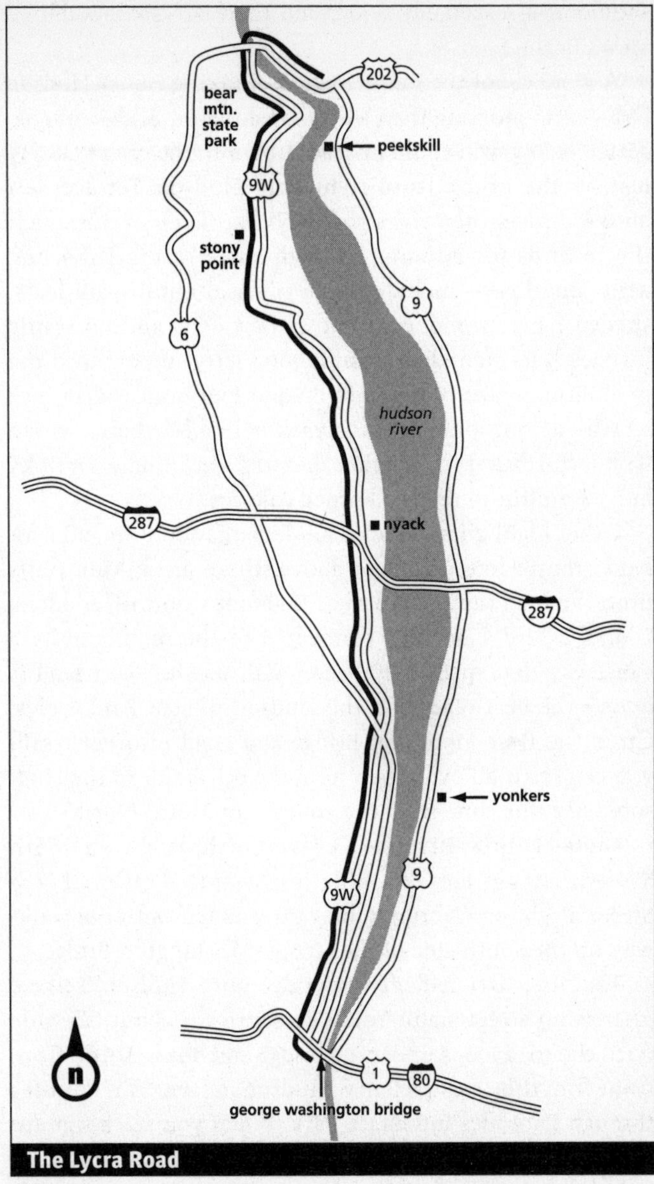

The Lycra Road

shoulder is reasonably wide, and there are some sublime views of the Hudson.

A word about the route: Instead of taking Henry Hudson Drive after crossing the George Washington Bridge, as suggested below, you could instead turn onto the easier US 9W just off the bridge (turn right onto Hudson Terrace, left onto Palisade, then right onto 9W). But keep in mind that the rewards for grinding through some of the Palisades' highs and lows—including one colossal climb—are leafy, shaded lanes, some awesome river views, and no traffic worries. Piermont Pier, a mile-long jetty jutting into the undulating wilds of the Hudson and Piermont Marsh, is a worthy detour for a picnic. Nyack is like Mayberry with a wonderful bakery; tradition dictates you inhale a sticky bun or muffin to replace burned calories.

Other highlights include Dunderberg Mountain, all dark bald granite looming high above (there are hiking trails from the road that rise to the 1,000-foot summit), and Iona Island, a bird sanctuary connected to the mainland by a causeway that spans a 200-acre tidal marsh. The island is one of the best places on the Hudson to spot bald eagles. Cross the Bear Mountain Bridge and head into Peekskill; you can see it all over again from the other side of the Hudson, only this time from the comfort of Metro-North.

Route: Follow Riverside Drive north. Right on 165th Street. Left on Fort Washington Avenue. Left on 177th Street. Right on Cabrini Boulevard, and left onto the walkway on the south side of the George Washington Bridge.

Take the first left off the bridge onto Hudson Terrace (there's no street sign). You'll go south for about 0.5 mile until the road loops under the bridge and heads north. Continue on this road, Henry Hudson Drive, for 8 miles through Palisades Interstate Park. When you see a sign for exit 2, go left under Palisades Interstate Parkway and turn right (north) onto US 9W.

Turn right on Rockland Road (toward the entrance to Tallman Mountain State Park). Right on Piermont Avenue. Right on Paradise Avenue to see Piermont Pier, or continue north on Piermont Avenue under the Tappan Zee Bridge. Left on Main Street, and right on Broadway in Nyack. The Runcible Spoon is on Broadway at High Avenue.

From here, there are two options. The more scenic route, if you don't mind riding on dirt, is to follow Broadway north to Nyack Beach State Park and ride along the Hudson until the path ends due to storm damage. Turn left at the fork (ignore the No Bikes sign; it pertains to the right fork), and left at the end of the bike path up a steep hill. Take the second right, just past the firehouse on the left. Rockland Lake State Park will be on your left. Turn right toward US 9W.

The second option keeps you on pavement. From the Runcible Spoon, take High Avenue to NY 9W and go north.

When options intersect: Continue through Haverstraw and Stony Point. For another off-road ride, bear right onto old NY 9W and continue on dirt path where the road ends. The path hugs the river and eventually returns to NY 9W. Continue and cross the Bear Mountain Bridge, then turn right toward Peekskill. Turn right on Main Street and curve around left onto Water Street, which takes you south to Railroad Avenue and Metro-North.

THE FORKS AND SHELTER ISLAND

Location: Riverhead, Long Island, 75 miles east of Manhattan

Distance: 63 miles

Difficulty: Easy

Heads up: Crabby Jerry's (631-477-8252) and Claudio's Clam Bar and Wharf (631-477-1889) are staples on the

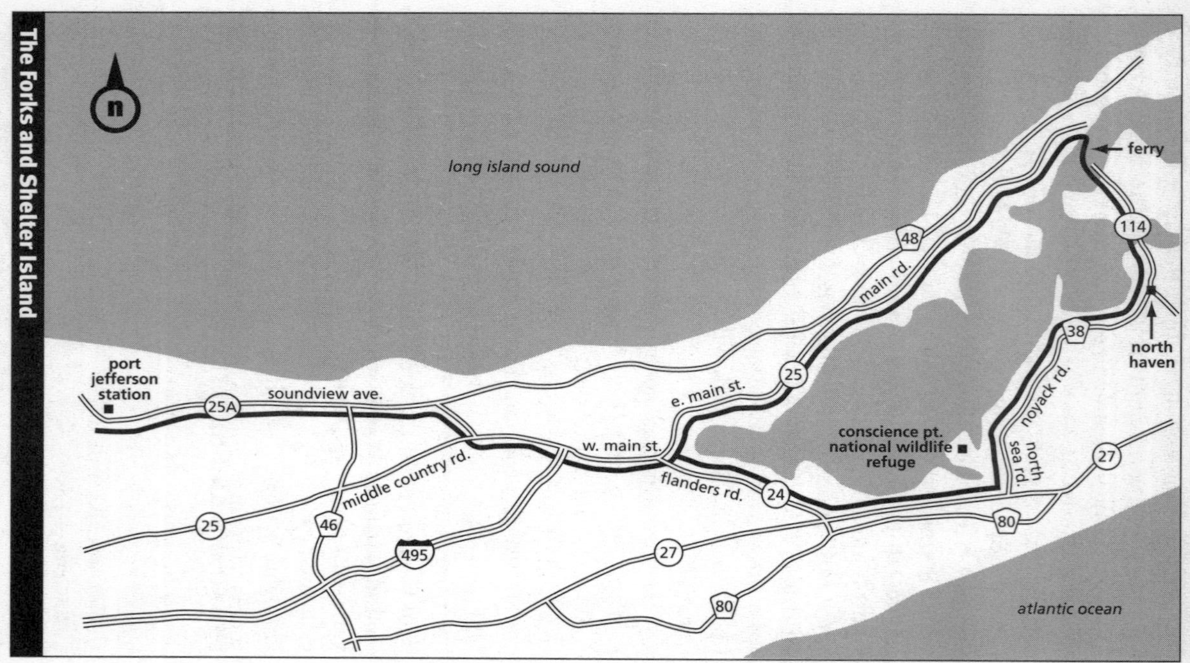
The Forks and Shelter Island
n
long island sound
port
jefferson
station
25A
soundview ave.
middle country rd.
25
46
495
w. main st.
e. main st.
25
main rd.
48
ferry
114
north
haven
38
noyack rd.
north
sea rd.
conscience pt.
national wildlife
refuge
flanders rd.
24
27
80
27
80
atlantic ocean

wharf in Greenport. On Shelter Island, try Baggio's Pizza (631-749-0595) at 53 North Ferry Road (NY 114) or Planet Bliss (631-749-0053) at 23 North Ferry Road. The latter has a front-porch hangout and a great fuel-up Sunday brunch.

Maps and resources: Hagstrom map of Long Island. The Country Time Bike Shoppe (631-298-8700) on NY 25 in Mattituck, and Piccozzi's (631-749-0045), a Shelter Island bike shop, are helpful.

Description: In an ideal world, this 2-day journey would be a thoroughly sensual experience. The local wines. The smell of marsh and saltwater. Shelter Island's mist. There are hints of that—enough to make this ride special. The route traverses Long Island's North Fork, crosses Shelter Island, and loops back via the South Fork in 2 days. There are a slew of vineyards clustered on the North Fork. There's a 2,100-acre nature preserve on Shelter Island where you should wander away from your saddle. There are sublime spots along the way to take in views and scour your lungs with salt air.

The drawbacks? Traffic whooshes by nonstop. It's the Long Island serenade. The area looks very appealing on a map, but many roads rarely afford more than selective peeks at the water.

Best to focus on Long Island's attributes. Look for vineyards east of Riverhead; many of them invite you to sit outside and have a picnic. Pindar (in Peconic, 516-734-6514) is an award-winner, but the entire industry on Long Island seems to generate buzz. Greenport is Sag Harbor minus the crowds, and Orient Point, a worthwhile detour, has gorgeous beaches and stellar fishing.

Shelter Island, huddled behind Gardiners Bay between the North and South Forks, is a resort-type escape that is beginning to rival the Hamptons for real-estate prices. Check out Mashomack Preserve, right off NY 114. Or detour to Ram Island Drive, which travels along a 3-mile peninsula nosing into Gardiners Bay. On the South Fork, leave time to roam around the Elizabeth Morton National Wildlife Refuge, a spit of sand with a pristine beach, cedar woods, and marshlands.

Route: RIVERHEAD TO GREENPORT (25 miles)

Ride east on NY 25 to Greenport. Camp at McCann Trailer Park (631-477-1487) on Moore's Lane in Greenport, which is nicer than it sounds, or for something more comfortable, consider Top O' the Morning (NY 25, 631-734-5143) in Cutchogue, Home Port Bed & Breakfast (2500 Peconic Lane, 631-765-1435) in Peconic, or the Ram's Head Inn (631-749-0059) at 108 Ram Island Drive on Shelter Island.

RETURN TO RIVERHEAD VIA THE SOUTH FORK (38 miles)

Take the North Ferry (631-749-0139) from Greenport to Shelter Island. Follow NY 114 south through Shelter Island; there are signs to the South Ferry (631-749-1200) for the 7-minute ride to the South Fork. In North Haven, take NY 114 until it forks, and bear right on Long Beach Road, which becomes Noyack Road; continue to the village of North Sea. Turn left on North Sea Road. Turn right on Millstone Brook Road and ride to the end. Turn left on Barker Island Road. Bear right on the Montauk Highway (NY 27) and bear right again onto North Shore Road. Pass under the Sunrise Highway. Turn right on CR 80. Turn right on NY 24 to Riverhead, and return on the Long Island Rail Road.

Directions: By train, take the Long Island Rail Road (718-558-3022) to Riverhead.

COVERED BRIDGES RIDE

Location: New York's Dutchess County and Connecticut's Litchfield Hills, 75 miles north of Manhhattan

Length: 54 miles

Difficulty: Moderate to strenuous, with rolling hills and a few lengthy climbs

Heads up: Villager Restaurant (Main Street, Kent, 860-927-3945); Stosh's Ice Cream (US 7, Kent Station Square, Kent, 806-927-4495)

Maps and resources: Hagstrom maps of Dutchess and Litchfield Counties. The Bikesmith bike shop (860-927-1330) is at 338 Kent-Cornwall Road (US 7) in Kent, CT.

Description: Somewhere north of Chappaqua, the suburban hubbub fades into rolling agrarian splendor. The country roads in Dutchess County, New York, and Litchfield County, Connecticut, carry you past fields of corn and sunflowers, working dairy farms, and authentic town greens. True, some of the perfection is a bit self-conscious, New York weekenders having swept in with their thick wallets. But the shady lanes still pass through colonial-looking villages that are apt to have, say, a covered bridge. This ride features two covered bridges, actually—the only two passable ones in Connecticut, both of them historic beauties that span the Housatonic River. (See "White Water," page 199.)

The bulk of the trip is on US 7 in Connecticut, a scenic road that apes the Housatonic's course. The Appalachian Trail follows the river from Bulls Bridge into Cornwall, too, though it's mostly in the woods. Highlights include Kent Falls State Park, which features not one waterfall but a series of falls that tumble 200 feet. It's a good spot to wade in and dunk your head. In Cornwall the Berkshires begin flexing their muscles, but the river valley saves you from climbing. Farther north, you'll pass Lime Rock, the famed

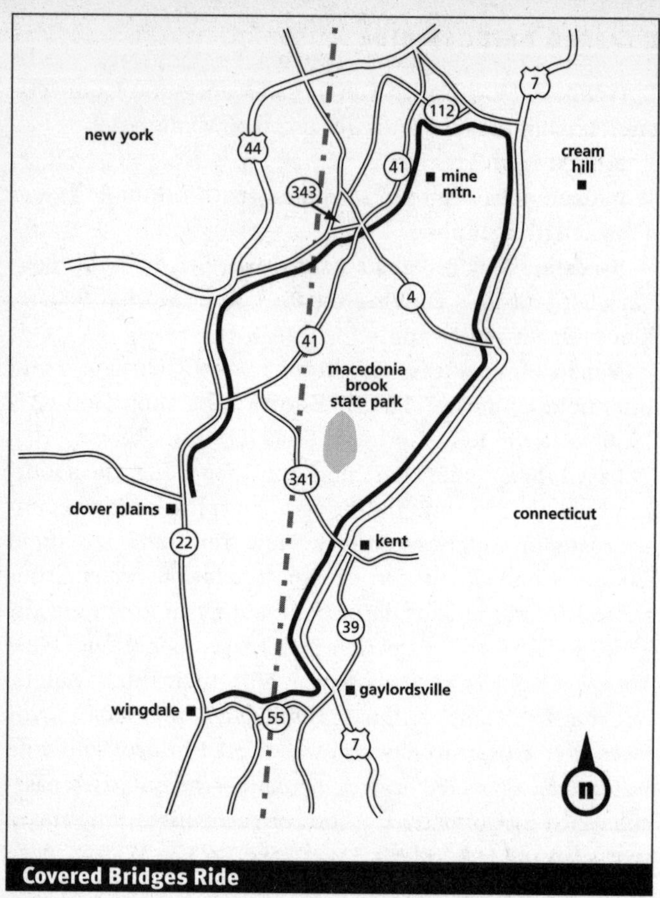

Covered Bridges Ride

racetrack where Connecticut resident Paul Newman burned rubber. The hills increase as you head west back into New York, but it's just too beautiful to complain.

Route: From the station, turn left (north) onto NY 22/55. Stay on NY 55 east when NY 22 splits off. Turn left on Dog Tail Corners Road. Cross into Connecticut, and in Bulls Bridge turn left on US 7 north. Ride through West Cornwall and turn left on CT 112 west. Turn left on CT 41 south. In

Sharon, take CT 343 west to Amenia. Turn left on NY 22-343 south to Dover Plains. To get to the train station, turn left onto Main Street, then left onto Railroad Avenue. The station is on the left.

Directions: By train, take Metro-North to Harlem Valley–Wingdale. Return from Metro-North station at Dover Plains.

By car, take the Taconic State Parkway to NY 55 east. Turn left on NY 21 to Wingdale. To return to your car, take Metro-North south from Dover Plains to Harlem Valley–Wingdale.

THE JERSEY SHORE

Location: Highlands to Island Beach State Park, New Jersey

Length: 62 miles or less, depending on how far into Island Beach State Park you ride. Shorter option: 40 miles or less, depending on how far you ride into Island Beach.

Difficulty: Flat and easy, especially in the off-season when traffic slows to a trickle

Heads up: Keep on Eatin' Clam Bar (1600 Ocean Avenue, Belmar, 908-681-6300) is a classic clam shack; bring your own brewskis. Mueller's Bakery (80 Bridge Avenue, Bay Head, 732-892-0442) has great sweets. Or try the Bay Head Gourmet Deli (82 Bridge Avenue, Bay Head, 732-892-4664).

Maps and resources: Tyres Bicycles in Seaside Park (732-830-2050); Hagstrom map of Monmouth County; Bruce Springsteen's *Greetings From Asbury Park, N.J.* and *The Wild, The Innocent and the E Street Shuffle.*

Description: Bruce Springsteen's songs about fortune-tellers, boardwalks, and dusty arcades still echo around the weather-beaten towns of the northern Jersey Shore. Truth be told, this isn't the most idyllic ride in this chapter, but

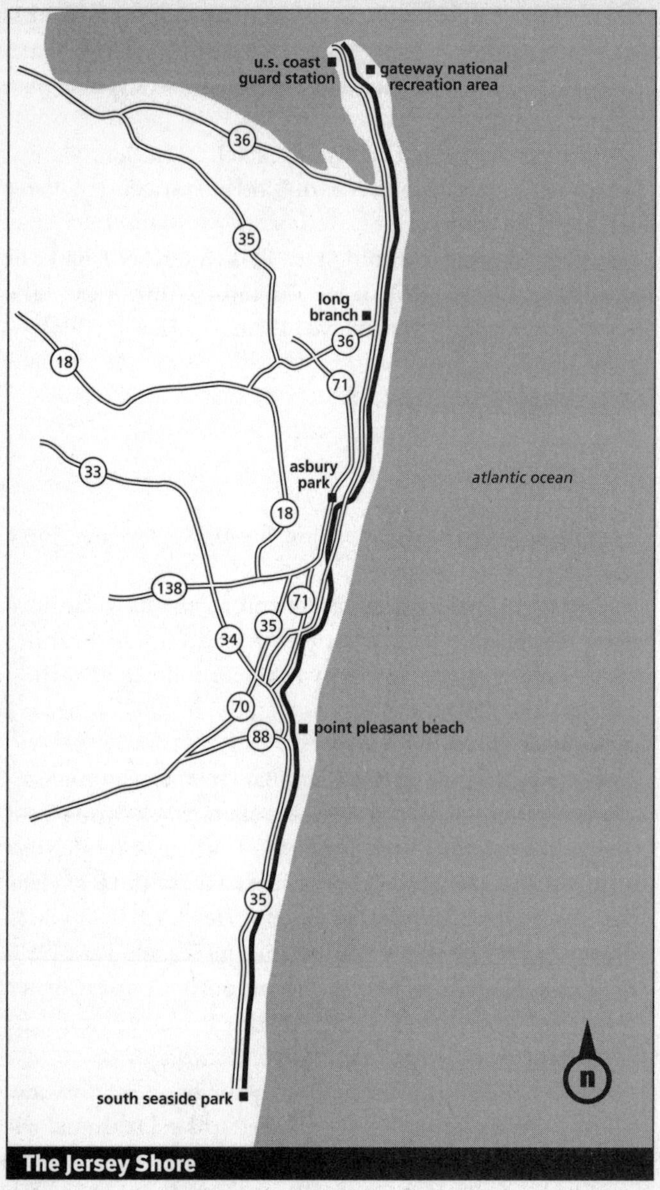
u.s. coast guard station
gateway national recreation area
36
35
long branch
36
18
71
33
asbury park
atlantic ocean
18
138
71
35
34
70
88
point pleasant beach
35
n
south seaside park
The Jersey Shore

it's pure Americana, alternately seedy and scenic, pristine and shopworn.

You'll ride through kitschy amusement-park towns such as Point Pleasant Beach and Seaside Heights, all buzzing neon, honky-tonk carnival rides, and greasy food. But there's also genuine nature. Barnegat Peninsula is a narrow, 22-mile-long strip of land separating the Atlantic Ocean from Barnegat Bay; its pretty towns include Bay Head, the Nantucket of the Jersey Shore. And at the ride's southern terminus is Island Beach State Park (732-793-0506), a pencil-thin, nearly 10-mile-long barrier peninsula. The park is everything the resort towns aren't. It has a 3,000-acre wildlife preserve, nature trails in its northern half, and 6 miles or so of largely uninhabited beach with the Atlantic on one side and a bayside marsh on the other. Consider starting your ride by exploring Sandy Hook; its dune-humped beaches stretch for 7 miles northward to New York, drawing legions of sunbathers and surfers in summer and bird-watchers and beachcombers in the off-seasons.

This is a mix-and-match ride. You can shorten it at any stage by using the shoreline New Jersey Transit train. Traffic makes summer a grueling time to do this ride. If you can't resist midsummer's pull, try to go midweek. And don't let colder weather deter you from this beach ride; during one late-fall trip to Asbury Park, a friend and I ran into a company shooting a Robert DeNiro film on the dilapidated beachfront boardwalk and arcades.

Route: Ocean Avenue takes you along the shore most of the way south, with a few minor detours. In Asbury Park, Wesley Lake interrupts the main drag; bear right on Lake Avenue, turn left on Main Street, left on Evergreen, and right back onto Ocean. South of the town of Spring Lake, after you cross Wreck Pond, turn right on Chicago Boulevard and left on Manasquan Turnpike, which will take you over the Manasquan River to Point Pleasant Beach. Follow

NJ 35 along the barrier island until the road ends in Island Beach State Park.

To return to New York, ride back on NJ 35 to Bay Head. Take a left on Osbourne Avenue for the Bay Head train station.Take New Jersey Transit (973-762-5100) to Penn Station. Conover's Bay Head Inn (646 Main Avenue, Bay Head, 732-892-4664) is an option if you want to crash.

Directions: By ferry, take New York Waterways (800-533-3779) to Sandy Hook during the summer only. Seastreak (800-262-8743) and the New York Fast Ferry (800 693-6933) provide daily service from Manhattan to Highlands.

THE FINGER LAKES

Location: Ithaca, New York, 225 miles northwest of Manhattan

Length: 92 miles

Difficulty: Moderate to strenuous, with some substantial climbs and descents

Heads up: Pack some PowerBars and peanut butter for the ride; there are long stretches between towns.

Resources: Finger Lakes Cycling Club (www.flcycling.org); The Bike Rack (414 College Avenue, Ithaca, 607-272-1010)

Description: This 2- or 3-day journey through a countryside that feels both remote and homey delivers miles of lakeshore riding. My girlfriend and I take swimming breaks at the parks, stop at the vineyards to pick up a bottle for the night's campfire, and buy tomatoes and fresh vegetables at roadside stands. This route focuses on our favorite lake, Cayuga, which at just more than 38 miles long is the longest of the five major Finger Lakes. The road nuzzles the

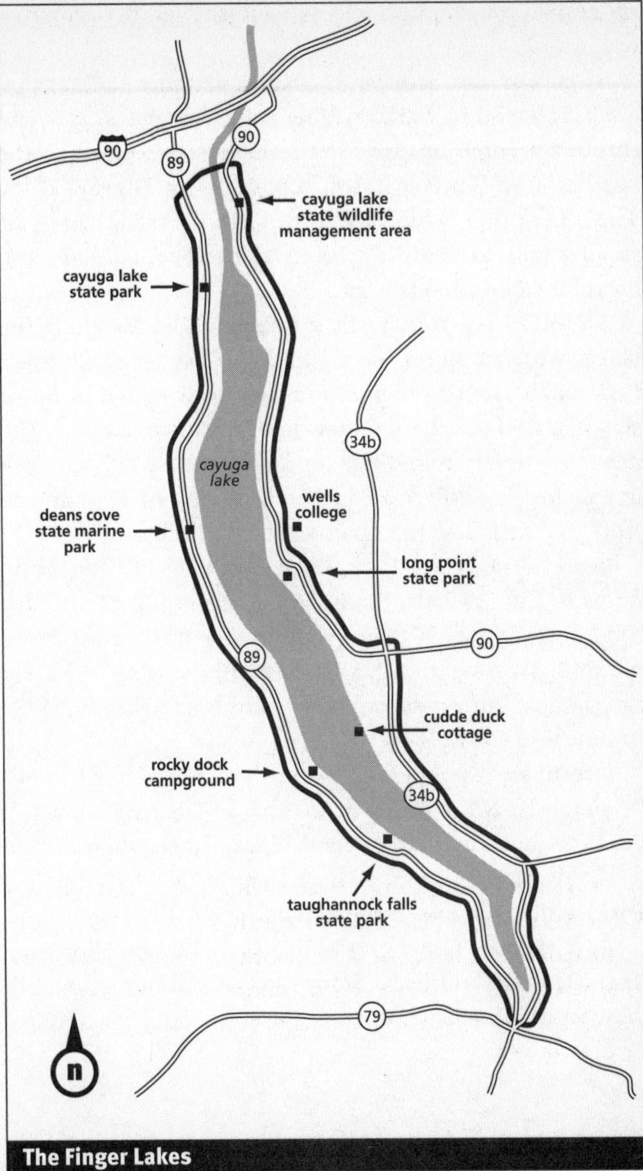

The Finger Lakes

shore, and the shoulder seems wide enough to accommodate a 747.

This is upstate writ large. Make a detour into Taughannock Falls State Park, where water cascades 215 feet through a gorge, making it the highest waterfall in the northeastern United States, topping even Niagara Falls. The hiking trail, which winds beneath overhangs and past smaller falls, is worth the effort alone. The lakes are also great for sailing and fishing.

The first day, ride north for about 34 miles along the lake's western shore from Ithaca to Cayuga Lake State Park. Grab a bottle of wine, and stop to swim and camp (or stay in one of the chain motels in nearby Seneca Falls). The next day, pedal around the top of the lake and head back down, logging either a long 58-mile day or stopping in Aurora, a little less than halfway back to Ithaca.

Route: From Cass Park, head north on NY 89 for 34 miles to Cayuga Lake State Park. Continuing north, turn right on NY 5/US 20. Turn right on NY 90. Turn right on NY 34B. Turn right on NY 34 in South Lansing and pedal into Ithaca. Turn right on NY 96 and bear right on NY 89 to return to Cass Park.

Directions: By car, take I-87 north to NY 17 west to NY 96 north to NY 96B north to Ithaca. Turn right on NY 96/13/34 and turn left several blocks later when NY 96 splits off the other routes. Bear right on NY 89 into Cass Park, which is a good starting point.

By bus, take Greyhound (800-231-2222) or ShortLine (800-631-8405) to Ithaca. From the bus station, follow NY 96 west to NY 89.

Where to Connect

Clubs and Organizations

- The New York Cycle Club (212-828-5711, www.nycc.org) runs weekly rides, weekend trips, training programs, and special events for novice and experienced cyclists.
- Transportation Alternatives (115 West 30th Street, Suite 1207, Manhattan, 212-629-8080, www.transalt.org) is an advocate for cyclists, pedestrians, and "sensible transportation."
- Time's Up (212-802-8222, www.times-up.org) is a nonprofit, volunteer-run environmental group; it runs monthly events including Critical Mass and "green" bike tours of places such as lower Manhattan and the South Bronx.
- The Five Boro Bicycle Club (891 Amsterdam Avenue, Manhattan, 212-932-2300, www.5bbc.org) organizes day-rides, weekend trips, and other special events.
- The Century Road Club Association (212-222-8062, www.crca.net) is the country's largest bicycle racing club.
- The Staten Island Bicycling Association (718-815-9290, www.sibike.org) organizes rides for cyclists of all skill levels.
- Westchester Cycle Club (888-245-3436, www.westchestercycleclub.org) is a recreational club that organizes rides to various destinations.

Shops

- Bicycle Habitat (244 Lafayette Street, Manhattan, 212-431-3846, www.bicyclehabitat.com) is among the city's best bike shops; they're knowledgeable, friendly, and can fix damn near anything—no small feat given what New York streets can do to your rims.

- City Bicycles (508 Ninth Avenue, between 38th and 39th Streets, Manhattan, 212-563-3373)
- Sid's Bike Shop (235 East 34th Street, between Second and Third Avenues, Manhattan, 212-213-8360)
- Midtown Bicycles (360 West 47th Street, between Eighth and Ninth Avenues, Manhattan, 212-581-4500)
- Bicycle Renaissance (430 Columbus Avenue, between 80th and 81st Streets, Manhattan, 212-362-3388)
- Larry's Cycle Shop (1854 Flatbush Avenue, Brooklyn, 718-377-3600)
- Castle Hill Bicycle Center (1010 Castle Hill Avenue, the Bronx, 718- 597-2083)
- Bicycle Place (45-70 Kissena Boulevard, Flushing, Queens, 718-358-0986)
- Bennett's Bicycles (517 Jewett Avenue, Staten Island, 718-447-8652)

Bike Rentals

Rental shops, which offer locks and helmets (usually for a small additional fee) with the bikes, are sprinkled throughout the city. A few options:

- Pedal Pushers (1306 Second Avenue, Manhattan, 212-288-5592)
- New York Rent-A-Car (146 West 83rd Street, Manhattan, 212-579-0119)
- Metro Bicycle (360 West 47th Street, Manhattan, 212-581-4500, and six other locations)
- Gotham Bikes (112 West Broadway, Manhattan, 212-732-2453)

- New York Rent A Bike (19 East 12th Street, Manhattan, 212-799-1100)
- Open Road Cycles, Inc. (256 Flatbush Avenue, Brooklyn, 718-857-8557)

Events

- NYC Century Bike Tour (212-629-8080, www.NYCCenturyBikeTour.com) features rides of 35, 50, 75, or 100 miles; they are held annually in late summer.
- Bike New York: The Great Five Borough Bike Tour (212-932-0778, www.bikenewyork.org) is one of the city's biggest sporting events, drawing about 30,000 people. That's an awful lot of Lycra; be prepared to wait more than an hour just to get to the starting point in Central Park. But the 42-mile ride is the quintessential tour of Gotham.
- The Tour de Bronx (718-590-2766, www.tourdebronx.org) is an annual free ride that includes 25- and 40-mile rides.
- The Bakery Bike Ride (212-828-5711) covers 40 miles of sugar highs, stopping in canoli shops in Little Italy in the Bronx and French bakeries in Queens.
- The Montauk Century Ride (212-932-2300, ext. 139; www.5bbc.org) runs all the way from the city to the tip of Long Island, cutting through the clog of Nassau County out into the vineyards, the oh-so-charming Hamptons, and, finally, the crashing surf of Montauk. If you can't handle the 130-mile haul, there are shorter routes of 100 and 62 miles.

Books and Maps

- Angelillo, Phil. *Short Bike Rides on Long Island.* 5th ed., Guilford, CT: Globe Pequot Press, 1998.

- Perls, Jeffrey. *Paths Along the Hudson: A Guide to Walking and Biking.* New Brunswick, NJ: Rutgers University Press, 1999.
- Walters, Sally. *30 Bicycle Tours in the Finger Lakes Region.* Woodstock, VT: Countryman Press, 1998.

Mountain Biking

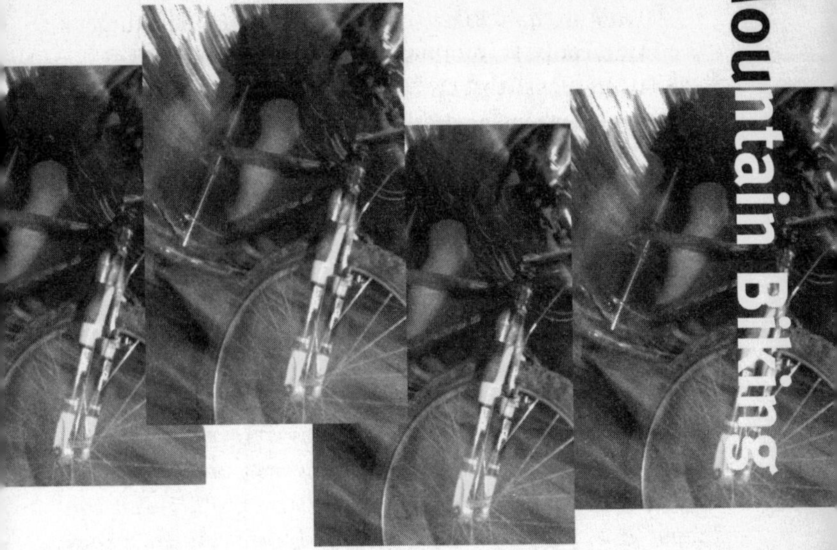

THIS BEING AN authentic guidebook, there's a lot we *can't* say about mountain biking in New York City. Officially, there is no mountain biking in New York City. It's banned on every unpaved path, trail, lawn, forest, and garden within city limits.

So we can't report on the park trails that don't get much use by hikers. You know, those hikers who would be under siege by marauding mountain bikes, if mountain biking were legal. Which, of course, it isn't.

And we certainly can't tell you that several of those same parks—Alley Pond Park in Queens, the Staten Island Greenbelt, and Floyd Bennett Field in Brooklyn, among others—seem to have a "don't

ask, don't tell" arrangement in which bikers quietly use trails, and park officials tacitly approve by not enforcing the rules. Far be it from us to report such a thing.

We *can* report that in 2002, fat-wheel aficionados have more trail options at destinations closer to the city than ever. There's plenty of molar-rattling singletrack just beyond the fringes, some of it freshly built. Westchester County and New Jersey both tout impressive networks of twisting, lunging trails laden with enough boulders, roots, and logs for even the most daring mountain goat. Long Island and Connecticut sites add to the profusion of options.

About the city ban: Officials apparently believe that mountain bikers are bug-eyed fanatics who've been lobotomized by adrenaline. The bikers I've met are thoughtful, friendly, and articulate enough to pass on trail information about great places you're not allowed to go riding. Or they *would* share the information if they'd gone themselves, which of course they haven't. The sport is, after all, illegal.

The city does plan to create mountain-biking trails, by the way, on what is now a toxic waste dump near Jamaica Bay. The landfill will be capped with plastic and soil, and trees will be planted. As soon as the trees grow, the site will be open to mountain bikers. It could be a gorgeous spot, but the conspiracy theorists among us wonder.

Go conquer the trails described here. And if you want to make the city more bike-friendly, contact the cycling activists at Time's Up (212-802-8222, www.times-up.org) and find out how to support them. But you didn't hear that from us.

Central Park by Moonlight

IF YOU READ this chapter's introduction, you're thinking, But offroad riding in Central Park is illegal. Exactly. Time's Up intends this monthly offroad jaunt around Central Park to be liberating, entertaining, and subversive. There's a great big world beyond the loop road, and this ride covers all sorts of interesting little corners of it. You'll circle various lakes, criss-cross footbridges and bridle paths, and tear up to Belvedere Castle. My favorite ride is the Halloween edition, when various wigged and masked riders startle the few remaining lingerers who haven't been chased out of the park.

The free ride takes place the first Friday of every month.

Short Hops

Westchester County, New York

For my money, some of the best mountain biking in the Northeast is just north of the city on Westchester's well-organized, well-maintained, county-supported trails. Go figure. The parks also have the support of the Westchester Mountain Biking Association (WMBA), a club that should be the envy of any city-bound biker. The group leads weekly rides, works in cooperation with the county government, and posts color-coded maps on its Web site, www.wmba.org.

SPRAIN RIDGE PARK

Location: Yonkers, 16 miles north of Manhattan

Length: Just under 5 miles

Physical difficulty: Moderate to strenuous

Technical difficulty: 2 to 4 helmets

Terrain: Challenging, technical singletrack with lots of logs, obstacles, rocks, climbs, and hairpin turns. The beginner trails are mellower, with lots of turns but few climbs.

Maps: WMBA Web site or at the park (914-478-2300)

Description: This park is a revelation: Just over 10 miles north of the Bronx, Sprain Ridge has a new network of trails (as of June 2000) that are as challenging as anything you'll find in the area. I rode it before the trail map existed, when the trail had seen so little traffic that a slick carpet of oak leaves covered the singletrack. The blazes are painted on trees so skinny it's hard to follow the route. (David DeLucia of the Westchester parks department, who designed the trail, inadvertently led two separate groups off the trail during rides that first year.)

Sprain Ridge has far too much going for it to stay a secret for long. The narrow trails seem designed to both vex and thrill. They cling to the crumbling flanks of ridges, contort around roller-coaster turns, and fall away to Wile E. Coyote drops. Unfortunately, the grunts of downshifting trucks and the persistent whoosh of traffic from the neighboring Sprain Brook Parkway accompany your efforts, but it's a small price to pay.

Route: The trail begins with a 4-foot climb at about a 70-degree incline at the corner of the lot near the access road. That sets the tone for the steep and rocky terrain, featuring some of the best singletrack around. The main trail here is fairly hellacious; as you wind around, you'll climb up from a basin along a loose, exposed ridge face, with a number of hard turns on the way. The trail loops around to the far corner of the parking lot, where you can follow a dead-end spur to an overlook. If you're not ready to bail out there, the trail continues around behind the park's swimming pool to a dirt road leading into the southern part of Sprain Ridge.

Directions: By train, take Metro-North to Scarsdale. From the station, turn right (west) on Popham Road. After a few hundred yards, dogleg right onto Ardsley Road. (You'll still be going west.) Turn left on Fort Hill Road. Turn right on Jackson Avenue. The park entrance is down the hill on the left. To get to intermediate and advanced trails, follow the driveway past the administration buildings and curl around the parking lot to the far left corner. A second entrance is at the far opposite corner of the parking area. To get to the beginner trails, go straight at the top of the hill (don't veer left toward the administration building) to the picnic area.

By car, take the Sprain Brook Parkway north to the Jackson Avenue exit; turn left off the ramp and drive 0.5 mile; the park entrance is on the left. See above for park directions.

Trail Wars

I HAD A FEELING something wasn't right. My girlfriend and I were circling the woods of Van Cortlandt Park on our bikes, looking for the start of the Old Croton Aqueduct Trailway. There was no sign of it—no sign of anything, in fact. The only people we encountered were four kids on bikes who'd never heard of the trail. Out on the street, a city cop had given us vague directions. I was baffled. I hadn't heard yet about the citywide ban on mountain biking, and I'd read that the aqueduct trail was open to bikes all the way down to this point, its southernmost section in the Bronx.

Finally, we got our answer: The trail was indeed open only to bikers once they left the city limits. It was an expensive lesson. Before long we bumbled into a park ranger who hit us with $50 fines for riding on the trails. There wasn't a single sign that noted the bike prohibition—or a single hiker to tip us off—even on a perfect Saturday afternoon in summertime.

Admittedly, mountain biking shouldn't be allowed everywhere. Fat tires can erode trails and endanger others. Trail-use conflicts are rampant around the country. But the New York City ban is also about fear. Kathleen Nutt, administrator of the Greenbelt Conservancy on Staten Island, said her park considered opening underused sections of the park to mountain bikers. Park officials decided against it, for fear the trails would be overrun.

An unwillingness to share is another core issue. "Possession of land is a very primal thing," says Dave Lutz, executive director of the Neighborhood Open Space Coalition and a longtime bicycle advocate. "Other advocacy groups think the land is theirs, and absolutely will not tolerate sharing it." Lutz has responded by developing greenways. An alternative-transportation group, Time's Up, stages noisy monthly protests to the city's unfriendly biking climate—and in the process has developed an antagonistic relationship with the city. The first time I talked to a high-ranking Time's Up official, the conversation was something out of *The Spy Who Came in from the Cold.* He suspected I was an undercover lackey for then-mayor Rudy Giuliani. "Of the biking groups out there," he later explained, "ours is the most political."

The bike ban on unpaved trails is exasperating for cyclists who crave pine needles and tree canopies as an antidote to diesel fumes. The frustration mounts when outlying city parks go to seed, or are largely unused, or are appropriated for golf courses. Bikers can settle for the greenways, which are wonderful, or they can organize and lobby for more. Boating groups creating waterfront access have proved that change is possible. Community gardeners have beaten back the city's threats to demolish their gardens. Whither bicyclists? Dave Lutz has a theory: "Not knowing how good it can be," Lutz says, "they don't know how to fight to make it better."

BLUE MOUNTAIN RESERVATION

Location: Peekskill, New York, 45 miles north of Manhattan

Length: 7 miles of trails, with several more "off the map" miles

Physical difficulty: Easy to strenuous

Technical difficulty: 1 to 4 helmets

Terrain: Ranges from wide, flat trails to highly technical singletrack laden with rock drops, roots, branches, and harsh climbs

Maps and information: WMBA Web site or (914) 737-2194

Description: If you can't find something engaging in this 1,600-acre, one-size-fits-all park, you better just go home and take up Yahtzee. It's no wonder Blue Mountain has a reputation for crowds on weekends; trails range from wide-as-an-interstate beginner stuff to freaky, hard-core expert rides. How taxing does it get? The climbs on Ned's Left Lung had me gasping and, at one point, walking. And 2 Crew Live and Yin Yang have some ferocious conditions along their switchbacks and drops. Mount Spitzenberg, at 540 feet, is a short but technical climb.

Then there's the notorious Y2K trail. In an online trail review, one rider advised would-be riders to bring extra tubes and patch kits. Another wrote: "There was one drop-off that just haunts me. I would drive back there just to see someone clean this. If you know what I'm talking about and want to show off, we'll be your audience!"

Route: Riders used to need orienteering skills to find their way around and out. But in 2000 the county began using blazes and numbered trail markers. Trails are designated for beginner (yellow), intermediate (orange), intermediate/advanced (blue), and advanced bikers (white, purple, and red, though some of the unmarked spur trails offer the real ferocious stuff). But even so the trail markers can still

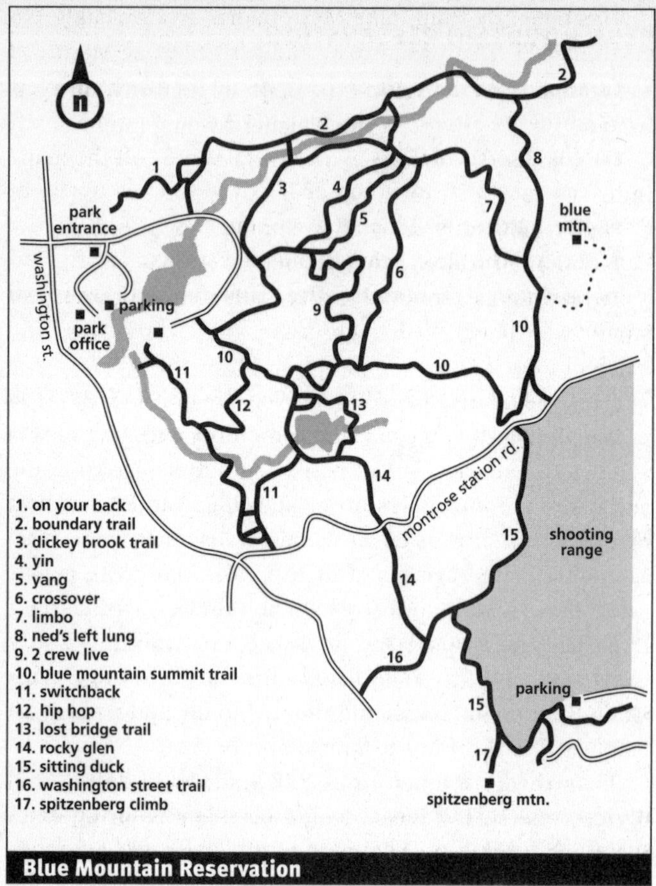

Blue Mountain Reservation

be confusing because of overlapping blazes, and some trails also have names. A full-color map, complete with trail names, can be downloaded from the Westchester Mountain Biking Association Web site (www.wmba.org/bluemt.html). Trail maps are available at the park, though they're hard to follow and not color-coded. I tracked my whereabouts by checking the trail marker numbers against the corresponding numbers on the map.

Directions: By train, take Metro-North to Cortlandt. Go north on NY 9A to Montrose, and turn right at Montrose Station Road. At the start of the seasonal highway, turn left on Washington Street. At the Welcher Avenue intersection, turn right into the park.

By car, take I-87 north to I-287; exit onto US 9 north. In Peekskill, exit at Welcher Avenue; turn right and follow Welcher into the park. Bear left past the entrance booth and follow the access road to the end. There's a parking fee in summer.

GRAHAM HILLS PARK

Location: Mount Pleasant, New York, 30 miles north of Manhattan

Length: 5.7 miles

Physical difficulty: Moderate to strenuous

Technical difficulty: 1 to 3 helmets

Terrain: Hard-packed dirt trails, mostly singletrack, with sporadic rocks and logs and some low-hanging branches

Maps: See the WMBA Web site, www.wmba,org.

Description: This little 431-acre park is like fast food—it's right off the highway and easy to swallow, but it doesn't sustain you for long. There are some challenges here, but mostly it's so-so stuff, with well-worn, fairly easy trails that allow you to sail through maple woods along a crisscrossing network of old stone walls. Its easy access and relatively small number of challenging spots make it ideal for beginners and intermediates looking to build their skills. And some of the trails are fun when you just want to tear-ass through the woods without knocking your rims out of true. Another asset: Graham Hills is for mountain bikers only, so you don't have to worry about hiker encounters.

The drawbacks? The trails have a tendency to link up

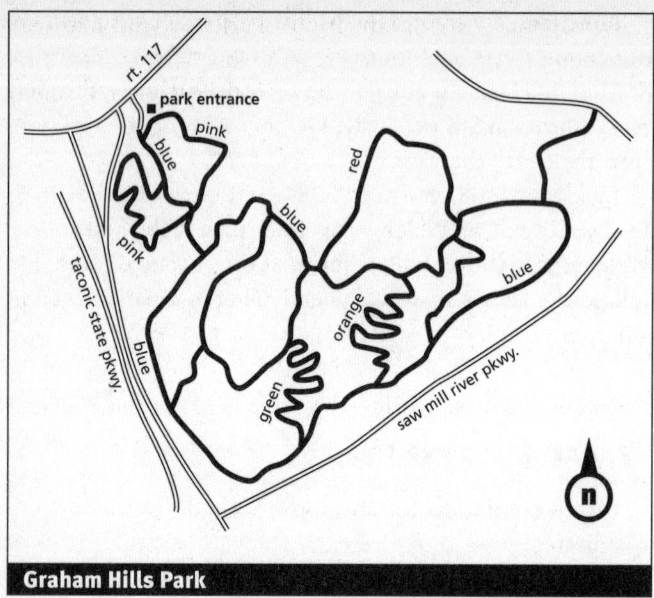

Graham Hills Park

near the top of the ridge, so you may find yourself repeating similar climbs. And the park is often packed with riders on weekends.

Route: The color-coded, looping trails (with markers that sometimes disappear) give no indication as to difficulty. For a trail with a little bite, bear right coming over the Eagle Scout footbridge onto the orange-blazed trail; it starts out narrow and fast, then gradually gets more root- and rock-covered. Ride along the fence and follow the pink blazes as the trail snakes up a steep ridge. It follows the ridgeline for a while, then plummets back to the valley floor. Follow the blue-and-yellow-blazed trail if you just feel like bombing through the woods.

Directions: By train, take Metro-North to Pleasantville. Go left from the station on Manville Street and continue to a stop sign. Turn right on NY 117; the park is on the left.

By car, take the Sprain Brook Parkway (the highway becomes the Taconic State Parkway just as you're exiting) north to the exit for NY 117. Turn right; the park is about 100 yards down on the right.

New Jersey

CHIMNEY ROCK PARK

Location: Martinsville, New Jersey, 41 miles west of Manhattan

Length: About 20 miles

Physical difficulty: Moderate to strenuous

Technical difficulty: 3 helmets

Terrain: You name it: singletrack, extremely rocky, lots of tree-fall, mud, and water holes on a mostly hard-packed trail.

Heads up: Reward yourself after the ride with a chocolate éclair at Valley Bakery on SR 525 in the center of Martinsville.

Maps and information: Call the park at (908) 722-1200.

Description: This 687-acre park, nestled between the first and second peaks in the Watchung Mountains, features a 20-mile honeycomb of trails in a pine and hemlock forest. You should know that the trails run along and through streams that spill into marshes and a 21-acre reservoir, so the terrain tends to get soupy. But the myriad obstacles and exceptionally rock-strewn runs make Chimney Rock a hotbed for fat-tire fanatics. They're a personable bunch; I've encountered riders willing to stop and share local insights even on unseasonably cold days.

One engaging trail hugs the edge of the reservoir; I spotted a red-headed woodpecker during a water break. Take some of the spur trails leading away from the reservoir for more switchbacks and obstacles. And for more protracted runs, explore the longer trails across the street from the parking area.

Route: To warm up, cross the street from the parking lot and follow the white-blazed trail (the only marked trail in the park), which is wide and easy for a stretch before getting increasingly rocky and technical. To loop back around after a mile or so, turn left shortly before the footbridge; the trail features a teeth-chattering series of bumps followed by a short stretch of engagingly technical singletrack. The trail eventually loops back to the white blazes. The trails connected to the parking lot are wet and rocky and unmarked, but the park is small enough that getting lost is not a concern. If you're willing to mix in some street riding, follow the reservoir trail from the back of the parking lot for about 3 miles. It spills out into the in-town portion of Chimney Rock Park, where there's a little baseball diamond and parking area.

Directions: By train, take the New Jersey Transit to Bernardsville. Follow SR 525 (Martinsville Road) to Martinsville—about 8 miles. Turn right onto CR 620, then left onto Newmans Lane. The parking lot is 0.7 mile down on the left.

By car, take the New Jersey Turnpike to I-78 west; take exit 33 and follow SR 525 (Martinsville Road) south toward Martinsville. Turn right onto CR 620, then left onto Newmans Lane. The parking lot is 0.7 mile down on the left.

Hitching A Ride

New York City has trains that are liberal about allowing bikes on board. City cyclists can even get their wheels on some buses and ferries headed out of the city. Here's the skinny.

Trains

- On the **subway**, bikes are allowed at all times; riders are asked to use the end-of-train cars. **PATH** subway trains to New Jersey also allow bikes without a permit, though there are restrictions on New York City–bound trains during rush hours.
- **Metro-North** (212-532-4900, www.mta.nyc.ny.us/mnr/html/mnrmap.htm) and **Long Island Rail Road** (LIRR, 718-558-8228) allow riders to bring a bike on with a permit. Pick up the permit at Grand Central Station (for both railroads) or Penn Station (for LIRR); there's a one-time nominal fee. No bikes during rush hours and on some holidays. Limit two bikes per car, eight per train.
- **New Jersey Transit** (973-762-5100, www.njtransit/state.nj.us/bikeperm.htm) gives free bike permits at Penn Station or by phone or Web site. No bikes during rush hours.
- **Amtrak** (800-872-7475, www.amtrak.com) allows bikes for a small fee per ride only if they're boxed and placed in baggage cars. Not all trains have baggage service, but you can put your bike on an earlier train and pick it up when you arrive. The exceptions: The Vermonter and Adirondack trains have roll-on service; no box required. Call for reservations.

Buses

- The **Academy** (212-971-9054) line, serving the Jersey Shore, takes bikes at no charge, as does **Asbury Park** (same number). Call for restrictions.

- **Olympia Trails** (212-964-6233) has no fee; call for details.
- **Bonanza** (212-947-1766) carries bikes for a fee.
- Several bus lines require bikes to be boxed or bagged, and you have to provide the container. They include **Adirondack/Pine Hill Trailways** (800-858-8555), **Martz Trailways** (800-233-8604), and **ShortLine** (800-631-8405).
- On **Peter Pan** (800-343-9999) and **Greyhound**'s northeast corridor route (800-231-2222), there's no fee, but you must take off the front wheel. You may have to box your bike, especially on holidays. On Greyhound's other routes, you'll be charged $15 and must provide your own box (or buy one from them for $10).
- **Hampton Jitney** (800-936-0440) and **Sunrise Coach Lines** (516-477-1200) charge $10 per bike; no box required.
- Several bus companies—including Liberty Lines, Carey Transport, and Red & Tan Lines—do not allow bikes.

Ferries

- The **Staten Island Ferry** (718-815-BOAT), **New York Fast Ferry** (800-NYF-NYFF), and **Harbor Shuttle** (800-254-RIDE) carry bikes at no charge.
- **New York Waterways** (800-533-3779) charges $1; bikes are not allowed on ferries bound for Wall Street and the Port Imperial–Weehawken line.
- **Seastreak** (800-262-8743), which serves Highlands and Atlantic Highlands, New Jersey, and Bay Ridge, Brooklyn, charges $3.

HARTSHORNE WOODS PARK

Location: Middletown, New Jersey, 46 driving miles south of Manhattan

Length: 11 miles of trails, but a few small sections are closed to mountain bikers

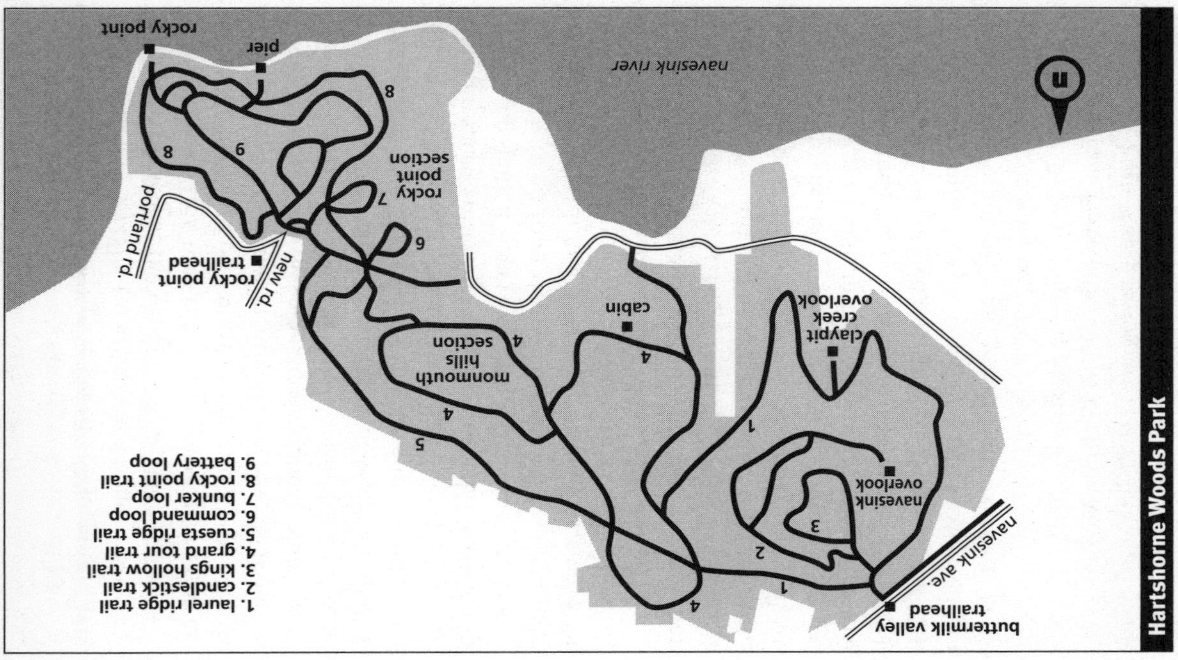
Hartshorne Woods Park
1. laurel ridge trail
2. candlestick trail
3. kings hollow trail
4. grand tour trail
5. cuesta ridge trail
6. command loop
7. bunker loop
8. rocky point trail
9. battery loop
buttermilk valley trailhead
navesink ave.
navesink overlook
claypit creek overlook
cabin
monmouth hills section
rocky point section
rocky point trailhead
new rd.
portland rd.
pier
rocky point
navesink river
n

Physical difficulty: Easy to strenuous

Technical difficulty: 1 to $2^1/2$ helmets

Terrain: Ranges from fire roads to challenging singletrack, with lots of technical ascents and drops

Maps: Available at the park (732-872-0336)

Description: This user-friendly 736-acre park stretches across the highlands on a northeastern nub of Jersey coast, just off the Sandy Hook peninsula and overlooking the Atlantic Ocean. The sight of the prominent bluffs rising over the water bewitched explorers dating back to Henry Hudson in 1609. The present-day park—with its impressive organization and layout—has far more to offer than compelling history. There are trails for all levels, including some advanced stuff that compares favorably with any of Jersey's top spots. The network of obstacles is formidable—the roots here jut from the ground like antlers—and there are hills that test limits of endurance and precision. Even the intermediate runs have plenty of puzzles to solve, sometimes with ridgeline views of the Navesink River.

Route: Intermediates will find plenty to occupy their attention on the Laurel Ridge Trail, a 2.5-mile loop through the park's Buttermilk Valley section. To get there, go to the far right trailhead from the parking lot; you'll face a short, hard climb to the ridge, where most of the ride takes place. There is a surprising number of obstacles during the first section, but then the trail narrows into speedy, freewheeling singletrack. Advanced riders should hit the Grand Tour Trail, which runs an epic 6 miles around a figure-eight design. Some of the hills are grueling and exacting. There are wide fire roads for beginners.

Directions: By ferry, take the Seastreak (800-262-8743) or New York Fast Ferry (800-693-6933) from Manhattan to Highlands. From the parking area, turn left on Bayside Drive. Turn right on Water Witch Drive and almost immediately right on Navesink Avenue. Bear left at the fork, staying on Navesink Avenue. The park is less than a mile down on the left.

By car, take the New Jersey Turnpike to the Garden State Parkway; take exit 117 and follow signs to NJ 36. Drive east to Navesink, and bear right on Valley Drive. After a short distance, bear left after a stone church on Navesink Avenue. The park is 0.5 mile down on the right.

ROUND VALLEY RECREATION AREA

Location: Lebanon, New Jersey, 52 miles west of Manhattan

Length: 9 miles, with an option to ride another 3 to 4 road miles to make a complete loop

Physical difficulty: Moderate to strenuous

Technical difficulty: 2 helmets

Terrain: Wide, hard trail, rocky at times, with steep climbs and drops

Heads up: When you finish, cool off in the sparkling 4,000-acre Round Valley Reservoir and check out the deer grazing nearby. And bring your fishing pole; the reservoir—180 feet deep—is stocked with trophy trout.

Maps and information: Available at the park office (908-236-6355)

Description: Riders who like hard-core singletrack loaded with booby traps can turn the page. This ride is about heart and thighs rather than technical skill. There's only one trail—the 9-mile, multiuse Cushetunk Trail—and heavy traffic over the years has left it wide and relatively worn. But if you fancy hair-raising drops and thigh-frying ascents amid some of the prettiest pine forest and lake scenery around, this is your spot. The massive downhill at the 2-mile mark—a ski-jump-type slope with small wooden steps built in at 3-foot intervals—is daunting. (Climbing it on the

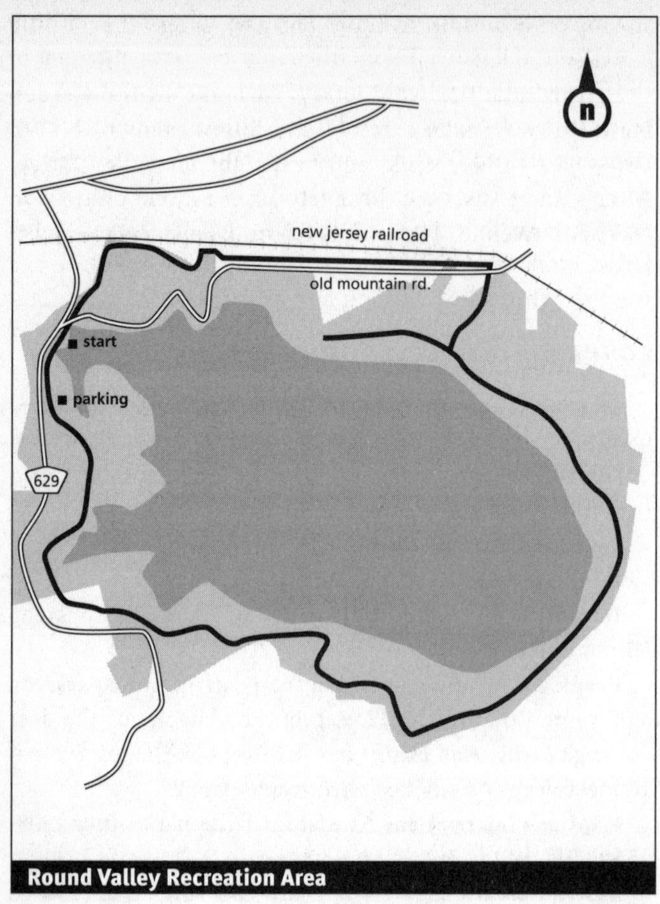

Round Valley Recreation Area

return trip is out of the question unless you're adept at steps.) There's another precipitous slope at mile 7 that will whip you into climbing shape.

Route: Part fire road, part doubletrack, the Cushetunk Trail more or less traces the outline of the Round Valley Reservoir; the trail connects hikers, bikers, and horseback riders to 85 wilderness campsites (see "Camping," page 360). If you finish the trail and are too gassed to ride back the same way, nearby paved roads can take you back in a fraction of the time: Take either spur trail near the end of the Cushetunk to Old Mountain Road. Turn left; when you reach Lebanon-Stanton Road (CR 629), you can either turn right and go into Lebanon for some Gatorade or turn left to complete the 13-mile loop.

Directions: By train, take the New Jersey Transit to Far Hills. From there it's about a 10-mile ride. Take SR 523 west to Whitehouse Station and pick up US 22 west. Follow signs into the park. Turn right after passing the visitors center. The trail begins at the boat ramp parking lot.

By car, take the New Jersey Turnpike to I-78 west. Take exit 20A to US 22 and follow the signs. Turn right after passing the visitors center. The trail begins at the boat ramp parking lot.

Long Island

STILLWELL WOODS PRESERVE

Location: Woodbury, Long Island, 32 miles east of Manhattan

Length: 4-mile singletrack loop with various spur trails

Physical difficulty: Moderate to strenuous

Technical difficulty: $2^1/2$ helmets

Terrain: It ranges from hard-packed singletrack to loose, sandy fire road. There are gullies and obstacles in some parts; other parts are wide open.

Heads up: After your ride, feast on a monster knish at Ben's Deli (516-496-4236), just off South Woods Road on Jericho Turnpike.

Description: This park has some peculiar challenges. Muddy trails often have closed signs, and eroded sections of trails are fenced or taped off. (Who obeys the signs is another question; I found the tape at one such barricade snipped.) The barriers are a testament, perhaps, to the popularity of the place, and not just with mountain bikers. Hikers and horseback riders also tromp these trails, the latter leaving the sort of obstacles you'd rather avoid.

Stillwell has plenty of decent singletrack to whip around amid dense, brushy, piney woods, if you can locate the trails around all the roadblocks. The main feature is a 4-mile, twisting, singletrack loop that provides some excellent technical riding. The thing is, it's one-way; if you come in from the wrong direction, a sign will admonish you to turn around.

Route: To get to the loop, ride under the train tracks and turn left. The loop is a lengthy run of moderate singletrack. For more hills, turn right at the first signpost and bear left where the trail splits. When you reach the fire road, look to your right. There are a couple of ski-jump-type ramps, and some of the dirt is fairly loose, so buckle in tight. There's more singletrack around there that's windy but relatively easy.

Directions: By train, take the Long Island Rail Road to Syosset. From the station, ride east on Cold Spring Road (toward the CVS pharmacy and firehouse). When the road forks, bear left. At South Woods Road turn right; the park is on the left.

By car, take the Long Island Expressway to exit 44N; follow NY 135 (Seaford Oyster-Bay Parkway) to Jericho Turnpike, and turn left. Turn left onto South Woods Road. The park is just over a mile down on the right; drive through the parking lot past the ball fields to get to the trailhead.

Information: Concerned Long Island Mountain Bikers (CLIMB, 516-271-6527, www.climbonline.org); Bicycle Planet (540 Jericho Turnpike, Syosset, 516-364-4434, www.thebicycleplanet.com)

BETHPAGE STATE PARK

Location: Farmingdale, Long Island, 36 miles east of Manhattan

Length: 4-mile "official" trail, with many more miles of interspersed singletrack

Physical difficulty: Easy

Technical difficulty: 1 1/2 helmets

Terrain: Soft, winding, almost obstacle-free singletrack and fire roads

Description: On my first visit here, I spent a lot of time trying to understand the map and figure out how to follow the white blazes marking the 4-mile mountain-biking loop so as to avoid hikers. After about 50 yards, I was confused. So I blasted off down a singletrack spur, and when I encountered another rider, I asked what was up. "I've been coming here for two years," she said, "and I still haven't figured it out." She described giving another rider directions to the parking lot, then coming across that same person—still lost—an hour later.

All you need to know about Bethpage is this: You can go essentially anywhere you want if you watch out for the weekend hikers. There are serpentine singletrack trails snaking all over the woods, and they are relatively free of speed bumps, so this is an ideal place for beginners. Forget the technical stuff; come here when you feel like running heats in the Indy 500. There are a few hills and gullies—I came across a guy jumping in one spot—but mostly you just wait for the checkered flag and deck it. Another plus: The park is very close to the train station.

Route: Enter from the picnic area parking lot and choose from the vast honeycomb of trails. You will probably get lost. Fear not: If you don't cross a paved road, you will eventually return to the parking lot. Try not to buzz by hikers at 25 mph. Generally they stay on the wide trails and are far fewer in number during the week.

Directions: By train, take the Long Island Rail Road to Bethpage. Take Central Avenue east and follow the signs into the park. Ride to the road's end at the picnic area parking lot; trails begin at opposite ends of the lot.

By car, take the Long Island Expressway to exit 44S; follow NY 135 (Seaford Oyster-Bay Parkway) to the Powell Avenue/Bethpage exit. Turn left off the ramp and left into the park. See above.

Information: Concerned Long Island Mountain Bikers (CLIMB, 516-271-6527, www.climbonline.org); park office (516-249-0701)

Connecticut

MIANUS RIVER STATE PARK

Location: Stamford, Connecticut, 37 miles northeast of Manhattan

Length: About 6 to 8 miles

Physical difficulty: Easy to moderate

Technical difficulty: 2 helmets

Terrain: Fire roads and winding singletrack with some rocks, roots, and log obstacles

Maps: Available from the Stamford Parks and Recreation Department (203-977-4641)

Description: This park is sort of a moving target. It straddles the border of Greenwich and Stamford, and as of this writing mountain biking reportedly is permitted only on the Stamford side. Silly, right? I know that plenty of bikers use the Greenwich parking lot. I also know that, practically

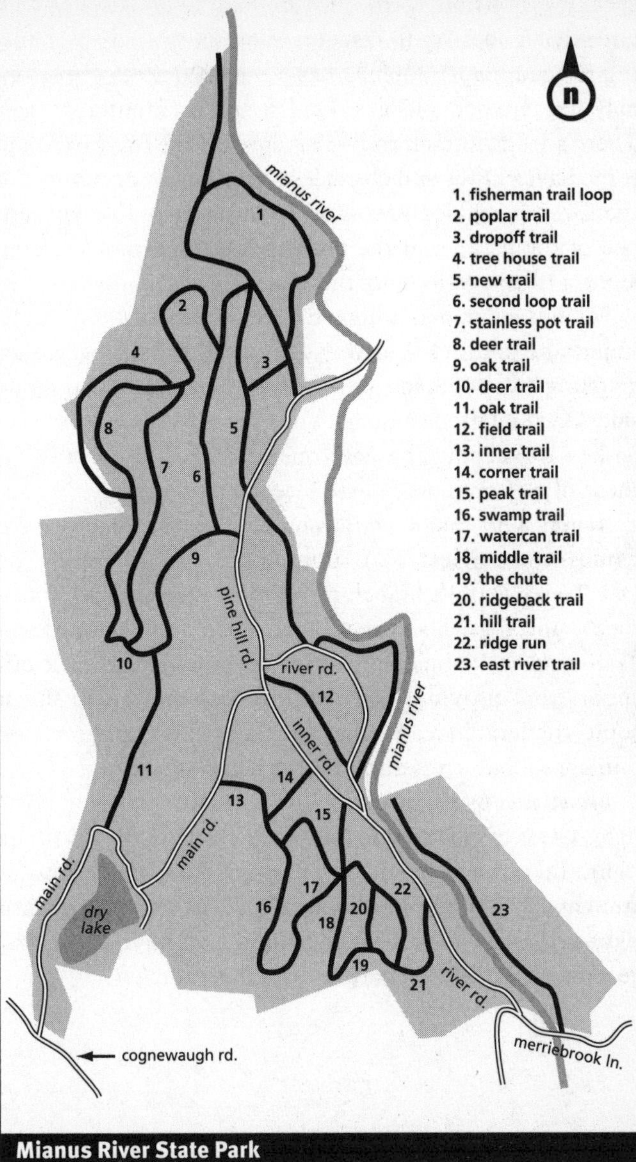
n
mianus river
1. fisherman trail loop
2. poplar trail
3. dropoff trail
4. tree house trail
5. new trail
6. second loop trail
7. stainless pot trail
8. deer trail
9. oak trail
10. deer trail
11. oak trail
12. field trail
13. inner trail
14. corner trail
15. peak trail
16. swamp trail
17. watercan trail
18. middle trail
19. the chute
20. ridgeback trail
21. hill trail
22. ridge run
23. east river trail
pine hill rd.
river rd.
inner rd.
mianus river
main rd.
main rd.
dry lake
river rd.
merriebrook ln.
cognewaugh rd.

Mianus River State Park

speaking, invisible town lines are hard to police (although Greenwich does try to discourage out-of-towners by refusing to send maps). Mianus has a nice 220 acres of reasonably dense woods, ledges, knolls, and rock outcroppings. There are singletrack trails that spur off the fire roads, and some have climbs and obstacles, including a fair number of roots, rocks, and logs. Most of the trails are in the southern end of the park, near the parking lots. One trail leads up along a ridge overlooking the Mianus River.

Mianus is popular among hikers and anglers, too, so it's important to mind your way. I stopped and apologized for startling two women out walking their dogs during one ride. Good relations among two- and four-legged users may be key to keeping the park open to bikes, especially for those of us from Somewhere Else.

Route: The major trails—more like fire roads—have names; the singletrack is impromptu and informal. The Oak Trail has trails branching off that are laden with roots, rocks, and logs. Fisherman Trail Loop and Second Loop Trail tend to be busy, but there are hilly singletrack offshoots that provide a chance to climb and bomb down some moderate-sized hills. Much of the singletrack is unmapped, but everything leads back to the fire roads.

Directions: By car, take I-95 to exit 4 and turn right at the light. Cross over US 1 and follow the road as it bends to the right. Take the first left on Stanwich Road and follow it straight for several miles, keeping left at stop signs. Turn right at Cognewaugh Road (look for the white signpost) and go about 0.5 mile; the parking area is on the left.

Meccas

THE CATSKILLS

Location: Minnewaska State Park and Plattekill Mountain, New York, 80 to 150 miles northwest of Manhattan

Description: You don't need to go all the way to the Adirondacks to get ski-mountain-length climbs and descents. Minnewaska State Park should be your warm-up ride. There's nothing narrow or technical at Minnewaska, but it works for just about anybody. Your day will go something like this. 1. Long, *long* climb. 2. Stop and stare at gorgeous views of the world below. 3. Tear down mountain (watch out for hikers). 4. Repeat. This beautiful spot tends to attract big crowds, but the trails are plenty wide.

Plattekill Mountain, on the other hand, is a ski resort with a chairlift. Between you and the bottom lies a system of dozens of trails—some of them suitable for beginners, many others featuring minefields of rocky, scary descents. It gets muddy and fiercely technical, so bring your goggles and strap your helmet down tight. If the going gets too rugged, there are fire roads to fly down. The crowds tend to grow here on summer weekends, especially when races are scheduled (check www.plattekill.com for updates). The lodge has food and a repair shop, and there's camping in the park.

JIM THORPE

Location: Jim Thorpe, Pennsylvania, 114 miles west of Manhattan

Description: Though it's rated as one of the top fat-tire destinations in the country by *Bicycling* magazine, Jim

Thorpe—a town—in eastern Pennsylvania's Poconos—has drawn the ire of first-time visitors. The reason? Some of its best, most advanced rides are unmarked and difficult to find. But this should not be a deterrent. Bone up on your map-reading skills before coming, and buy *A Guide to Mountain Biking in Jim Thorpe & the Western Poconos*. The payoff is terrific. The Mauch Chunk Trail, for one, offers 10 miles of hilly, technical terrain with some fast downhill runs. Another suggestion is the 2.5-mile Twin Peaks route.

Or sit back and take in the sights on the easy-to-follow classic routes. The 25-mile Lehigh Gorge Trail follows an old railroad bed past awesome 1,000-foot cliffs and Class III rapids. The same goes for the Switchback Trail, a 16-mile loop accessible right from downtown Jim Thorpe that works for most neophytes. The folks at Blue Mountain Sports (800-599-4421, www.bikejimthorpe.com) can provide maps, advice, and a shuttle service.

Where to Connect

Clubs and Organizations

- Transportation Alternatives (212-629-8080, www.transalt.org) is an advocate for cyclists, pedestrians, and "sensible transportation."
- Time's Up (212-802-8222, www.times-up.org) is a nonprofit, volunteer-run environmental group; it runs monthly events, including Critical Mass and "green" bike tours of places such as lower Manhattan and the South Bronx.
- Westchester Mountain Biking Association (www.

wmba.org) organizes rides and includes trail maps on its Web site.

- Concerned Long Island Mountain Bikers (CLIMB, 516-271-6527, www.climbonline.org) oversees trails on Long Island.

Shops

- Bicycle Habitat (244 Lafayette Street, Manhattan, 212-431-3846, www.bicyclehabitat.com) is one of the savviest, biker-friendly shops in the city.
- Bike Works (106 Ridge Street, Manhattan, 212-388-1077, www.bikeworksnyc.com) is one of the few shops in the city selling used bikes.
- CNC Bicycle Works (1101 First Avenue, Manhattan, 212-230-1919)
- A Bicycle Shop (345 West 14th Street, Manhattan, 212-691-6149, www.a-bicycleshop.com)
- R&A Cycles (105 Fifth Avenue, Brooklyn, 718-636-5242, www.racycles.com)

Event

- The Fat Tire Festival (www.wmba.org), a benefit for United Cerebral Palsy of Westchester, is held annually at Blue Mountain Reservation.

Books and Maps

- Kick, Peter. *25 Mountain Bike Tours in New Jersey.* Woodstock, VT: Countryman Press, 1997.
- Margulis, Michael. *Mountain Biking New York.* Helena, MT: Falcon Publishing Company, 1997.
- Matsinko, David. *A Guide to Mountain Biking in Jim Thorpe & the Western Poconos.* Self-published.

- Pierce, Joshua M. *Ride Guide New Jersey Mountain Biking*. Liberty Corner, NJ: Anacus Press, 1997.
- Sendek, Joel D. *Ride Guide: Mountain Biking in the New York Metro Area*. Liberty Corner, NJ: Anacus Press, 1998.

Rock Climbing

NEW YORK IS a vertical city. People come with the idea of the metaphorical ascent—in career, fortune, lifestyle. Manhattan's skyline is famously jagged and vertiginous, the Himalayas of cityscapes. So it's no surprise that even without a single mountain on the horizon, the city is home to an active rock-climbing community. It's a pretty colorful bunch, too. New York rock climbers tend to be artists, musicians, and poets; some have performed with the Metropolitan Opera and danced with the New York City Ballet. It's a laid-back, mostly noncompetitive crowd; the kind that substitutes the word "peace" for "good-bye."

Many local climbers are into bouldering, a sport

that took root in Central Park in the absence of any crags closer than the Shawangunks. (There are, of course, the artificial climbing walls, but they're a whole other animal, detailed in "Climbing Walls," page 163). Boulderers have been around since the 1960s, though the city briefly banned the sport in the '80s because of large crowds gathering at the crags. But since climbers Ralph Erenzo and Nick Fallacci negotiated an agreement with city officials, the city has embraced the sport. The Central Park Conservancy, which is responsible for the park's stewardship, offers climbing courses and maintains bouldering sites by clearing brush and spreading wood chips beneath the crags for cushioning. This chapter covers some of the highlights of Central Park bouldering. A membership in the City Climbers Club (212-974-2250, www.climbnyc.com) is effectively a permit to climb on these and other designated boulders. The club's Web site includes the full text of Fallacci's 1988 Central Park climbing guide. The Conservancy (212-348-4867, www.centralparknyc.org) is another valuable bouldering resource.

The other element of this chapter is conventional rock climbing. Most New York climbers are devotees of the aforementioned Gunks, though this chapter also touches on hot spots farther afield, such as the Delaware Water Gap and the Adirondacks. Rock climbing has become immensely popular, so it's fairly easy to find someone to hook up with on the City Climbers Club Web site or walls. All you have to do to get started is invest in some carabiners, ropes, and a harness, take a lesson or two, and start shredding those fingertips.

City Limits

BOULDERING IN CENTRAL PARK

On the west face of Rat Rock, the renowned bouldering outcrop in Central Park, someone has scrawled: "Time is the greatest challenge of all." That oracular statement is typical in bouldering, which is rock climbing minus the ropes, altitude, and protection. The regulars tend to be a studious, reverent, almost Zen-like group. Whereas tourists scarcely notice Central Park's deposits of ancient Manhattan schist, boulderers see in them challenge, frustration, triumph, intrigue, and legend. "Bouldering is a metaphor for life," says Eric Lee, a 31-year-old artist, musician, and climbing instructor who for the past decade has helped incubate the sport in Central Park. "It requires growth, persistence, and self-reliance, as well as trust in others."

A word on terminology: Boulderers call a route or traverse across the face of a crag a "problem." If the problem is unsolved—that is, no one has completed the route—it is called a "project." There are an infinite number of problems in Central Park because climbers love to invent new challenges. "It's a canvas," Lee says, "and there are always new possibilities." One climber, known simply as Yuki, is referred to as the sensei of Rat Rock because for more than a decade he has climbed only that rock, forever creating new problems. Some call bouldering "the essence of climbing." All you need is a pair of climbing shoes and a bag of powdered chalk, and a bouldering pad if you're attempting an ascent where falling could cause injury. Similar to power lifting, bouldering requires bold bursts of power rather than the endurance required for a daylong ascent. A boulderer might lunge for a hold in a way a rock climber would consider reckless—but being only a few feet off the ground, a boulderer hasn't got as much to lose.

Chill Out

Bouldering in New York is a cool-weather sport. It's best to climb when the temperature is around freezing. That's because your fingers aren't likely to grease up with sweat and slip off, as they would in the summer heat. Some boulders, in fact, can be climbed only in winter because the sun cooks their surfaces during the warm seasons. The challenge is to keep your body and hands warm enough between climbs. Some boulderers do chin-ups on the subway and jog to the rocks. Between climbs, they swap off use of a parka; you can't climb in a heavy winter coat.

RAT ROCK

Location: Central Park

Description: Rat Rock is ground zero for Central Park boulderers. The rock, named for a family of furry vermin that may or may not still live under it, has an impressive, sagging face, with quartz wrinkles. The north face is the most popular bouldering section, with more beginner-type problems; the midtown skyline—fronted by the stately Essex House facade—looms overhead. Rat Rock is only a few feet off the ground and has some prominent cracks, with a classic right-to-left problem that gets progressively harder. "This becomes a break-through spot," says Lee, who took me on a bouldering tour through Central Park. "At first, beginners can't do the whole thing. Not even close. But the movement is sequential. You rehearse a certain sequence, and eventually you put all the sequences together, and then you have it."

The east face draws a crowd of regulars. It's a tough, 17-foot-high outcrop with no substantial cracks, just tiny, crimpy fingerholds and a 10- to 20-degree overhang. There are more top-outs up high with more variations in the holds.

The west face presents a problem worthy of any X-Games. You start almost underneath the rock and haul yourself up and over. Rat Rock lore holds that only two people have conquered it, but that may be apocryphal; to the locals, it remains a prize. "The west face," Lee says, "opens doors to a whole new renaissance. You have to have a lot of open-hand strength, and it involves very powerful movements."

Directions: Located at the north end of the Heckscher Playground in the area of 61st Street

CHESS ROCK

Location: Central Park

Description: Named for its proximity to the Chess and Checkers House, this rock is an ideal beginner spot—a slab with an angled face that isn't quite vertical. There are two large cracks and waves of striations that provide ample holds. Here you can develop "foot-eye coordination"—a key to good climbing. "There are times when you can't get any higher with your hands, but you can step higher," Lee says. "Our legs are designed to support our weight. You always want to economize your energy by using your legs as much as you can." The rock tops out at 15 feet, so this is a good spot for beginners to start conquering those fear-of-heights butterflies.

Directions: Located between Wollman skating rink and the Chess and Checkers House at about 65th Street

Boulder Fever

ERIC LEE IS a typical New York climber. He loves bouldering, but he has other serious pursuits. He's hoping to sell some of his paintings to galleries, and he plays bass for a Japanese pop band, but at the moment he makes most of his money teaching climbing. The first time I met him, he wore thick brown-framed glasses and chipped black fingernail polish. His bleached hair spilled out from under a floppy hat. "Some people just get the bug," he says of climbing. "It's kind of like a fever."

Lee caught it around 10 years ago, when he met the impresario of Rat Rock, a Japanese climber known as Yuki. Under Yuki's tutelage, Lee prowled the Central Park boulders three or four times a week, year-round, for a decade. "I lived out West for a while, but it's funny," he says. "It wasn't until I came to New York that I really got into climbing." Gregarious and articulate, Lee helped convince the Central Park Conservancy to allow climbing at several new sites. He impressed the conservancy officials so much, they offered him a part-time job as a climbing instructor.

Part of his job involves teaching at-risk kids. "We use climbing as a model," he says. "It's about communication skills and self-reliance, but also trusting your partners. The results are pretty tangible. They'll try and try, and then somehow something happens—a minor mental adjustment allows them to make a movement they couldn't do before. Kids get really amped on that."

Lee demonstrates some moves on Rat Rock. He's wiry and catlike; he glides up boulders as if he's hovering over them. In the past few years, a new wave of boulderers has swarmed the park—people claiming first ascents, soliciting publicity, renaming routes. "We get old and crusty about it, seeing how hip and trendy it is," says Lee, only 31. He grins. "It's never been about egos. Bouldering is more social than rock climbing because the climbers remain in a small space, working together on a problem. The thing is, if you take any given problem, chances are somebody did it long before any of us got here. It's not important to lay personal claims to them, but to add to the sport, the lore."

Regardless, bouldering is a sport with a wide-open membership. As Lee says: "Anyone can come down here and get their calluses."

CAT ROCK

Location: Central Park

Description: The diehards flock to this crag in winter because the south-facing wall is too cooked by the sun to climb the rest of the year. "My best day it was twenty-eight degrees, about 4 P.M. The sun had gone behind the buildings, and the rock was just starting to cool down," Lee says. We visit in late November with the temperature in the 40s. Lee puts his hand on the rock—named for feral cats living beneath it—and says it's still too warm. The lights from Wollman skating rink allow boulderers to cling to the rock well into the night. Though it's an appealing site—it often draws crowds of spectators from the rink and offers a sweet view of midtown—this is no place for newbies. With the exception of an east-facing slab, the numerous problems are advanced, and the holds are small and technical. Just to the east is Tooth Rock, a small training boulder good for toughening your hands.

Directions: North of the Wollman rink, between 63rd and 64th Streets

The Legend of Hepatitis Rock

THE MASSIVE CHUNK of cantilevered schist known as Hepatitis Rock is wedged into the rear of a small grotto in the Ramble, north of Central Park Lake. Boulderers came up with the name after stepping over the leavings of its various homeless visitors. "It was so nasty we thought we were going to get hepatitis just from hanging out in there," Eric Lee says.

Since boulderers discovered the rock several years ago, they've solved two problems, named Hepatitis A and B. Hepatitis C, though, is another story. It's a project some believe can't be solved. The climb begins at about 5 feet and tops off at about 12. In that span, there are virtually no holds. There was a single, crimpy hold, but it broke off during an early attempt. The climber still has the hold, prompting vigorous debates about whether it should be glued back on. So far, the hold hasn't been reattached. What remains is a small circular scar.

Word of the unconquerable project has spread rapidly through climbing channels, fueled by titillating online discussions. Hepatitis C is now the big prize in the international bouldering community. Can Hepatitis C be mastered? Lee thinks so. He thinks it will involve about four Spiderman-like moves. "It can be done," Lee says, "but it's going to take some extreme finger strength and technique."

CITY BOY (AKA THE NATIVE)

Location: Central Park

Description: Shrubs and overhanging trees obscured this boulder a couple of years ago, until boulderers convinced the park to do some clearing. The climbers scrubbed the horizontal, low-lying boulder with wire brushes to clean off a moss bloom. It was well worth the effort: City Boy is an angular left-to-right traverse that gains steepness the farther along you go. The 20-foot problem concludes with an overhang. "It's a beauty—totally uncontrived," Lee says. There's a jutting section of rock in the middle that serves as a rest area.

Directions: Along the loop road in the area of 107th Street, above Lasker skating rink. Coming from the south, the boulder is on the left just off the loop road's shoulder.

Rock of Ages

THE WRINKLY, DISTINGUISHED-looking outcrops jutting from the ground in Central Park and Fort Tryon are called Manhattan schist. The 450-million-year-old rock was formed when the planet's shifting continents rear-ended each other; one shelf was crushed, restructured in a 1,100°F cauldron 9 miles underground, and eventually burped back up to the surface. It's popular among local boulderers for its hard, solid faces.

WORTHLESS BOULDER

Location: Central Park

Description: During the 1980s, a previous generation of boulderers named this prominent chunk of schist Rap Rock, and named the problems after songs by Public Enemy and Run DMC. When climbers were temporarily evicted, the place fell prey to drug dealers and prostitutes, becoming a repository for syringes, crack vials, a corpse, and other undesirable items. Climbers and park personnel reclaimed it several years ago, and now there are chalk stains all over the rock. Worthless presents some knotty challenges: It's about 10 feet tall and precipitously steep, with a substantial overhang. "ADD" is a popular problem that runs straight up the middle of the rock face. "This is definitely a destination for the diehard," Lee says.

Directions: At 110th Street at the north end of the park, between Seventh and Lennox Avenues. The rock is up a small embankment where the road bends west.

Adventure in Staten Island

IT WAS ONLY a matter of time before the adventure-race craze hit New York City. The High Rock 10K Adventure Challenge, held for the first time in 2001, is a spin-off of made-for-TV events in places such as Patagonian Argentina. One hundred two-person teams have to run together at all times through a course in Staten Island's Greenbelt while tackling five "mystery events" which, along with the course, are kept secret until race day. (*Survivor* creator Mark Burnett would be proud.) The events test teams' problem-solving ability, adaptability, and strength, but most of all, teamwork.

In the first race, they included the Carry or Drag Challenge, in which one team member hauls another more than 100 meters uphill, and the Pasta for Two Challenge, in which teams ran three-quarters of a mile, jumping over a 4-foot stream and ascending 200 feet—all while carrying a single piece of dried pasta. If the spaghetti broke, the team was assessed a penalty run. Another doozy involved tying a string around a rope that was suspended nine feet in the air.

To register, download a race application from the New York Adventure Racing Association Web site (www.nyara.org) and send a check for $50 to NYARA High Rock Challenge, 219 Wardwell Avenue, Staten Island, NY 10314. Or register online at www.active.com (keyword: High Rock).

110TH STREET ROCK

Location: Central Park

Description: This huge piece of schist is an interesting training tool for climbers of all skill levels. The 35-foot slab is outfitted with three bolt anchors that the Central Park Conservancy uses to set up top ropes for climbing programs. Several enormous cracks offer practice spots for placing protection—a valuable exercise for climbers training for the Gunks. And for boulderers there are ample opportunities for free-solo climbs up the face. Lee lists 5 to 10 advanced routes, including some problems along the bottom left corner.

Another unnamed boulder off to the right—Lee calls it the Millennium Falcon—has a climb with a scary overhang. And there are a number of projects a little farther up the hill. (They've yet to be conquered, in part due to access issues; the site also happens to be a default bathroom zone for the homeless population.)

Directions: At 110th Street and Adam Clayton Powell Boulevard (the north-central end of the park)

STONE BRIDGE BOULDER

Location: Central Park

Description: This classic in the Ramble, north of the Loeb Boathouse, is sometimes off-limits; the conservancy occasionally fences it off to prevent erosion problems on the hillside. The rock is smooth and contoured—not nearly as sharp to the touch as many other boulders. There's a classic route up the middle of its face. To ratchet up the difficulty, avoid "stemming," or reaching out for bigger holds to the sides. When the adjacent streetlamp is working, this is another after-hours climbing site. Don't ever climb the bridge, which is a historic landmark.

Directions: From the loop road on the west side, take the path at about 76th Street, just above Central Park Lake. Cross the footbridge and bear right; the boulder is on the right just past the stone arch.

FORT TRYON

Location: Manhattan

Description: Climbers have long eyed this prominent uplift in Manhattan's northwest corner for its climbing potential. The Central Park Conservancy has two bolted anchors at the top of a 60-foot crag it uses for the grand finale of its 6-week climbing course. But this remains largely unsolved terrain in the higher grades. There's a boulder just off the exit for the Henry Hudson Parkway that offers what looks like compelling problems, but the seldom-climbed rock needs to be cleaned. "Somebody needs to rappel down with a wire brush and remove some of the loose rock," Lee says.

Directions: By subway, take the A train to 190th Street. Contact the Central Park Conservancy for detailed directions and permit information for the bolted anchors.

Short Hops

Climbing in ranges such as the Shawangunks requires far more commitment than bouldering in terms of both risk and equipment. In addition to the usual assortment of protection, carabiners, ropes, and so on, it's always a good idea to pack rain gear and rappelling equipment in case the weather turns nasty. And always wear a helmet; falling rock is a problem even in the heavily trafficked Gunks.

SHAWANGUNKS

Location: New Paltz, New York, 84 miles north of Manhattan

Outfitters: Rock & Snow (New Paltz, 888-255-1311), Mountain Skills Cimbing School (845-687-9643); High Angle Adventures (800-777-2546, www.highangle.com.)

Information: Mohonk Preserve (845-255-0919)

Description: If Central Park's boulders are a local climbers' playground, the Gunks are their Madison Square Garden—*the* place to overlay technique onto grand scale. This is a mixed blessing. The Shawangunks are considered one of the top climbing destinations in the East, and there's a lot of teeth-gnashing over the biblical hordes that descend on the Gunks, located a convenient 90 miles north of the city. The thing is, the Gunks' cachet is richly deserved. The twinkling white quartz conglomerate cliffs are so superior—with so many generous cracks, horizontal holds, and stuntman overhangs—it's absurd to think of heading anywhere else if you're going to haul out your gear for the day. There are routes for all skill levels, and a massive Chinese menu of options; the essential *Shawangunk Rock Climbs* lists roughly a thousand possibilities, all within a relatively compact area.

The Shawangunks, which range up to 260 feet, stretch for 8 miles over a series of ridges loosely connected to the Appalachians to the south. The 5,600-acre Mohonk Preserve contains the most popular climbs, including the

Trapps and Near Trapps areas. Here, if you sleep late on summer or fall weekends, you may find you're out of luck. The preserve recently instituted a 350-car limit; even if you get in, you'll probably wait in line at the cliff base. Summer can be oppressive, so go in spring and fall; then at least you're not dealing with the crowds *and* the heat. Better still, arrange weekday trips. Fridays and Mondays are often library-quiet, even sandwiched around a busy weekend. Another option on a busy day is the Plattekill area—just 2 miles south and west of the preserve on US 44/NY 55—a good top-roping spot that draws more modest crowds.

Directions: By bus, Adirondack/Pine Hill Trailways (800-858-8555) runs several express buses daily to New Paltz. That's significantly cheaper than taking Metro-North to Poughkeepsie and getting a cab.

By car, take I-87 north and cross the Tappan Zee Bridge. Take exit 18 and go west on US 44/NY 55; the cliffs are about 5 miles west of New Paltz.

DELAWARE WATER GAP NATIONAL RECREATION AREA

Location: Delaware Water Gap, Pennsylvania, 75 miles west of Manhattan

Outfitter: Pack Shack Adventures (Delaware Water Gap, PA, 570-424-8533, www.packshack.com) runs a climbing school that offers private, semiprivate, or group lessons.

Books and maps: Pick up a copy of *Climbing Guide to the Delaware Water Gap* at the Pack Shack. Also, the Kittatinny Point Visitors Center (908-496-4458) has climbing guides.

Description: The Gap ranks a solid second to the Shawangunks in terms of day-trip climbing options. The Delaware River created the site when it carved a 1,200-foot gorge through the Kittatinny Ridge. The two sides of the gap—Mt. Tammany in New Jersey and Mt. Minsi in Pennsylvania—offer more than 200 climbs that run the gamut of pitches and difficulty levels. Newcomers should know there is some truth to the persistent rumors of loose rock. "The Jersey side is actually an extension of the conglomerate rock in the Shawangunks, but it's a little bit softer," says John Greene, owner of Pack Shack Adventures. National park regulations prevent climbers from cleaning it as much as they normally would. For that reason—and because top-roping isn't a great option; traverses tend to wind around obstacles—it's a good idea to hook up with a guide or some locals the first time out. Or start with the moderate, shorter climbs at Ricks Rocks in New Jersey, north of the Gap.

Both sides offer crags ranging from 120 to 220 feet, but Tammany has cleaner, more established routes. Minsi is a little tougher to access; getting to the climbs sometimes involves hobbling across the scree. There are also 20 or so ice climbs during winter freezes.

Directions: The Tammany approaches are off the Cliff Trail, just above the westbound lane of I-80 near the Kittatinny Point Visitors Center. For Minsi, go through the Gap on I-80, through the tollbooth, and take exit 4. Drive through Delaware Water Gap and turn left on PA 611; park at the second of two areas immediately after the Point of Gap tourist area.

RAGGED MOUNTAIN

Location: Southington, Connecticut, 99 miles northeast of Manhattan

Outfitter: For gear and advice, stop at Prime Climb (203-265-7880, www.primeclimb.com) in nearby Meriden.

Books: *Ragged and Free,* a booklet published by the Ragged Mountain Foundation (www.raggedmtn.org), covers a number of Connecticut's top climbing spots. Also look for a new guidebook by foundation member David Fasulo.

Description: It isn't a huge area, but Ragged Mountain is still a good option, with easily the best crags in Connecticut. The traprock—the term widely used here to describe volcanic basalt—is relatively smooth and hard, but there's not much jointing and the cracks are steep and discontinuous. "Traprock is a very subtle kind of climbing," says John Peterson, a longtime Ragged Mountain climber. "The rock has a lot of delicate small-scale features, like tiny ripples, so you have to take some time and think about what you want to do. It's very intellectual."

The main cliff, which rises about 90 feet, has about a hundred good routes. Because of the rock's subtleties—and the challenge of placing protection—leading requires a bit more expertise here than on other cliffs. Many climbers resort to top-roping, but if you plan to settle on that option, bring extra webbing; the trees are about 20 to 30 feet back from the cliff's top lip. Ragged Mountain is also an ideal hiking spot. On clear days, the trails deliver spectacular views all the way to Massachusetts and Long Island Sound.

Sleeping Giant State Park in Wallingford, which has a big peak with seven or eight excellent climbs, is another intriguing spot.

Directions: By car, take I-95 north to I-91 north to I-691 west. Take exit 5 and follow CT 71 north out of Meriden. Drive for several miles, past CT 364, and turn left on Reservoir Road. The trailhead is about 2 miles down Reservoir Road. There are no designated parking areas, and on-street parking is prohibited on Reservoir Road, Carey Road, and Andrews Street, but okay elsewhere, unless a sign says otherwise, just don't block driveways or mailboxes.

THE HIGH PEAKS OF THE ADIRONDACKS

Location: Keene Valley, New York, 271 miles north of Manhattan

Outfitters: The Mountaineer (518-576-2281, www.mountaineer.com) and Adirondack Rock and River (518-576-2041, www.rockandriver.com) both offer advice and instruction in the Keene Valley region.

Books and resources: *Climbing in the Adirondacks: A Guide to Rock and Ice Routes in the Adirondacks* is a thorough guide. The Adirondack Mountain Club (800-395-8080, www.adk.org) is a catchall resource.

Description: To put the vastness of the Adirondacks into perspective, consider that new walls are still being discovered even after scores of climbing expeditions over the course of half a century. The park's 6 million acres take in more than 40 mountains that top out at over 4,000 feet, and much of the terrain is pretty remote by easterners' standards. Some climbing trips in the High Peaks will feel like full-on expeditions, requiring long hikes on vague trails, thrashing through trees and around boulders amid swarms of mosquitoes, to crags where top-roping is almost impossible.

Panther Gorge, for example, is a near-mythical spot that is virtually uncharted. There are two choices for getting there: hike 10 miles from Elk Lake, or drop into the ravine from a trail between mounts Marcy and Haystack. There's no chalk residue, no guidebook advice, nothing.

Don Mellor's seminal guidebook *Climbing in the Adirondacks: A Guide to Rock and Ice Routes in the Adirondacks* divides the "Dacks" into seven regions: Cascade Lakes, Keene Valley, Poke-O-Moonshine, Wallface, the Northwest, Whiteface, and the Southern Adirondacks, the modern-day frontier. Not all the crags are wild and woolly. The most concentrated and popular climbs are in the Keene Valley and Poke-O-Moonshine areas; many are just off roads or parking areas. They include Chapel Pond, a 700-foot wall that serves as a mandatory crucible for aspiring High Peaks climbers. It features six or seven pitches, but the rock has clean, reliable holds. (It's only a 5-minute walk from the Chapel Pond parking lot, too.) There is little sedimentary rock in the Adirondacks, so you'll see few of the horizontal holds that make the Gunks so popular. And come prepared. The weather is notoriously mercurial.

WHITE MOUNTAINS

Location: North Conway, New Hampshire, 346 miles northeast of Manhattan

Outfitters: Eastern Mountain Sports (www.emsclimb.com) runs a climbing school. Also, try International Mountain Equipment (603-356-6316) in North Conway and Ragged Mountain Equipment (603-356-3042, www.raggedmt.com) in Intervale.

Books and resources: *Rock Climbs of the White Mountains* and *An Ice Climber's Guide to Northern New England* are both solid resources. Also, the Web site Climb New Hampshire (www.climbnh.com) has lots of good info.

Description: This giant granite range takes awhile to get to—northern New Hampshire is not a day trip from New York City—but adventure climbers will find all they could ever want. The names alone—the Old Man of the Mountain, Franconia Notch, Mt. Washington—evoke majesty. The weather is wicked, the rock unpredictable, the scenery dazzling.

North Conway is probably the epicenter of climbing activity, offering access to Whitehorse and Cathedral Ledge. The former is a mammoth 800-foot granite slab with a wide range of ratings; many guides bring their students here for the reliable belay and rappel stations. Cathedral Ledge is a gorgeous granite crag with multiple-pitch climbs.

The crags at Franconia Notch, meanwhile, ratchet up the intensity level a bit. Cannon Cliff, a 1,100-foot wall with some loose rock and a bed-of-nails surface, is among the most extreme areas. There are a number of classic routes here, including Pinnacle Ridge, one of the few ridge climbs in the East. An expedition in the Whites demands extra preparation. You need several ropes to launch a big-wall expedition such as this, and that also means you should be ready to spend a night on the crag or to get off in a hurry in case the weather turns quickly, as it is wont to do.

Where to Connect

Clubs and Organizations

- The City Climbers Club has a Web site, www.climbnyc.com, with numerous resources, including a bulletin board listing partners and carpools to the Gunks. It also runs instruction at its own wall (see "Climbing Walls," page 164).
- The Central Park Conservancy's adventure program (212-348-4867, www.centralparknyc.org) offers climbing instruction.
- The Chinese Mountain Club of New York (www.cmcny.org) organizes various outings; membership is open to anyone.

Shops

- Eastern Mountain Sports (20 West 61st Street, Manhattan, 212-397-4860; and 611 Broadway, Manhattan, 212-505-9860) stocks climbing supplies.
- Paragon Sports (867 Broadway, Manhattan, 212-255-8036) carries climbing and mountaineering gear.
- Tent and Trails (21 Park Place, Manhattan, 212-227-1760), a slender reed of a store, carries all climbing essentials.

Books and Maps

- Mellor, Don. *Climbing in the Adirondacks: A Guide to Rock and Ice Routes in the Adirondacks*. Lake George, NY: Adirondack Mountain Club, 1995.
- Steele, Michael. *Climbing Guide to the Delaware Water Gap*. Delaware Water Gap, PA: Pack Shack Adventures, 2001.
- Swain, Todd. *The Gunks Guide* Evergreen, CO: Chockstone Press, 1998.
- Webster, Ed. *Rock Climbs in the White Mountains of New Hampshire*. Eldorado Springs, CO: Mountain Imagery, 1996.
- Wilcox, Rick. *An Ice Climber's Guide to Northern New England*. Burlington, VT: Huntington Graphics, 1997.
- Williams, Dick. *Shawangunk Rock Climbs*. Golden, CO: American Alpine Club Press, 2000.

Climbing Walls

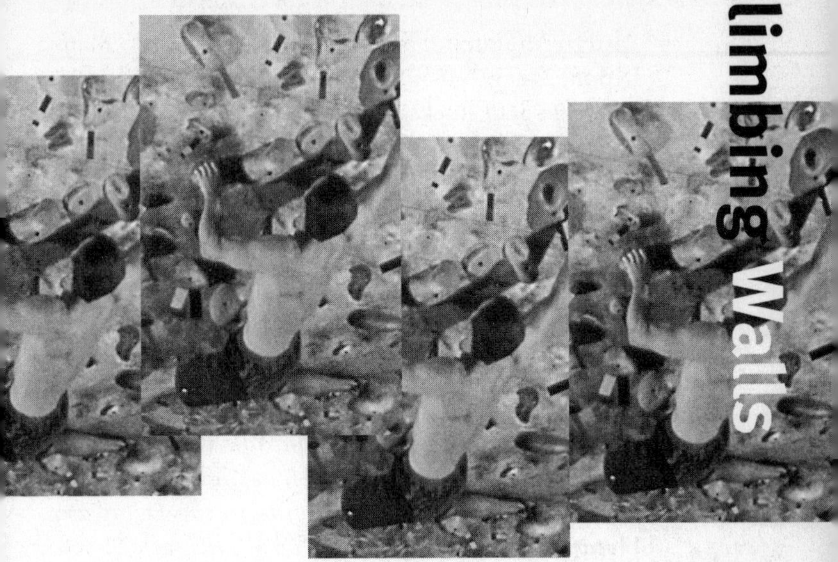

I HAD NOT DONE MUCH climbing before I attempted a wall one evening at the City Climbers Club. Twenty feet up, I felt stiff and unsteady. Sweat trickled down my sides, more from the effort of not looking down than from exertion. Still, I felt edgy in a good way. I was having a blast.

Many New Yorkers have gone through similar initiations in the past decade. Back in 1989, when the City Climbers Club convinced the city to create a volunteer-run climbing wall in the 59th Street Recreation Center, it was a true novelty. Now? Climbing the dimpled, contoured walls—holds nailed onto them like spots on a leopard—became the fitness rage of the 1990s, and now climbing

walls are practically as de rigueur for Manhattan health clubs as the common dumbbell. This is a good thing for New Yorkers, because most of us can't just sally off to the Shawangunks anytime. (Just keep in mind that training on artificial walls isn't the same as climbing outdoors, where there are far more variables.)

The city is pretty egalitarian when it comes to climbing walls. There are expensive spots, of course, but two places —the City Climbers Club and ExtraVertical—make the sport accessible to those who just want to show off for their out-of-town guests. Those who take climbing seriously find that it's an ideal way to merge skills of balance, poise, strength, coordination, and flexibility.

City Limits

THE CITY CLIMBERS CLUB WALL

Location: Manhattan

Outfitter: There's a modest day fee for admission to the gym (Parks and Recreation Center, 533 West 59th Street; 212-974-2250, www.climbnyc.com), and an annual membership costs a fraction of what the big gyms charge.

Description: It's no longer the biggest, but it is New York City's first, and still *the* climber's climbing wall in Manhattan. There's no swank here in the rather run-down, city-owned Parks and Recreation Center. To get to this wall, you have to ascend a flight of stairs, walk through mildewed locker rooms, and mount a second flight of stairs to find the hidden-away climbing area.

The modest quarters are close and informal but friendly, and the beta (climber-speak for advice) flows freely. Every available space is used. A bouldering cave is tucked under a locker area. On a small patch of wall outside the cave is the city's only campus board, a strength-training device designed to add meat to climbers' fingers.

When the place first opened, the back wall was the only one set up for climbing. Someone had to free-climb it to set up rope for top-roping. Now all four walls are covered; they range from 20 to 25 feet high, with 11 belay stations. There are more than 30 routes, but the beauty of the wall here is that a creative group of route-setters is constantly rearranging the holds. Many routes simulate conditions similar to what you'll find outdoors.

Directions: By subway, take the A, B, C, D, 1, or 2 train to Columbus Circle and walk west. The center is between Tenth and Eleventh Avenues on the north side.

EXTRAVERTICAL

Location: Manhattan

Outfitter: ExtraVertical (61 West 62nd Street and Broadway, 212-586-5382, www.extravertical.com) offers day or package rates.

Description: This is a remarkable spot—an open-air climbing destination on Broadway, just up the street from that bastion of culture, Lincoln Center. The concept here is that a climbing wall can lure anyone off the street—even refined folks fresh from a *La Boheme* matinee. One climbing wall is actually on the sidewalk at the entrance to ExtraVertical. "Take the challenge," a sign urges. In summer, crowds gather to cheer climbers up the 50-foot wall. "This is the only facility where anybody, no matter who they are or what their level of experience is, can walk in off the street and climb," says Ralph Erenzo, ExtraVertical's managing partner. "This is grassroots. Climbing for the people."

To that end, ExtraVertical offers a walk-in "challenge climb" package: $10 for two climbs, including equipment and shoes. It's built for crowds; the main wall inside an open-air atrium stretches 32 feet up and 45 feet across. There are 5 ropes outside and 10 inside. More experienced climbers can practice leading here, though rock rats say the routes aren't challenging enough. That's not surprising, even though the main wall was imported from the first ESPN Extreme Games. Above all else, this is an Everyman climbing destination.

Directions: By subway, take the A, B, C, D, 1, or 2 train to Columbus Circle; walk north two blocks on Broadway.

CHELSEA PIERS

Location: Manhattan

Outfitter: The wall is in the Sports Center (Pier 60, 23rd Street and the Hudson River; 212-336-6000, www.chelseapiers.com), where admission is by day fee or membership.

Description: This sprawling, glittering complex is home to New York City's über-wall: a 10,000-square-footer that was one of the biggest in the country when it opened, and it is still considered one of the best. The highlight is a 46-foot-high, 100-foot-wide simulated cliff with an overhanging roof. There's also a 10-foot-high, 73-foot-long bouldering wall. That adds up to about a hundred different routes to solve. Climbers, who tend to be artsy rather than Wall Street types, complain that they get priced out—and at $50 a pop for nonmembers, they've got a point. There's a cheaper wall in the Field House, but it was designed for kids, so it's substantially smaller.

Directions: By subway, take the C, E, 1, or 2 train to 23rd Street; walk west to the river.

NORTH MEADOW RECREATION CENTER

Location: Manhattan

Outfitter: There's a day fee and an annual fee, both nominal, for admission to the North Meadow facility (located midpark at 97th Street, 212-348-4867, www.centralpark nyc.org). Public access is limited; call for information.

Description: Given that the Central Park Conservancy runs this center, it's no surprise that the focus here is on bouldering, a sport that thrives on the park's crags. The 12-foot-high walls cater to boulderers' training whims, with a variety of bends and overhangs on the highly contoured walls and scores of holds that narrow down to tiny crimps. There's a little cave in one corner—an excellent place to work on a sitting start, a technique unique to bouldering. Climbers have set up any number of traverses, and routes evolve.

Directions: By subway, take the C train to 96th Street and walk east, or take the 6 train to 96th Street and walk west.

MANHATTAN PLAZA HEALTH CLUB

Location: Manhattan

Outfitter: The Plaza (482 West 43rd Street; 212-563-7001, www.mhpc.com) offers day fees and memberships.

Description: It sounds more like a corporate sweatbox than a rock-hound magnet, but the Plaza is for real. The club converted a racquetball court into a wall in the '90s, and it got so popular that management added a second wall in an adjacent room in 2000, bringing the total wall space to more than 5,000 square feet. Better yet, the second wall was constructed by Entre-Prises, the world's largest climbing-wall builder. The firm, which also erected the wall at

Chelsea Piers, is known for creating surfaces with the look and feel of natural rock. The Plaza also boasts some impressive versatility. There's a 40-foot overhanging ceiling for lead climbing; a squeeze chimney, which is two parallel walls where you climb with hands and feet on opposite sides; a bouldering cave; and an area with some cracks where plenty of routes have been set up. The drawback is the wall is now located in the middle of a busy gym thoroughfare, and the comings and goings make it tough to concentrate.

Directions: By subway, take the A, C, E, N, R, Q, 1, 2, 3, or 7 train to 42nd Street and walk west. The club is between Ninth and Tenth Avenues.

REEBOK SPORTS CLUB/NY

Location: Manhattan

Outfitter: The wall (160 Columbus Avenue at 68th Street, 212-362-6800, www.phillipsclub.com/reebokTS.html) is open to members only.

Description: There's a 40-foot-high, 21-foot-wide climbing wall where qualified climbers can work on both top-roping and leading.

Directions: By subway, take the 1 or 2 train to 66th Street and walk north, or take the C train to 72nd Street and walk south.

CRUNCH

Location: Manhattan

Outfitter: Crunch's facilities (1109 Second Avenue at 59th Street, 212-758-3434, www.crunchfitness.com) are open to members only.

Description: The international chain offers a relatively narrow strip of wall, visible from the street. It's not much of a destination for hard-core climbers, but it's fun to try out.

Directions: By subway, take the 6 train to 59th Street and walk east.

Where to Connect

Clubs and Organizations

- The City Climbers Club (www.climbnyc.com) offers instruction. Or just go and hang out; advice is free.
- The Central Park Conservancy's adventure program (212-348-4867, www.centralparknyc.org) offers climbing instruction.

Shops

A few places to find rock-climbing gear:

- Eastern Mountain Sports (20 West 61st Street, Manhattan, 212-397-4860; and 611 Broadway, Manhattan, 212-505-9860)
- Paragon Sports (867 Broadway, Manhattan, 212-255-8036)
- Tent and Trails (21 Park Place, Manhattan, 212-227-1760)

Sea Kayaking

HELICOPTERS CHATTER OVERHEAD. Seaplanes buzz by. A blue-whale-sized barge rumbles past, churning up a wake that could have starred in *The Perfect Storm*.

Say this about sea kayaking on the Hudson River in New York City: If you dip a paddle in here, or any other waterway in Gotham's vast mosaic of rivers, harbors, and bays, you don't have to go looking for adventure. It finds you quickly enough. There are tidal rips, strong currents, powerful headwinds, whip-crack sea squalls. It's unbelievably fun. "When you're in the harbor, you're in touch with natural forces in a way that you can't experience otherwise in Manhattan," says Randy Henriksen, owner of New York Kayak Company.

"It's just you and basic elements: wind, currents, tides. There's so much sensory data coming in, you can't think about anything else." Like the city itself, a paddling trip here is alternately exhilarating and jarring. There's also a startling otherness to it.

From the cockpit of a sea kayak, the din fades, and the cityscape—Wall Street, Battery Park, the bridges and monuments—widens to wondrous I-Max dimensions. Beyond the harbor are salt marshes and beaches where seals hang out in winter, where the only man-made sounds might be jumbo jets roaring into the sky.

Sea kayaking is relatively new and unknown here; among all its other charms, there's a sort of pioneering feel to it. This will change as the sport creeps into the mainstream over the next decade. The water is cleaner than it has been for more than a century, and a burgeoning number of paddling and rowing clubs are pushing to open boathouses from the Harlem River to the far reaches of Jamaica Bay.

This chapter touches on other paddle sports, such as canoeing and kayak sailing. You won't see many canoes in New York City waters, and for good reason: They're not built for big, swirling tidal currents. But they're fine for exploring the city's milder backwaters—eccentric, blossoming places such as the Bronx River and the Gowanus Canal, where only a few years ago a paddling trip required an iron stomach as much as a sturdy upper body.

No matter what you're paddling, the important part is just to do it. Neighborhoods in the city morph every few moon cycles. The waterfront? That's New York's last great frontier.

City Limits

THE HUDSON RIVER

Location: Manhattan

Length: Trips can range from short outings to day-long journeys.

Difficulty: Moderate

Water: The current is strong, so plan your trip around it. There is also an abundance of commercial vessel and ferry traffic, so use caution or go with an experienced guide.

Heads up: Once you are on the water, there is little access to the city looming above. Plan accordingly. Never paddle alone, and plan your route carefully.

Outfitters: Manhattan Kayak Company (212-924-1788, www.manhattankayak.com) and New York Kayak Company (212-924-1327, www.nykayak.com) run guided excursions from Chelsea Piers to the Intrepid Sea Air Space Museum and Battery Park, among other Hudson River destinations. The Downtown Boathouse (212-385-8169, www.downtownboathouse.org; 212-385-2790 for updates on hours of operation) runs free trips on weekends to either the Statue of Liberty or the Intrepid Sea Air Space Museum. Space is limited, and boats are filled by lottery; you must get to the pier by 8 A.M. to be eligible. Guests should take the free paddling lesson at least once to get a feel for the kayaks.

Description: Like the Montana sky and the Himalayas, the Hudson offers a lesson in perspective. I'm almost six-foot-seven, but I feel Lilliputian out here in a sea kayak. The water is wide and muscular, the traffic is abundant, even the piers loom high overhead. The Hudson is essentially a drowned river (see *Go With the Flow*, page 175)—engulfed by the Atlantic Ocean—and it behaves like an estuary, changing directions with the tides. Chances are you'll have to do some hard work, but the trick is to minimize it. To paddle north from Chelsea to the Intrepid Sea Air Space Museum, as I did with the Manhattan Kayak Company, you'll probably wrestle the current on the trip there so you can ride it home. That means crossing the path of the New York Waterways ferry as it chugs back and forth to New Jersey, while battling a current that can easily hit 6 knots. The first time I did this I felt like a turtle crossing an expressway. Eric Stiller, owner of Manhattan Kayak and a guide on my outing, shepherded us over toward the edge of the city, out of the strongest water midriver. We ventured out of the eddies only when there was no choice.

I checked the skyline to gauge my progress; when the Empire State Building was behind me, I knew I was close. Heading back downstream, I reaped the rewards of all that work: The current swept us along, making the return all but effortless. Try to go on a clear evening, when the setting sun ignites the water's surface and midtown's glassy veneer. When night comes, the city is a galaxy that hovers portside.

Once you gather some experience, paddle from the outfitters to the Statue of Liberty. The kayak liberates you from the T-shirt stands, queues, and tourist families wearing foam crowns. Kayakers typically circle the statue, then glide back upstream on the incoming tide. One caveat: Only ferries can land at Liberty and Ellis Islands, so even though you may feel like a visiting conquistador, you can't plant a flag in front of the statue. If you need to disembark, go to Liberty State Park in New Jersey.

Directions: Manhattan Kayak Company is at Pier 63 at West 23rd Street, just north of Basketball City in the Chelsea Piers complex. New York Kayak Company is at 601 West 26th Street, 12th floor. Take the C, E, 1, or 2 train to 23rd Street. Walk west to the river, or take the westbound M23 bus to the last stop. For the Downtown Boathouse at Pier 26, between Canal and Chambers Streets, take the 1, 2, A, or C train to Chambers Street; walk west to the river, then six blocks north.

Go with the Flow

THE HUDSON CAN be a treacherous place for paddlers. The river is a highway of commerce, and many barge operators can't see kayaks in their path. One veteran paddler estimates that ferry traffic more than doubled between 1998 and 2000.

But the real perils are nature's doing. The natives who first occupied Manhattan called the Hudson *Muhheakunnuk*—"the river that flows two ways." When the tide comes in, it backs the river up almost as far north as Albany. During ebb tide, the current roars southward, ending its 315-mile run beyond the Verrazano Narrows, where it pours into the ocean. For this reason, you need to check which way the tide is headed before dropping a boat in the water. The removal of many piers in Manhattan has intensified the flow through the city.

It's important to remember, too, that you can't always plan for the elements. Sea squalls and thunderstorms occasionally blow in with little warning, and there are few places to exit the water. One group of Manhattan Kayak Company paddlers once sprinted back to Chelsea from the George Washington Bridge with streaks of lightning zigzagging across the cityscape.

For tide reports, go to www.tides.com. Under "support," click on daily predictions and select the mid-Atlantic region. For location, type in "Hudson River Entrance."

Prying Open the Riverfront

THOUGH SEA KAYAKING is becoming more popular, it remains hindered by paddlers' limited access to the water. There are 578 miles of coastline in New York, but much of it is owned by the Port Authority and various commercial interests who don't want to deal with the cost or liability of a boat launch.

That's why waterfront-access groups such as the Downtown Boathouse (212-385-8169, www.downtownboathouse.org) are so crucial. The organization started in the early '90s as a loosely connected group of kayakers brought together by the desire to store their boats at a shabby but structurally sound boathouse at Pier 26 in Tribeca.

After a few years, members decided on a more philanthropic concept. They solicited donations of used boats, and in 1995 the club obtained a license to make free kayaking available. Volunteers offer a "30-second lesson," then let you paddle a sit-on-top kayak around a protected embayment. "Our business model is cheap boats, lousy life jackets, cranky staff," jokes Graeme Birchall, who helps run the public program. "But it's free." From 1995 to 1999, the number of users increased from 100 to 11,000.

The club opened a second boathouse in 2000 at Pier 64 on West 23rd Street in Chelsea and hopes to keep going. But the boathouse at Pier 26 is slated for demolition, and the city has not yet indicated how its replacement will be used. (A for-profit vendor is among possible scenarios.) How can you help? Buying a $50 membership helps pay for public programs and equipment. More significantly, if membership rolls swell, that might help convince the city to leave the Downtown Boathouse as it is: free and accessible to all.

CIRCLING MANHATTAN

Location: Manhattan

Length: 7 to 11 hours, covering roughly 30 miles

Difficulty: Strong intermediate skills are a minimum.

Water: A variety of conditions, but strong current throughout. You'll pass under 10 bridges, including the Brooklyn, Williamsburg, and Queensboro.

Outfitters: The Manhattan Kayak Company and New York Kayak Company both lead circumnavigations (see contact information above). A trip costs $200 and up, depending on whether you purchase it as part of a package.

Description: This is the holy grail of the New York kayaking scene: a circumnavigation that requires decent conditioning and solid paddling skills.

Kayakers usually start from the Downtown Boathouse, circle around the Battery, and head up the East River. The East—not actually a river at all, but a tidal channel—has some of the most aggressive currents you'll face, culminating at Hell Gate, the Dantean mishmash of water that results from the East River's confluence with Long Island Sound. There's little room for miscalculation. "It's actually very simple," says Peter Wallace, president of East River Community Recreation and Education on the Water. "If you're late even by an hour with the tide, don't fight it because you're going to lose. But if you ride with it, nobody has a problem."

There's a tricky section where you may have to beat your way through the swirling currents of the Harlem River, another tidal channel that links the East and Hudson. Some paddlers have reported hearing organ music and cheers from Yankee Stadium as they battled the elements. But once you make the U-turn around the tip of the city at Inwood Hill Park and get the George Washington Bridge in your sights, you've got it made unless there's a ferocious headwind. Just

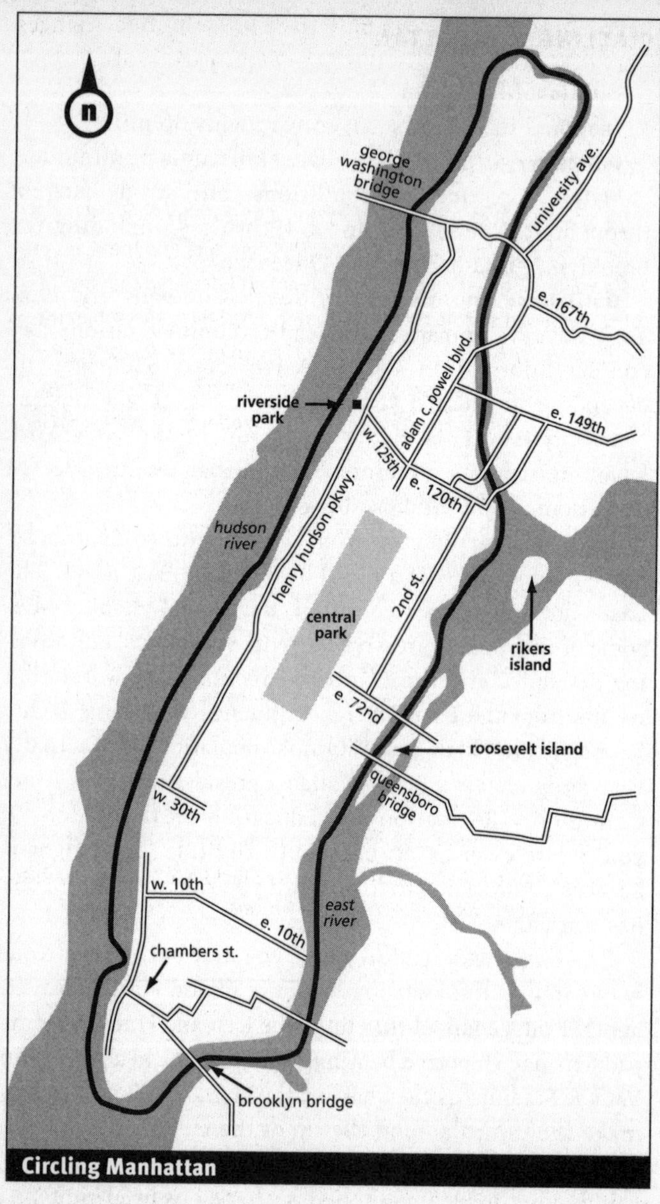

Circling Manhattan

don't pause too long to enjoy the view; the tide changes every 6 1/2 hours (see *Go With the Flow*, page 175).

Iron Man

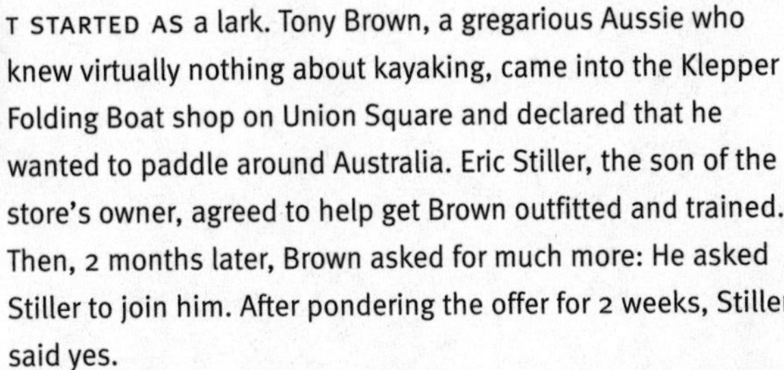

T STARTED AS a lark. Tony Brown, a gregarious Aussie who knew virtually nothing about kayaking, came into the Klepper Folding Boat shop on Union Square and declared that he wanted to paddle around Australia. Eric Stiller, the son of the store's owner, agreed to help get Brown outfitted and trained. Then, 2 months later, Brown asked for much more: He asked Stiller to join him. After pondering the offer for 2 weeks, Stiller said yes.

The enormity of the trip—about 10,000 miles—didn't sink in until the pair set off in 1992. Their inexperience didn't help. "I was like a good 10K runner trying to run a marathon in Death Valley," Stiller says, "and Tony was like someone putting on a pair of running shoes for the second time." Among the toughest moments: a sleepless 6-day, 5-night crossing of the Gulf of Carpenteria. "In hindsight it's fun, and when you're preparing for it you're thinking it's going to be great, but when you're actually doing it, it's a totally different story," says Stiller, founder of Manhattan Kayak Company. Though they didn't finish, they covered 4,500 miles in 5 months—the longest two-man kayak trip in recorded history. Stiller recounts his exploits in his book, *Keep Australia On Your Left*.

CANOEING THE BRONX

Location: Bronx

Length: Trips can be tailored to whatever amount of time you have, but plan on 3 to 4 hours to get a thorough look at just over 2 miles of water.

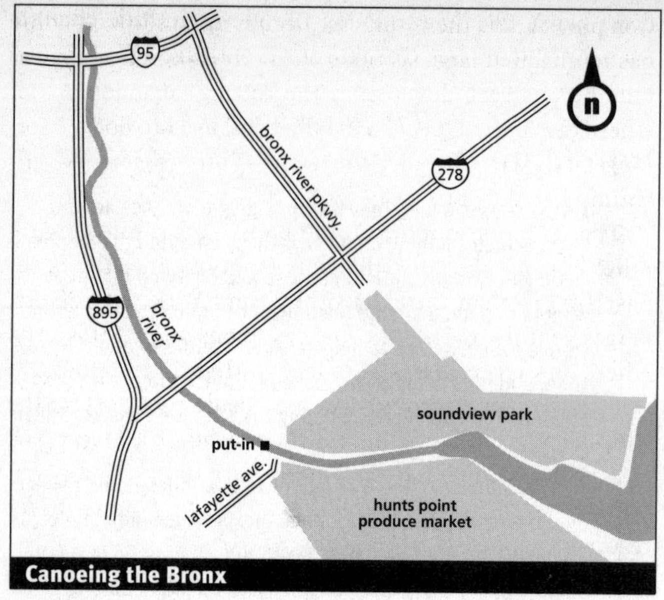

Canoeing the Bronx

Difficulty: Beginners will do fine.

Water: Mild, with almost no current; watch for headwinds near the East River

Outfitter: The Point (940 Garrison Avenue, the Bronx; 718-542-4139), a nonprofit community development organization, recently built a temporary boathouse and launch; canoe rides are free by appointment. Ask for Nino DeSimone, a native of the Bronx's Little Italy and an avid diver and maritime scientist.

Description: Only a few years ago, it would have been easy for paddlers and neighbors to dismiss the Bronx as hopeless. The city's only wild, freshwater river winds under highways and train trestles, past an abandoned highway, factories, and urban decay. At some points, you still have to steer your boat around junk cars. But the city and surrounding communities have made the river a reclamation project, and the results are beginning to show. Wildlife has reinhabited large sections of the river. Egrets and great blue herons gaze down from the rotting, abandoned pier where the *Bronx Queen*, a fishing boat, used to dock. Foot-long trout dart through the waters. Blue crabs and gill shrimp live down there.

There's more solitude on the Bronx—which flows for 8 miles through the borough before emptying into the upper East River—than on most other New York City rivers. Barges venture up only the lower sections at high tide. And where the river passes through Starlight Park, massive weeping willows, cottonwoods and locust trees replace the back sides of buildings. Local kids attached a ladder to one tree so they can plunge into the world's unlikeliest swimming hole. It's only anecdotal evidence of a Bronx River resurrection, but it's compelling.

From the boat launch at Hunts Point, you can paddle as far north as Devoe Avenue and East 177th Street, just south of Bronx Zoo. When it gets too shallow, head back downstream. South of the Hunts Point boat launch, the river quickly gets wider and stronger, and a mile south of Hunts Point it spills into the open expanse of the East River, with La Guardia Airport, Shea Stadium, and Riker's Island looming in the distance. Stronger wind and currents often make the lower section more challenging.

Directions: By subway, take the 6 train to Hunts Point Avenue; walk under the Bruckner Expressway, bear left on Lafayette Avenue, and walk to the river.

The PATH to the River

MOST KAYAKING TRIPS present logistical challenges. Paddlers need vehicles to shuttle between the take-out and put-in. The metro area's vast public transportation network—teamed with a folding kayak—gives city paddlers a distinct advantage. For example, you can launch from the Downtown Boathouse (see *Prying Open the Riverfront,* page 176) in Tribeca, then paddle down the Hudson to the Statue of Liberty, through the Kill van Kull, and up the Passaic River to Newark. When you're done, fold up your boat into a 35-pound backpack and jump on a PATH train back to the city.

New York Kayak Company founder Randy Henriksen grew up in Minnesota paddling canoes, but they were ill-suited for New York's rougher waters. Hence the folding kayaks he sells out of his Chelsea shop. "If not for folding kayaks, I wouldn't be here," says Henriksen, who moved to New York to write fiction in 1985. "I intended to leave a long time ago."

Launching Pads

SPACE IS MONEY in Manhattan. After all, this is a city where parking spots are passed down like heirlooms. So, because you're unlikely to be able to shoehorn your 17-foot fiberglass sea kayak into your studio apartment, the question arises: What now? And, more to the point, how much is it going to cost?

Manhattan Kayak Company charges around $600 per boat per year. But there are other, more creative solutions. You can store your kayak at the Downtown Boathouse if you volunteer for the community-service programs, but it takes more than a few token appearances. The club president divvies up kayak slots among the most dedicated volunteers. To volunteer, stop in during public-access hours or visit the Web site. The Downtown Boathouse will let you launch your kayak from their dock, provided you have the necessary gear and can establish that you know how to navigate the Hudson's mercurial waters. Look for the cramped storage scene to improve in coming years, with boathouses popping up all over the city.

PADDLING THE GOWANUS CANAL

Location: Brooklyn

Length: A paddling trip can last anywhere from 20 minutes to 3 hours, depending on your pace and the number of side channels you explore. The put-in is near the head of the canal's 2.5-mile length, so you can venture either upstream, near the northern terminus at Butler Street, or downstream, toward Gowanus Bay in New York Harbor.

Difficulty: Easy

Water: This flatwater excursion isn't tricky until you get out into the bay, where winds can pick up.

Outfitter: The Gowanus Dredgers Canoe Club (718-243-0849, www.waterfrontmuseum.org/dredgers) keeps two canoes chained next to the water on Second Street. If you've never been on the canal, ask Owen Foote or another member of the Dredgers to take you out for a free tour. A $100 membership buys you a copy of the keys to the canoe locks. You can then use the canoes at will by signing them out on the club's Web site.

Heads up: The canal is largely sealed off from the Brooklyn neighborhoods it passes through. Once you push off, there are few places to get out of the canoe and onto dry land. Plan accordingly.

Books: *Heartbeats in the Muck: A Dramatic Look at the History, Sea Life, and Environment of New York Harbor* details some of the canal's colorful history.

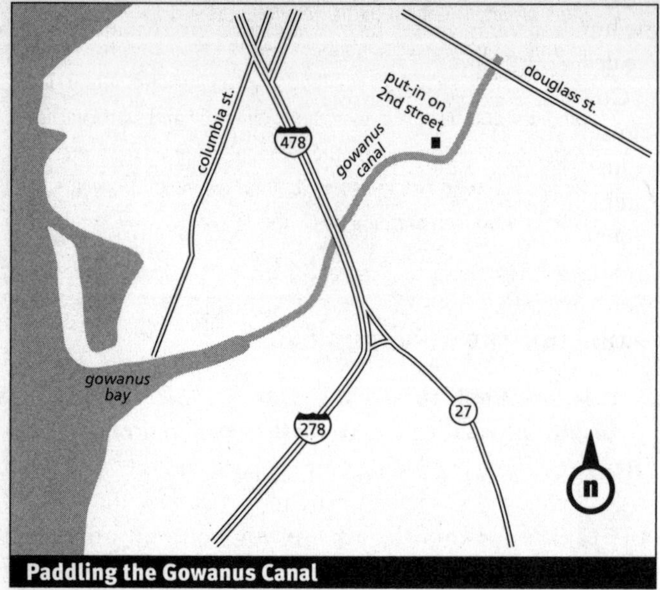

Paddling the Gowanus Canal

Description: For anyone remotely interested in New York's history and waterfront, this is a must-see. You'll paddle past old, rusting cranes and working gravel-crushing operations. When the water drops at low tide, you can drift between the rotting support beams of a half-sunken barge. The long-polluted but fast-recovering canal in Brooklyn's Carroll Gardens and Red Hook neighborhoods is a fascinating collision of decay and resurrection. At times the canal is a wasteland of litter, vacant buildings, and barbed wire, and its history of abuse will raise the hair on the back of your neck. On my excursion, our canoe passed bits of trash that had settled in a slick gray grime. A latex glove floated by.

But recent improvements in water quality are also apparent. The canal walls are lined with fiddler crabs. Gowanus advocates are working to reintroduce a native species of oyster (they grew as large as dinner plates a couple hundred years ago). The water can be greasy as you paddle deeper into Brooklyn, but where it mixes with seawater in Gowanus Bay it's a shimmering blue. Try to go when the sun sets over the gritty, flat-topped buildings of Red Hook; at just the right angle you can see the Statue of Liberty's torch and Staten Island across the open water.

Directions: By subway, take the F or G train to Carroll Street; exit to the front, cross Smith Street, and veer left, then turn right on 2nd Street and head downhill to the canal.

Eau de Gowanus

THE GOWANUS CANAL used to stink. There's no way to put it delicately. A busy shipping channel built in the 1800s, it was heavily polluted by an industrial stew of petroleum and dyes; printing plants poured in so much waste that the canal was nicknamed Lavender Lake. So in 1911, the city opened a tunnel equipped with a large propeller to flush cleaner water through from New York Harbor. But the tunnel's propeller shaft broke in the 1960s, and city engineers decided not to fix it, concluding that a sewage-treatment facility in Red Hook would reduce the stench in the neighborhood. It didn't work that way. The canal water stagnated, and a gravy of sewage, petroleum, and dead fish settled on the bottom. Most days it reeked of rotten eggs.

The Gowanus has improved immensely since the city repaired and reopened the tunnel in March 2000. The canal sends off the familiar old stench only at low tide, when contaminated sediment is exposed. But high tide in the bay is now actually a pleasant olfactory experience; sometimes the only scent wafting over the canal is of fresh bread from a nearby Italian bakery.

The Gowanus Dredgers Canoe Club formed soon after the

tunnel was repaired, and the group now has two canoes stationed on the canal to give rides to anyone willing to check it out. "We're called the Dredgers because we hope someday the canal will be dredged," says Owen Foote, one of the founders. "I hope that's in my lifetime, but realistically it will probably be in my children's lifetime. And I don't have any kids."

The debate over the canal's future breaks down into several camps. Some envision the neighborhood returning to its industrial roots, whereas Foote's group envisions a blend of housing, small businesses, and galleries. Still others see it gentrified and artsy, with gondolas and outdoor cafes—like the Venice of New York.

During my outing with Foote, the Venice concept seemed a little absurd. The only eatery on the canal now is "a pathetic little Nathan's," as Foote puts it, attached to a Home Depot and faced away from the water so the canal doesn't ruin customers' appetites. Foote shrugs. Once the canal is cleaner still, it'll be fine just as it is, he suggests. "You can get twelve or fourteen people together with a couple of canoes, and nobody bothers you," Foote says. "For now, it's just us out here."

JAMAICA BAY

Location: Brooklyn and Queens

Difficulty: Easy to moderate.

Water: There are tides and winds to be aware of here. Best to go with someone from the Sebago group the first time.

Outfitter: The Sebago Canoe Club (718-331-8577, www.sebagocanoeclub.org) has a launch on Paerdegat Basin in Brooklyn, where it offers annual clinics on canoe and kayak sailing and sea kayaking. Alternatively, you can launch from Floyd Bennett Field with a car-top boat permit; call (718) 338-3799 and allow 7 to 10 working days.

Maps: USGS Map 12350 will help you negotiate the marshy maze.

Description: Members of the local Sebago Canoe Club sometimes rig sails to their canoes and kayaks to help them cover more of this section of the Gateway National Recreation Area. There are, after all, 18 square miles of marshes and more than a dozen islands of phragmite and spartina grasses. All the more chance to hang out with birds, ranging from ubiquitous ruddies and buffleheads to rarer species such as black-bellied plovers and oystercatchers. The flats are loaded with mussels and other mollusks (though it's illegal to harvest them because the bay was so polluted for so long) as well as box turtles and hognose snakes.

If you want just to paddle, leave the open water and explore tidal mudflats, winding channels, and salt marshes amid flocks of shorebirds. You can actually get lost in marshes such as Elders Point and Pumpkin Patch, where disorienting mazes of towering marsh grasses and bulrushes obscure the surrounding cityscape. Some channels lead to open water; others are dead ends. Departing 747s from nearby JFK International Airport keep this from being an entirely Thoreau-like experience, but between takeoffs an enormous quiet fills the marsh. A great place to explore, but bring a compass.

Directions: By subway, take the L train to Canarsie/Rockaway Parkway; connect to the B42 bus to Rockaway Parkway and Avenue N, then walk southwest on Avenue N about 15 blocks to Paerdegat Avenue North. The club is located between Diamond Point Yacht Club and Paerdegat Athletic Club.

By car, take the Belt Parkway to exit 13 (Rockaway Parkway), follow the parkway 0.5 mile, turn left on Avenue M, and follow until it ends on Paerdegat Avenue North. Turn left; the club is on the right.

Short Hops

THE MEADOWLANDS

Location: Secaucus, New Jersey, 7 miles west of Manhattan

Difficulty: Easy to moderate. The marsh is calm, but if you venture onto the Hackensack River you'll need to know how to handle some current.

Water: Swampy flatwater. Watch for strong headwinds on the river.

Outfitter: The Hackensack Meadowlands Development Commission (201-460-1700, www.hmdc.state.nj.us) offers guided trips on Mill Creek and may open a canoe concession. The Hackensack River Canoe & Kayak Club (www.geocities.com/hrckc) and the Wanda Canoe Club (201-836-8139, www.ci-ridgefield-park.nj.us/village/wandacanoeclub.htm) both run paddling trips in the area.

Books: There are no paddling guides, but to whet your appetite try *The Meadowlands: Wilderness Adventures on the Edge of a City* and *Fields of Sun and Grass: An Artist's Journal of the New Jersey Meadowlands*.

Description: Save the I-think-my-paddle-just-struck-Jimmy-Hoffa cracks. Yes, the legendary North Jersey swamps are known as a "wilderness" of superhighways, toxic waste, and Himalayan mounds of trash. But you'll be surprised to find the Meadowlands also contain reasonably healthy estuaries and rivers and grasses that shelter flocks of migrating and native birds such as green herons and northern harriers. Fish and shellfish have returned. This is testimony to nature's restorative powers, and to the work of the Hackensack Meadowlands Development Commission (HMDC), which is trying to simultaneously protect the ecosystem and improve its economic prospects. In summer 2001, HMDC and the city of Secaucus opened a canoe launch on the Mill Creek Wildlife Management Area, a 260-acre wetland adjacent to the Hackensack River.

A paddling trip out here is an exercise in the surreal. There are swaying grasses and a stirring quietude only 5 miles from Manhattan's skyline, visible in the distance. "You feel like you're on the *Amazon Queen*," says Katy Weidel, a landscape architect at HMDC. It also can be surprisingly adventurous. There are substantial currents, especially if you venture out onto the tidal Hackensack River.

Directions: Provided by HMDC

NASSAU COUNTY

Location: Island Park, Long Island, 28 miles southeast of Manhattan

Difficulty: Easy (though the kayak surfing takes some practice)

Water: Usually quiet and smooth on the bay; the surf clinic involves modest surf

Outfitter: Empire Kayaks in Island Park (516-889-8300, www.empirekayaks.com) rents standard and tandem kayaks.

Description: If you don't want to dodge barges on the Hudson but can't travel far, Island Park is a just-beyond-city-limits oasis. Put in from Island Park, which is protected from open water by Long Beach on Nassau County's south shore, and you can explore tidal channels and marshes speckled with shorebirds and several island beaches accessible only by boat. In Reynolds Channel, the locals buzz about the proliferation of crab, bluefish, and huge fluke. And if you just can't do without civilization for long, paddle over to Long Beach's 2-mile boardwalk and restaurants.

On alternate Wednesday evenings, Empire Kayaks offers

either a sunset tour or a free kayak-surfing clinic. When surfing, expect to get tossed from the sit-on-top kayaks into the foam a few times until you learn how to lean into the waves just as they crest and break. But once you get it—and the breakers carry you into shore rather than dump you—the *Hawaii Five-0* theme loops endlessly in your head. The outfitter also runs occasional sunrise tours, which begin in the gloom at 5:30 A.M. and end with the early-morning sky aflame.

Directions: By train, take the Long Island Rail Road to the Island Park station. Walk or take a cab 1 mile up Long Beach Road. Turn left on Empire Boulevard; the outfitter is at the end of the street on the left.

By car, take the Long Island Expressway (I-495) east to Van Wyck south; head east on the Southern Parkway to exit 20S; then go 2 miles and turn onto Sunrise Highway (NY 27) headed west. Turn left on Long Beach Road; turn left onto Empire Boulevard. Empire Kayak is at the end of the street on the left.

LONG ISLAND'S NORTH SHORE

Location: Sea Cliff, Long Island, 29 miles east of Manhattan

Difficulty: Easy

Water: Conditions are usually smooth, with no breaking waves. The harbor is fairly busy with sailboats, so stick close to shore leaving the harbor.

Outfitter: Sea Cliff Kayakers (516-220-5434, www.seacliffkayakers.com) offers kayak rentals, instruction, and guided sunset paddling trips that are free if you have your own boat.

Description: Sea Cliff is classic North Shore. J. P. Morgan, among other old-money magnates, bought up huge chunks of waterfront property in the 19th century, and there has been relatively little subdividing since. The result: No condos are shoehorned ass-to-elbow along the chastely developed shoreline. What you find here is smooth Long Island Sound paddling, wooded shores, and plenty of birds. Once you kayak out of Hempstead Harbor, you've got the best kind of tough decision to make: You must either go west, toward several old mansions and the Theodore Roosevelt Bird Sanctuary, or east to the Welwyn Preserve, a 204-acre estate built by oil merchant Charles Pratt. Its freshwater swamps and ponds, nature trails, and salt marsh are now home to nesting osprey and plenty of cormorants, herons, and egrets. You can pick out the Nassau County park by the regiment of tulip trees standing at attention more than 100 feet above the shore.

On a slow day you might get to paddle with Sea Cliff Kayakers owner Melissa Halliday, a town native who returned home and started the business in 1999 after long detours through Northern California and Ecuador. She's a font of local history.

Directions: By train, take the Long Island Rail Road to Sea Cliff. Arrange in advance with Halliday for transportation. Or walk up the hill on Sea Cliff Avenue and continue about 1 mile. Turn right on Prospect Avenue and left on Cliff Way to the beach.

By car, take the Long Island Expressway to exit 39 and follow Glen Cove Road north for about 4 miles. Bear right at the sign for Sea Cliff/Cedar Swamp Road. At the traffic light, take the immediate left turn onto Sea Cliff Avenue and drive into Sea Cliff. Where Sea Cliff Avenue ends, turn right on Prospect Avenue. Turn left on Cliff Way and follow it to the bottom of the hill and around a hairpin turn. Turn left after passing the Sea Cliff Beach Pavilion. Sea Cliff Kayakers is on the beach to the far right of the pavilion.

NORWALK ISLANDS

Location: Norwalk, Connecticut, 46 miles northeast of Manhattan

Difficulty: Easy

Water: This sheltered stretch of water is usually quite tame.

Outfitter: The Small Boat Shop in Norwalk (203-854-5223, www.thesmallboatshop.com) offers full-day guided trips June through October that are discounted if you bring your own kayak. Year-round instruction is also available.

Description: The chain of a dozen or so uninhabited islands off the coast of Connecticut in Long Island Sound is a birder's paradise. You have to paddle 1 to 3 miles to reach them, but it's a relatively easy open-water crossing if there's no headwind. The four largest islands are the biggest attractions. Sheffield and Chimon Islands are part of the Stewart B. McKinney National Wildlife Refuge, which includes three other islands, tidal salt marshes, and some mainland properties. Nearby Shea and Cockenoe Islands, which are administered by the towns of Norwalk and Westport, respectively, are open for camping by permit.

The bird life is abundant, especially during the spring and fall migrations; 68-acre Chimon Island is home to about 135 species of birds, including the endangered roseate tern and the piping plover, a threatened species. The island hosts one of the largest wading bird colonies in the Northeast, with a mixed rookery of herons, egrets, and glossy ibis that has grown to more than 1,000 pairs from only a handful 40 years ago. The island, accessible only by boat, has a 3-acre beach, forests, and thick, shrubby landscapes. In autumn, it might be just you, the birds, and the deer. In winter, if you're dressed warmly, it's worth paddling to nearby Smith Reef, between Norwalk and Darien, to check out the harbor seals wintering in the Sound.

Directions: By train, take Metro-North to South Norwalk; exit to the right out of the parking lot onto Monroe Street and walk toward the water. At the second traffic light, turn right on Water Street, then left into Rex Marine Center; the shop is at the end of the gravel driveway.

By car, take I-95 north to exit 14; go right off the ramp. At the fourth traffic light, turn right onto Water Street, then left into Rex Marine Center.

North Fork by Night

SALT MARSHES BECOME fascinatingly spooky after dark. The wind dies and all the croaks, chatters, and hoots get a little louder. Look for jellyfish and other swimmers that glow green in your wake, or when touched by a paddle. Don't worry, it's not nuclear spillage from the nearby Brookhaven reactor but bioluminescence, a natural phenomenon. Two outfitters, Cornell Marine Learning Center (631-852-8660) and Eagle's Neck Paddling Company (631-765-3502, www.eaglesneck.com), run full-moon paddling trips.

Meccas

THE HAMPTONS

Location: East Hampton, Long Island, 105 miles east of Manhattan

Difficulty: Easy

Water: Generally quiet and unspoiled

Outfitter: Main Beach Surf & Sport in Wainscott (631-537-2716, www.mainbeach.com) rents single and double kayaks. Rowboats, rowing shells, sea cycles, and sailboats are also available.

Description: Yes, we know about the jangling cell phones, the Monopoly money, the frenetic air-kissing. But the pristine salt marshes, tidal ponds and estuaries, and roaring surf provide refuge for paddlers of all persuasions. And if you want some glitter, a sea kayak can actually improve your chances of spotting celebrities at their multimillion-dollar digs. Paddle a kayak on Georgica Pond in East Hampton and the seasonal shorebirds you might glimpse include osprey, egrets, Martha Stewart, and Calvin Klein.

Georgica Pond is a 290-acre freshwater refuge for piping plovers and least terns, both threatened species. Mute swan pairs have been seen nesting there. Shallow and spring-fed, Georgica is separated from the Atlantic only by a thin strip of beach, so kayakers can drag their boats across the sand and shove off into the surf—or abandon ship for a while and go after some of the abundant (and highly edible) crab population.

The region is pocked with similar oases: Shinnecock Bay, Sagaponack Pond, and Hook Pond among them. Another option is to head over to nearby Cedar Point and paddle a meandering estuary loaded with mussels; eventually you'll spill out into a pond, where at high tide you can follow submerged deer trails.

Directions: By car, take the Long Island Expressway to the Sunrise Highway (NY 27) east; the outfitter is at 328 Montauk Highway (NY 27).

THE MAINE ISLAND TRAIL

Location: Portland to Machias, Maine, 310 miles northeast of Manhattan

Difficulty: Ranges from intermediate to expert, depending on the region

Water: From quiet coves to the open Atlantic

Outfitters: The Maine Island Kayak Company (800-796-2373, www.sea-kayak.com) of Peaks Island, and Coastal Kayaking Tours (800-526-8615, www.acadiafun.com) of Bar Harbor are among many outfitters running a variety of trips.

Description: This is the crown jewel of East Coast sea kayaking: a collection of about 100 astoundingly rugged and beautiful public islands scattered along 325 miles of Maine coast from Casco Bay to Machias. Penobscot Bay, just one of dozens of highlights, is home to old schooners, craggy cliffs, lighthouses, and bird sanctuaries; pods of whales migrate through. Stonington has an evocative Down East harbor. And then you have the foreboding cliffs and crashing surf of Acadia National Park.

If you're planning a trip, invest $45 in a Maine Island Trail Association membership (207-596-6456, www.mita.org); it buys you access to privately owned islands not accessible to the general public and a guidebook that helps you find your way around.

Where to Connect

The Basics

Try an introductory paddling session to get a feel for the city's powerful, swirling waters before planning an excursion. The Downtown Boathouse offers a free introduction to the sport (see *Prying Open the Riverfront,* page 176).

For more detailed instruction, Manhattan Kayak Company (212-924-1788, www.manhattankayak.com) offers a free 45-minute classroom session in July and August on the basics of paddling, followed by a supervised tryout at its Chelsea facility. The company also offers a full slate of beginner, intermediate, and advanced instruction.

New York Kayak Company (212-924-1327, www.nykayak.com) has some distinguished credentials: Len Hartley is one of only fourteen instructors in the world to hold the British Canoe Union's top coaching certification, the BCU equivalent of a black belt. The BCU began certifying sea kayak instructors in the 1960s, much like the Austrian Ski Patrol pioneered the training and certification of ski instructors. Hartley's fundamentals courses cover subjects such as leaning, turning, and edging.

Clubs and Organizations

- The Downtown Boathouse (Pier 26 and Pier 64, Manhattan, 212-385-8169, www.downtownboathouse.org)
- Floating the Apple (212-564-5412, www.floatingtheapple.org) has opened boathouses in Manhattan, the Bronx, and Brooklyn; it builds and rows sturdy Whitehalls and aims to restore "universal access onto the public waterways."
- East River CREW (Community Recreation and Education on the Water, Manhattan, 212-427-3956, www.maxpages.com/eastrivercrew) is working to replace a boathouse on East 90th Street where a 1999 fire claimed a pier and historic fireboat facility.
- The Red Hook Navy in Brooklyn (212-352-9330, dave.lutz@treebranch.com) is working on a boathouse project in the renovated Valentino Park.
- Sebago Canoe Club in Brooklyn (718-331-8577, www.sebagocanoeclub.org) organizes paddling, rowing, and sailing trips around metropolitan New York.
- Rocking the Boat in the Bronx (718-466-5799)
- The New York Restoration Project (Manhattan, 212-258-2333, www.nyrp.org), Bette Midler's brainchild, recently built a floating boathouse on the Harlem River to house community rowing programs.

- The Hudson River Watertrail Association (www.hrwa.org) is a nonprofit group working to establish a trail from the mouth of the Hudson to the Great Lakes and the St. Lawrence Seaway, providing overnight facilities every 10 to 12 miles.
- The Hackensack River Canoe & Kayak Club (Bogota, NJ, www.geocities.com/hrckc) runs paddling trips in the Meadowlands.
- The Wanda Canoe Club (Ridgefield Park, NJ, 201-836-8139, www.ci-ridgefield-park.nj.us/village/wandacanoeclub.htm) is a storied canoe racing organization based on the Hackensack River.
- The Appalachian Mountain Club's New York–North Jersey chapter (212-986-1430, www.amc-ny.org) conducts paddling trips and clinics.

Shops and Outfitters

- Manhattan Kayak Company (Pier 63 at West 23rd Street, Manhattan 212-924-1788, www.manhattankayak.com) offers a variety of services, from instruction to guided trips to "kayak polo." Founder Eric Stiller is determined to see the sport grow in the city. Don't bet against him.
- New York Kayak Company (601 West 26th Street, Manhattan, 12th floor; 212-924-1327, www.nykayak.com) sells foldable kayaks and offers instruction and guided trips. Owner Randy Henriksen clearly has a passion for the boats.
- Paragon Sports (867 Broadway, Manhattan, 212-255-8036) sells kayaks and gear.
- Kayak Sleepy Hollow (888-321-4837, www.kayakhudson.com) runs tours on the Hudson 2 miles north of the Tappan Zee Bridge.

Events

- The Meadowlands Cup Race (201-941-4738) is an annual two-person canoe race at Laurel Hill Park in Secaucus, NJ.
- Mayday on the Bay is an annual 3-mile race around Garrett Marsh in Nassau County. Contact Empire Kayaks (516-889-8300, www.empirekayaks.com).
- Kayak Round the Island Benefit (609-285-2060, www.capemaybeach.com/kayakround.html) features races of 10 and 20 miles in the Wildwoods in New Jersey.

Books

- Adams, Arthur G. *The Hudson River Guidebook*. Bronx, NY: Fordham University Press, 1996.
- Mittelbach, Margaret, and Michael Crewdson. *Wild New York*. New York, NY: Three Rivers Press, 1997.
- Quinn, John R. *Fields of Sun and Grass: An Artist's Journal of the New Jersey Meadowlands*. New Brunswick, NJ: Rutgers University Press, 1997.
- Seitz, Sharon, and Stuart Miller. *The Other Islands of New York City*. 2d ed. Woodstock, VT: Countryman Press, 2001.
- Stiller, Eric. *Keep Australia on Your Left*. New York, NY: Forge Books, 2000.
- Sullivan, Robert. *The Meadowlands: Wilderness Adventures on the Edge of a City*. New York, NY: Anchor Books, 1998.
- Waldman, John. *Heartbeats in the Muck: A Dramatic Look at the History, Sea Life, and Environment of New York Harbor*. New York, NY: Lyons Press, 1999.

White Water

NEW YORK CITY lacks the hilly terrain that it takes to create rushing rivers. Blame it on the last great freeze some 20,000 years ago, when the Wisconsin ice sheet bulldozed everything in sight, leaving much of the local terrain as flat as a manhole cover. That's the bad news.

The good news: Head out of New York in any direction except east, and within a couple of hours you can find enough hissing, churning water to satisfy even the most fearless steep-creeker. To the south, New Jersey's rocky creeks roil when it rains; drive several hours more and you reach West Virginia's monster rivers. To the west are the scenic runs of the Delaware Water Gap. To the northeast is the Housatonic, a moderate river where you

can practice surfing and rolling without worrying about getting sucked into any boat-eating holes. And when the snow melts off all those mountains in the Adirondacks, several upstate rivers thunder with Class IV and V water.

If you're not an experienced paddler, it's best to get your first taste of white water in the relative safety of a raft. (Rafting is available on all entries here except the Tohickon.) And although the first three rivers in this chapter are suitable for intermediate-level and sometimes beginner kayakers, the average weekend wetsuit warrior will want to tackle the final two, the Hudson Gorge and the Gauley, in a guided raft; these runs should be attempted in kayaks only by elite paddlers. In most cases, timing is all-important. Plan to go in spring, when snowmelt creates torrents of water, or after a major rainfall.

You will expend a bit of effort getting to white water, but the payoff is commensurate. Ask anyone who has dropped into a roiling hole, hung on through the torrent, and popped out the other side. You're never the same again.

Short Hops

UPPER DELAWARE RIVER

Location: Pond Eddy, New York, 101 miles northeast of Manhattan

Length: 10 miles

Difficulty: Fine for beginners in rafts; for kayakers, conditions range from beginner to advanced

Outfitter: Kittatinny Canoes (800-356-2852, www.kittatinny.com) offers rafting trips and kayak rentals and will often throw in a campsite with the fee. Pack Shack Adventures (570-424-8533, www.packshack.com) and Adventure

Sports (800-487-2628, www.adventuresport.com) offer multiday canoe/camping trips to the south, in the milder currents of the Delaware Water Gap, where there's also excellent March runoff paddling on the Paulinskill and Pequest Rivers.

Description: The Delaware is the northeastern paddler's version of Old Faithful—it reliably spouts good water, whatever the climate. The river is regulated by releases from five reservoirs, so you can expect consistent rapids even through dry summers. The Upper Delaware Scenic and Recreation River—just north of the Delaware Water Gap, about 90 minutes from Manhattan—is where you'll find the best hydraulics. Most rafters and paddlers focus on a 10-mile section from Pond Eddy to Matamoras, which features two Class III rapids: Staircase, a series of descending ledges, and Butler's Rift, where in high-water conditions a standing wave rises like a threatened cobra, swelling as high as 8 feet. (Another high-water note: When the river is swollen, you can start at Barryville, which adds 7 miles and another series of holes and haystacks.) The locals always look forward to the run over Skinner's Falls, so named for a legendary logger who rode logs to be used as ship masts down to Philadelphia.

The Upper Delaware has mostly fun and easy stuff—Class II, with some Class III mixed in when the water is high—so it doesn't require a lot of scouting or technical skills. And there's plenty to entrance you between rapids. Resident bald eagles roam the thermals above the spectacular shale cliffs known as Elephant's Legs.

Directions: By car, take I-80 west to exit 34B; follow NJ 15 north to US 206 north, cross the Milford Bridge, and pick up US 209 north to Port Jervis. Turn at the second light onto NY 97 and follow it 14 miles to Pond Eddy.

TOHICKON CREEK

Location: Point Pleasant, Pennsylvania, 78 miles southwest of Manhattan

Length: 3.75 miles

Difficulty: You should have intermediate kayaking skills and the ability to roll. The Tohickon features mid- to upper-level Class III water, increasing to Class IV in high-water conditions. If you're a first-timer, don't put in if it's running higher than 4 feet unless you're going with a group of locals. If it's too high, go across the Delaware to the Lockatong and Wickecheoke. For updates on river levels, check www.pa.water.usgs.gov.

Outfitters: Bucks County River Country (Point Pleasant, PA, 215-297-2000, www.canoeonline.com) rents kayaks, canoes, and rafts.

Description: The creeks along the border of New Jersey and Pennsylvania just south of Trenton have turned local paddlers into Weather Channel addicts. When it rains, the streams roar, and the locals scramble for their boats.

The best of the bunch are the smaller creeks—New Jersey's Lockatong and Wickecheoke, and Pennsylvania's Tohickon—that spill into the Delaware about 80 miles south of the Water Gap. The Tohickon is the local favorite, a white-knuckle wonder located just over the state line in Ralph Stover State Park. During scheduled water releases on the third weekend in March and the first weekend in November, the creek offers nearly 4 miles of Class III and IV water filled with ledges, holes, and surfing waves. As one longtime paddler observed, "It's like you just took yourself to West Virginia." There are additional sporadic releases, but most locals just pray for rain up north in Bucks County. There's no time for warm-ups here; from the put-in, the action starts only a couple hundred yards downstream at a huge surfing hole called Fish or Swim.

The deep canyon draws lots of climbers; if you have time to look up, you'll see them top-roping the steep walls.

If the conditions are just right, try for what the locals call "the hat trick": all three rivers in the same day. Another local alternative is Scudder's Falls, a Class III play hole in the Delaware River above the I-95 bridge near Trenton.

Directions: By car, take the New Jersey Turnpike to I-78 west; take exit 15 and go south on SR 513 to Frenchtown. Take NJ 29 south to Ralph Stover State Park, which has river access. Take out at the small park in Point Pleasant, or at River Country's property. They'll shuttle you back to your car for a $5 fee that gets donated to the local fire department.

Shiver Me Timbers

THE BEAUTY OF spring paddling is that melted snow bloats the rivers. But the water temperatures can be beastly, often in the 40° to 50°F range. Outfitters provide wetsuits, but still, if you wind up out of the raft, the chill will penetrate your bone marrow. Keep calm, and remember to stay on your back and keep your feet out in front of you. You don't want to be hugging rocks, known in river-rat parlance as "romancing the stone."

HOUSATONIC RIVER

Location: West Cornwall, Connecticut, 104 miles northeast of Manhattan

Length: 4 miles

Difficulty: Mostly Class II—fine for intermediates and

beginners who've had some lessons—under normal conditions. Spring runoff on the Housy is for more experienced paddlers.

Outfitter: Clarke Outdoors Shop (West Cornwall, 860-672-6365, www.adventuresports.com/canoe/clarke) offers kayak rentals and self-guided four-, six-, or eight-person rafts and runs a shuttle service. Instruction is also available.

Heads up: The Housatonic Downriver Race is held annually in May. Contact Clarke Outdoors for information.

Description: The Housy winds down from the Berkshires and through industrial western Massachusetts before hitting its stride in postcard-perfect Litchfield County. Start your trip at West Cornwall's 160-year-old covered bridge, home of the river's biggest and most consistent water. The rapids rise nearly to Class III froth after a good rain or dam release, but provide fine surfing in spring under normal conditions. Over the next 4 miles there are numerous small waves and play spots on what is also an extremely popular catch-and-release trout fly-fishing section. Hang out in a series of haystacks where the river doglegs right 0.25 mile beyond the covered bridge; there's a huge eddy just below. And spend some time in the roiling hole next to the Housatonic Meadows State Park campground, a couple of miles to the south. Also, there's a short but intense practice run, called Rattlesnake Slalom, to the north in Falls Village.

During the drier stretches of summer, the river gets some help from the hydroelectric dam in Falls Village, so you should coordinate your paddling with the water releases. Consider going on weekdays in summer; the weekend armada of tubes, canoes, rafts, and kayaks looks like the crowd at a Jimmy Buffett concert. Other local options: In spring, check out the rafting run at Bulls Bridge in Kent (Zoar Outdoors, 413-337-8436). Or for Huck Finn–style relaxation, kick back on a tube at Satan's Kingdom State Recreation Area in Canton (Farmington River Tubing, 860-693-6465).

Directions: By car, from New York, take I-684 to I-84 east. Take exit 7 and follow US 7 north to Cornwall. Clarke Outdoors is a mile south of the covered bridge. To get to the put-in, go north on US 7, turn right on CT 128, and cross the covered bridge, then turn left. Take out at the Housatonic Meadows picnic area just above the intersection of US 7 and CT 4.

HUDSON RIVER GORGE

Location: North Creek, New York, 236 miles north of Manhattan

Length: 14 miles

Difficulty: No experience necessary on rafting trips, except on the Moose, where participants must have previously rafted Class IV water. Kayakers should be advanced paddlers able to handle all types of water.

Outfitters: Among others, Hudson River Rafting Company (800-888-7238, www.hudsonriverrafting.com), Middle Earth Expeditions (518-523-7172, www.adirondackrafting.com), and Wild Waters Outdoor Center (518-494-7478, www.wild-waters.com). Rafting trips generally start at about $75, though prices vary by season.

Heads up: The Hudson River Whitewater Derby (800-896-5428, www.whitewaterderby.com) is held annually in May in North Creek.

Description: New Yorkers used to seeing a miles-wide, sealike Hudson will hardly recognize the hellacious torrent roiling through the gorge. In fact, locals claim that this stretch of the Hudson is one of the top ten single-day white-water runs in the country. That may be hometown hyperbole, but there's no doubt that the gorge's run of Class

IV and V water delivers by anyone's standards. Most outfitters start with a warm-up on the Class III Indian River, which falls 150 feet over 3 miles. The Hudson then drops a vertiginous 500 feet during its 14-mile run through the gorge—a steeper drop than the Colorado River's descent down the Grand Canyon.

Plan to go in spring, when snowmelt has the river raging. And leave time for a jaunt on the Moose River, which swells to a ferocious Class V and is renowned as the most intense rafting trip in the Adirondacks. In fact, rivers emanate out of the "Dacks" like spokes on a wheel. It takes a little time and gasoline, but you can also notch the Ausable and Schroon in a couple more days. Where else can you run four white-water rivers in a single park?

Directions: By car, take I-87 to exit 23; follow NY 28 north to North Creek.

Meccas

GAULEY RIVER

Location: Summersville, West Virginia, 500 miles southwest of Manhattan

Length: 25 miles

Difficulty: In the Upper Gauley, take a raft unless you have superior kayaking skills. The optimal level is 2,000 to 3,000 cfs; avoid it when flow levels top 5,000 cfs. Strong intermediate skills are necessary to run the Lower Gauley between 5,000 and 15,000 cfs. For daily flow information, call the Summersville Dam at (304) 872-5809 or check the USGS Web site: www.waterdata.usgs.gov/nwis-w/WV.

Outfitters: New and Gauley River Adventures (800-759-7238, www.gauley.com) and Class IV River Runners (800-

252-7784, www.raftwv.com) are among numerous outfitters; call 800-225-5982 for a complete list. Rafting trips start at about $80.

Heads up: The Gauley Festival (914-586-2355) is held annually in September in Summersville.

Description: It's a long haul from New York City, but excluding the Gauley from this chapter would be like leaving the Appalachian Trail off a list of epic hikes. Most river rats rank the Gauley's 25 tumultuous miles among the world's ten best white-water runs. Consider the sheer numbers: Between the Upper and Lower Gauley, there are more than 100 rapids, over half of them Class III or higher.

The 12-mile Upper Gauley, with its multitude of Class IV and V rapids, is Mother Nature's ultimate mosh pit. This hair-raising collection of wrenching twists and drops includes world-famous rapids such as Insignificant, Pillow Rock, and Iron Ring. Needless to say, if you're kayaking you need lots of technical know-how; these are definitely not good places to be counting fish. The Lower Gauley is wider and less exacting, but a thrill nonetheless. There's a raft-pinning boulder at the bottom of the aptly named Mash, and another rapid, Pure Screaming Hell, is vigorous and nearly as long as eternity.

High season on the Gauley is autumn, when the Army Corps of Engineers releases 2,500 to 2,800 cfs (cubic feet per second) from three giant tubes at the base of Summersville Dam. The water release is a show in itself, like three monstrous fire hoses opened to full blast. In spring, the river is almost as turbulent and less crowded.

Directions: Summersville is off US 19 in central West Virginia.

Where to Connect

Clubs and Organizations

- Manhattan Kayak Company (Pier 63 at West 23rd Street, Manhattan, 212-924-1788, www.manhattan kayak.com), in its quest to become a full-service kayak outfit, offers rolling clinics every other week at Chelsea Piers. White-water instruction and kayak polo also offer ways to learn to maneuver. Founder Eric Stiller also offers paddling excursions to the Delaware, Housatonic, and other sites.
- New York Kayak Company (601 West 26th Street, Manhattan,12th floor, 212-924-1327, www.nykayak.com) also offers instruction.
- The Canoe and Kayak Club of New York (845-424-3169, www.kccny.org), based upstate, is another way to hook up with other paddlers.
- HACKS, aka the Housatonic Area Canoe and Kayak Squad (www.bestweb.net/~keech/hacks), offers competition and training opportunities.

Shops

- Paragon Sports (867 Broadway, Manhattan, 212-255-8036) is the place in the city to buy kayaks and gear; ask for Anatoli, the resident paddling expert.
- Eastern Mountain Sports sells kayaks, but not in the city; you have to go to the Carle Place store (516-747-7360) on Long Island.
- The Jersey Paddler in Brick, NJ (888-225-2925, www.jerseypaddler.com), is a major retailer with online shopping.
- Campmor in Paramus, NJ (800-226-7667, www.campmor.com), has paddles and accessories.

Books and Maps

- Adams, Arthur G. *The Hudson River Guidebook*. Bronx, NY: Fordham University Press, 1996.
- *Appalachian Mountain Club River Guide: Massachusetts, Connecticut, Rhode Island.* Boston, MA: Appalachian Mountain Club, 2000.
- Davidson, Paul, Ward Eister, Dirk Davidson, and Charlie Walbridge. *Wildwater West Virginia.* Birmingham, AL: Menasha Ridge Press, 1995.
- Gertler, Edward. *Garden State Canoeing: A Paddler's Guide to New Jersey.* Rockville, MD: Seneca Press, 1992.
- ———. *Keystone Canoeing: A Guide to Canoeable Water of Eastern Pennsylvania*. Rockville, MD: Seneca Press, 1993.
- Letcher, Gary. *Canoeing the Delaware River*. New Brunswick, NJ: Rutgers University Press, 1997.

Fishing

YOU RISE EARLY on a spring morning to get to a Westchester trout stream so that your fly is dancing on water when the sun pokes up over the hills. You have lunch and return to the city for your afternoon siesta: fishing for bluefish from a park bench on the East River. Toward the latter part of the day, you arrive at Sheepshead Bay in Brooklyn, where you hop an overnight party boat to test your will against 350-pound mako sharks and swordfish.

Not bad for 24 hours. Fishing is the city's most democratic and ubiquitous adventure sport. It requires little investment, has many options, is productive from any borough almost year-round, and, with the exception of fly-fishing, doesn't

require a lot of technical know-how. You can even get dinner out of it, though you'll want to be careful about what goes in the frying pan. More on that later.

There's such an embarrassing wealth of fertile fishing grounds that fishing junkies—"sharpies," in angler-speak—sometimes don't know which way to turn. Go for Hudson stripers or stream trout? Deep sea or surf? Things get particularly exciting in spring, when fish churn up the rivers to breed. There's another intense surge in late summer and fall, when blues and stripers, along with weakfish, fluke, porgies, and others, rush to city waters in pursuit of a meal. Many people jump on charters to chase the teeming schools, but when the fish make a run, any spot where anglers can legally access water (some are vigorously policed against trespassing) is fair game. As you might expect, the fishing community is an intense, excitable, and colorful bunch. One charter captain calls himself "the Duke of Fluke." Johnson Motors advertises that their outboard is "so trustworthy you'd let it take out your 16-year-old daughter." Wall Street fishing fanatics hire charters to squeeze in a half day, hopping off the boat at the World Financial Center before the opening bell.

A final word: Purists may question my decision to combine two distinct fishing disciplines, bait and fly-fishing, in one chapter. (Read David James Duncan's *The River Why*—one of the best novels ever written about the sport—to learn why this may be blasphemous.) The bottom line is, fishing is a vastly complex and specialized sport, and unfortunately I can only skim the surface here. For more detailed information, consult any of the weekly fishing mags or visit area tackle shops, especially Capitol Fishing Tackle in Manhattan, a local institution.

City Limits

NEW YORK HARBOR AND THE EAST RIVER

Location: Manhattan

Fish: Striper, bluefish, weakfish, and flounder, among many others

Season: Anytime except January and February; best in fall and spring

Onshore: The 69th Street Pier in Bay Ridge, Brooklyn, is a classic. Liberty State Park in New Jersey and Gantry Plaza State Park in the Long Island City neighborhood of Queens are two newer additions to the fishing scene that are gaining popularity.

Charters: Two captains base their operations in the harbor: Shastay of New York Harbor Sportfishing (201-451-1988, captshastay@aol.com) and Tony DiLernia of Rocket Charters (212-529-6910, www.rocketcharters.com). Fin Chaser Charters (718-317-1481 or 718-356-6436, www.finchaser.com) out of Staten Island also has lots of experience in the New York Bight.

Heads up: Licenses and permits not required

Description: When Joe Shastay Jr. calls fishing on the harbor "dynamic," he's not exaggerating. Working Bay Ridge Flats or Dimond Reef off the Battery, Shastay has to simultaneously find fish and steer his charter boat clear of commercial traffic, air traffic (a landing seaplane once nearly shaved off the tips of his fishing rods), and the flotsam that mangles about 10 boat propellers a year. The thing is, he wouldn't be out here if lots of fish weren't plying these waters, including the first of the striped bass headed up the Hudson to spawn each spring. Stripers and bluefish feed in fast-moving waters of the harbor and the East and Hudson Rivers, and there are only 6 minutes of slack when the tide changes directions. Shastay, who runs New York Harbor Sportfishing, has been fishing here longer than anyone else and has kept copious records of the successful fishing holes. Other boats have been known to follow him around the harbor, waiting to see where he stops. The best time of year is October and November, when there are "so many fish you get tired of catching them," Shastay says. But April and May are fun, too, because that's when the stripers come through.

If you want to go it alone, long stretches of the city's shoreline are accessible to the enterprising angler.

Directions: Shastay picks up customers at various points in Manhattan. For Rocket Charters, by subway, take the 6 train to 23rd Street and walk 6 blocks east to the East River.

Family Ties

KEVIN BRADSHAW KNEW his life's calling before he could read. His father and grandfather were both fishing boat captains out of Brooklyn's Sheepshead Bay, and Bradshaw was 5 years old when he first fished off the family boat. At the ripe age of 8, he cast out a line with three hooks and reeled in three codfish—about 18 pounds worth of wriggling flesh. He kept catching fish that day until he couldn't move his arms. "The fishing was fantastic," says Bradshaw, now 55 and the captain of the family boat, the *Dorothy B VIII*. "It was right after World War II, and nobody had been out there fishing for years."

His family has lived off the sea's bounty since 1920, when Bradshaw's grandfather, a painter, contracted lead poisoning, and his doctor prescribed fresh air. Bradshaw's grandmother bought him an 18-foot fishing boat, and the couple began taking out neighbors. It soon blossomed into a business; the family is now on its eighth boat, a 90-footer.

But when Bradshaw took over in 1975, the oceans were under siege; foreign commercial fishing boats used sonar and trawlers to scoop up mass quantities of fish. When foreign access was restricted, American commercial interests adopted the same practices. The results are predictable. Whiting used to be so plentiful they washed up in the surf on Coney Island, and Bradshaw picked them up in flip-flopping bunches. Now, overfishing has all but eliminated whiting as a reachable game fish. Bradshaw used to fish year-round; now there are only enough fish for 7 months of business. "I've seen the fishing at its peak, and I've seen it at its worst," Bradshaw says. "I've seen 40 or 50 boats in Sheepshead Bay dwindle to 13 or 15."

An avid nature-watcher, Bradshaw supplements his business with ecotourism and birding trips. He loves seeing 60-foot finback and minke whales churning below the surface. He loves watching gannets dive like missiles from 200 feet in the air to scoop up a fish. The ocean is Bradshaw's life. His challenge is to find a way to keep the *Dorothy B VIII* afloat. "I don't have any choice," Bradshaw says. "I don't know anything else."

THE HUDSON CANYON

Location: Manhattan

Fish: Just about anything and everything, from tuna to sharks, depending on the season

Season: Many captains skip only the harshest winter months. If you're prone to seasickness, go in summer, or pick your days in spring and fall carefully.

Charters: *Dorothy B VIII* (718-646-4057, www.dorothyb.com) is the boat to go on if you're interested in learning while you fish (see *Family Ties,* page 214). Other options include the *Sea Queen IV* (718-646-6224) and the *Tampa VII* (718-769-5363), but if you walk along Emmons Avenue you can choose from more than a dozen.

Heads up: Licenses and permits not required

Description: About a hundred miles south of New York Harbor, the floor of the ocean suddenly drops away into a 3,300-foot abyss. The Hudson Canyon is actually a gorge carved by the Hudson River back when much more of the world's water was trapped in ice. When the glaciers melted after the last ice age, the canyon was flooded. Now it puts the "deep" in deep-sea fishing. To fish the canyon, you'll want to hop on a party boat—so named because they're equipped for parties of two dozen or more anglers—in Sheepshead Bay, Brooklyn. The charters, which carry all the necessary gear and bait, line up along Emmons Avenue and usually depart early in the morning to take advantage of the calmer conditions. (Some run overnight trips as well.)

There are stunning runs of sea bass out there in August, and the tuna season unfolds in earnest around October. In November and December, when the seas are too turbulent to venture far from home, the captains pursue winter flounder in Jamaica Bay. Or they work Wreck Valley, the shipwrecks beyond the Verrazano Narrows that act as fish magnets.

Directions: By subway, take the Q train to Sheepshead Bay; walk to the water.

By car, take the Belt Parkway to exit 9A. Turn right off the ramp and right on Emmons Avenue. The charters will be lined up on the left along the waterfront.

Eating the Catch

STRIPED BASS, BLUEFISH, and American eels in the Hudson, East, or Harlem Rivers or Jamaica Bay can be contaminated with PCBs, so anglers are advised to eat no more than a half pound of these species per week. Children and women of childbearing age should not eat any.

The New York Department of Health also suggests choosing smaller fish and fish with lower fat content, and removing fatty deposits (where toxins accumulate) before eating. For updates, call the health department's Environmental Health Information Line at (800) 458-1158.

HUDSON RIVER STRIPERS

Location: Manhattan to Troy, New York

Season: March through June, with the peak around the first week of May

Charters: Use New York Harbor Sportfishing (201-451-1988, captshastay@aol.com) early in the season. Osprey Marine in Kingston (845-255-8737, www.ospreymarine.com) and HookHer (845-795-2620, www.hookherfishing.com) in Newburgh are among the established upstate charters.

Heads up: Licenses and permits not required on the Hudson up to the Troy Dam

Description: A few years ago, when the Hudson was still an egregious mess, charter boat captains and the big-game anglers they rely on all but ignored the river. Then fishermen began to "discover" 40-pound striped bass in the Hudson. "Suddenly it went from a hard-core group of regulars to a phenomenon," says John Waldman, a scientist with the Hudson River Foundation and author of two books about the river and New York Harbor. Whereas only a handful of charters plied the waters of the central Hudson a decade ago, more than 200 do today. The fish, of course, were there all along; the Hudson is the second-biggest striper spawning ground on the East Coast, after Chesapeake Bay. The prize fish are probably more plentiful now than they've been in several decades, thanks to a commercial lockdown in the 1980s, Waldman says. In any case, it's no wonder they're so popular: The beautiful, sleek purple-and-brown fish put up a Homeric battle.

The stripers show up in New York Harbor in March to begin their upriver trek to their spawning grounds. In April and May—the time you're most likely to find the 40-pound monsters—try between Croton Point and Kingston. In June you can still catch them near the Troy Dam, the tidal Hudson's northernmost point. There are plenty of places to catch stripers from shore; look for areas with relatively shallow water, which tend to warm up faster. But if you're not intimately familiar with the Hudson's banks, it's wiser to go out with a charter captain who has the mobility to look for the schools.

SURF CASTING LOWER NEW YORK BAY

Location: Queens and Staten Island

Fish: The weakfish stock has grown steadily over the past decade, and bluefish runs can be astounding. Fluke are also in abundance.

Season: Spring through fall

Heads up: For surf casting, you need a fishing pole 7 feet or longer. A $25 parking permit is required year-round at Crooke's Point. They're available at the Great Kills Visitors Center (718-987-6790). At Breezy Point, the park service issues off-road parking permits for $25 at Fort Tilden's

Building 1; a four-wheel-drive vehicle is required. The permit allows you to park on Breezy Point Tip Beach between September 1 and March 14; the beach is closed the rest of the year for nesting birds, though you can still walk out and fish. For information on other Gateway parking areas, stop by Fort Tilden or call (718) 318-4300.

For Crooke's Point, tackle is available at Michael's Bait & Tackle (187 Mansion Avenue, 718-984-9733). Great Kills Bait & Tackle (4044 Hylan Boulevard, 718-356-0055) will outfit you and share some of the latest gossip. For Breezy Point, use Bernie's Bait & Tackle (3035 Emmons Avenue, Sheepshead Bay, 718-646-7600).

Description: This massive bay is nature's own hatchery. Stretching 7 miles from the Breezy Point Tip across to Sandy Hook in New Jersey, this is one of the world's largest open-mouthed bays. For anglers it can be like the Atlantic Ocean without the powerhouse currents. The muddy bottom, the channels, and the brackish water make it prime spawning and feeding ground for blues, weakfish, and fluke, and all the lesser species down their food chain.

Crooke's Point in Staten Island's Great Kills Park is perfectly situated for surf casting. The gorgeous stretch of beach with waving dune grasses juts out past Great Kills Harbor into a wide-open channel favored by fluke. If it's elbow-to-elbow, try the municipal fishing pier at Lemon Creek Park on Prince's Bay (located at the end of Sharrott Avenue on the far west end of the park).

Across the bay, the seawall in Rockaway is packed in summer when word spreads that blues and stripers are moving through. At the Breezy Point jetty, though, there's more than a mile of beach where you can wade into the foam and make the most of that 10-foot surf-casting pole. Depending on what's happening, you can choose from the bay side of the jetty, the ocean side, or the jetty itself. A Russian fisherman I met there talked of hauling in

70-pound sharks. It's the only place around where you can drive on the beach (though not in summer when endangered birds are nesting).

Directions: By car, for Crooke's Point, take the Staten Island Expressway (I-278) to the Hylan Boulevard exit and drive south to the Great Kills entrance. Crooke's Point is at the park's southern tip. For Breezy Point, take the Belt Parkway to exit 11S; follow Flatbush Avenue over the Marine Parkway Bridge. Bear right off the bridge and drive to the end of the peninsula. If you're not driving onto the beach, park at the 222nd Street lot and take the path that branches off from the dirt road to the beach. At the water, turn left to go to the jetty.

For Keeps

SO YOU'VE REELED in a fluke, but you're not sure it's a keeper. As long as it's at least $15^1/_2$ inches (by 2000 regulations), you can reserve a spot in the frying pan for your catch, and up to seven more for that day. For other size and daily take-home limits—the regulations change roughly every year—call 800-REGS DEC (734-7332) or pick up a DEC flyer at park visitors centers.

CITY ISLAND

Location: Bronx

Fish: Primarily blackfish, though the bay also has runs of blues, striped bass, porgies, flounder, and fluke

Season: Fall and late spring are the best

Heads up: Licenses and permits not required

In City Island, tackle is available at Jack's Bait & Tackle and City Island Bait & Tackle. Rosenberger's Boat Livery on City Island (718-885-1843) rents out skiffs and offers helpful hints, gratis.

Description: For an afternoon that combines relaxation with some lively fishing, the sheltered, historic waters of City Island are tough to top. Rent a skiff at Rosenberger's Boat Livery on a sunny day and head out to the shallows. The blackfish that cruise these waters put up a wicked fight; even at a relatively modest 4 pounds, they tug like Clydesdales. They feed off the shell beds in May and June, but the bigger runs will likely come in fall, when the water temperatures drop into the low 60s. The word from those in the know: For bait, try hermit crabs, or the more inexpensive green crabs, shelled and halved or quartered. Ignore the dainty nibbles, which are probably something too small to bother with. When you feel a thud reverberate through your line, start reeling like hell; that would be the blackfish crushing the bait. Settle in near the shell beds between City Island and Hart Island, or head out to Execution Lighthouse and look for areas with about 40 to 50 feet of water. Flounder, bluefish, and fluke also cruise these waters.

Directions: By subway, take the 6 train to Pelham Bay Park station. You can walk or take the BM29 bus to City Island. Or bring a bike and use the greenway path.

By car, cross the Triboro Bridge and go east on I-95 to the Pelham Bay/Orchard Beach exit; follow signs to City Island.

Short Hops

FLY-FISHING THE CROTON RIVER

Location: Brewster, New York, 57 miles north of Manhattan

Fish: Brown and rainbow trout

Season: Spring through fall

Heads up: In addition to a state fishing license, you'll need a reservoir permit (free) to fish the New York City water supply; they're available at Department of Environmental Conservation (DEC) offices at 1250 Broadway, 8th floor, in Manhattan, (212) 643-2215.

Description: There is much to be grateful for in the network of streams, rivers, and reservoirs in Westchester and Putnam Counties. The vast watershed fills New York City's drinking glasses and offers some pretty plum flyfishing to boot. We highlight the Croton for two reasons: It is accessible by train, and it is in Brewster, a rare, pretension-free zone in tony Westchester. If you go early on a weekend morning, you might find Jonathan McCullough, a Manhattan book editor, matching wits with the Croton's wily browns and rainbows. Herein, McCullough discusses this trout retreat:

> As you leave the train station, there's a main street to the right of the northbound tracks. I can't say that economic times have been overly kind to Brewster, but I think it's a very nice little town, a sort of stepsister to the towns of greater means along the Harlem line. There's a library on the right, and you come to a little valley with teeny little businesses on the right. A curious white neo-federalist house with flaking white paint and a fine two-story colonnade appears on a hill to the left. As you go down into the swale, a bridge comes into view. It's about two-thirds of a mile from the train stop.
>
> There's fishing to be had around the bridge, but I would recommend that you take a left after crossing the bridge and walk upstream until the road intersects with the river. This is probably a one-mile hike. There is a hole there with very selective trout. I think

the best thing to do is dredge with a size ten or twelve Hare's Ear at the head of the pool.

The water slows down and pools up at a right angle to the road. There, little bass nip at the surface and waste your time. Midstream there is a place where trout occasionally eat things just subsurface, but they are canny, cunning fish. There are also places to fish further upstream, and I believe there's a dam with a spillway one or two miles up.

From Grand Central to the stream is a little over two hours. I would recommend this for a summer weekday afternoon when you get out of work early for some reason. Just off the train there's a little whistlestop on the right that serves a tasty burger and the people are cheerful. Kids. A lunch-lady type behind the register. Locals. All were fairly tolerant of my neoprene waders and bulky fly rod.

Directions: By train, take Metro-North to Brewster. See directions in Description, above.

Queens Trout

FRESHWATER TROUT HAVEN'T lived in a Gotham zip code for more than 50 years, but the New York City chapter of Trout Unlimited, an advocacy group, plans to restore a local species to Alley Creek, a small, spring-fed stream in the Douglaston section of Queens. Restoration work, including adding vegetation to reduce the stream's summer temperatures, is scheduled to start in 2002. The idea came from a 16-year-old junior Trout Unlimited board member. "He kept saying we should take a look at it, and we ignored him at first," says chapter president Susanne Weiser. "And then we finally went and took a look, and he was right. We're convinced it was once a trout stream."

Don't go running for your fly rod yet, though. Until further notice, this is a "lab stream" project—for research only.

CONNETQUOT RIVER STATE PARK PRESERVE

Location: Oakdale, Long Island, 56 miles east of Manhattan

Fish: Brook, brown, and rainbow trout

Season: February through mid-October. It's catch-and-release until April; thereafter the limit is two trout. (You have to stop fishing once you've kept two.)

Heads up: In addition to a state freshwater fishing license, you'll need a 1-year visitation permit (free by writing P.O. Box 505, Oakdale, NY 11769), though rangers may give you a 1-day pass if you show up without one. Call (631) 581-1005 a week ahead for platform reservations. There is a year-round vehicle entrance fee.

Description: The park has 30 developed sites with platforms; once you make a reservation you'll be assigned an area for 4 hours. This is a good thing because you're assured no one will poach your spot; it's a bad thing if your stretch of the shallow, languid, and relatively narrow river is quiet—but that's not usually a problem. The hatchery here raises brook, brown, and rainbow trout, so there are no worries about a slow year. The fish are stocked when they're 9 inches or longer, and the rainbow and brown trout grow up to 15 pounds once they hit the spring-fed stream water. Alternatively, there are trout in a 10-acre spring-fed pond; boat rentals are available. Oh, and all you spinning-rod-and-reel guys? Sorry, this is fly-fishing only, thank you very much. No lead, weighted flies, barbed hooks, or bait allowed.

Directions: By car, take exit 44 off the Southern State Parkway onto NY 27 (Sunrise Highway); because the park is on the north side, you have to go 0.3 mile past the park entrance and make a U-turn.

SAUGATUCK RIVER

Location: Westport, Connecticut, 49 miles northeast of Manhattan

Fish: The whole spectrum. Stripers are always popular, but there are trout in the mix as well, along with bluefish, smaller pickerel, and sunfish later in the season.

Season: Spring through fall

Heads up: A state license is required anywhere north of the Kings Highway Bridge, the freshwater demarcation line. Licenses are available from any town clerk's office.

Tackle is available at Longshore Marina (203-226-3688).

Description: There's an 11-mile stretch from the Saugatuck's mouth on Long Island Sound to the Samuel Senior Dam in Weston that locals believe is among the best trout water in Connecticut. Here's why: The state stocks fish just to the north, and seagoing species swim up from the south. That translates into an alluring mix of striped bass, blues, snappers, weakfish, river trout, and bass. One of the highlights is the spring migration at the river's tidal terminus; striped bass chase baitfish up to Wood's Dam (the first dam that fish encounter coming north from the Sound) and gorge. Fish it from the Bridgeport Hydraulic Company property on the east side.

The trick here is to arrive early; public space is fairly limited, and this is one of the region's most popular fisheries. A canoe or kayak will increase your chances of getting to spots sealed off by private land ownership along the river. Case in point: Lee's Pond, above Wood's Dam, holds some of the biggest trout on the river, but to get there you need to paddle from Ford Road, about 0.25 mile north of the

Merritt Parkway bridge. If you're stuck on shore, try the River Road Bridge and Keene Park, and the Skerlick fishing area at the lower end of Ford Road; there are cool, deep pools, and the merger of the Saugatuck's west branch.

Directions: You can access various points by taking I-95 north to exit 17, just south of the river. Your best bet is to buy a Fairfield County map or get some advice at a tackle shop as to which section to attempt.

Meccas

MONTAUK POINT

Location: Montauk, Long Island, 116 miles east of Manhattan

Fish: Nearly everything that swims: sharks, dolphin, tuna, stripers, eel, cod, and much more

Season: Early spring to early winter

Charters: *No Time* (718-281-0689) and *Jay-Mar* (516-763-1756) are among the dozens of charter boats in and around Montauk. Party boats include *Viking Fleet* (631-668-5700) and *Lazy Bones* (631-668-5671). To go your own way, try Uihlein's Boat Rentals (631-663-3799).

Heads up: No license required; New York State four-wheel-drive permits, sold at Belmont Lake State Park (631-667-5055), let you drive on Montauk Point, Hither Hills, and Napeague. A Suffolk County outer-beach permit and green key—available at the Suffolk County Park administration office (631-854-4949)—give you access to other beaches.

Tackle is available at Star Island Yacht Club (631-668-5052) and Montauk Marine Basin (631-668-5900).

Information: The Montauk Surfcasters Association

(www.surfcasters.org). The Web site On Montauk (www.onmontauk.com) has a lengthy list of charter fishing boats.

Description: Fishing is religion here, and no wonder: There are far more good fishing spots than churches. On the north side are the jetties at Montauk Harbor and all around Shagwong Point to North Bar, False Bar, and Montauk Lighthouse. To the south are Turtle Cove, Caswells and Ditch Plains, and, to the west, Hither Hills and Napeague State Parks. Whew. Better get busy. During the fall runs, the waters around Montauk Point seethe with stripers, blues, and sometimes albacore. The fish blitz the lighthouse and the south side, making the annual migration off Montauk Point the stuff of legend for surf casters.

The offshore fishing is equally enticing. A series of offshore canyons 70 to 100 miles from the South Fork are home to the sort of serious game stuff—swordfish, white and blue marlin, and yellowfin that reach 200 pounds—that ends up on guys' den walls. There are 8-foot-long blue and mako sharks that at 300 to 350 pounds are as heavy as NFL linemen. This is true adventure. I once hooked a shark that looked about a hundred pounds and felt as though my forearms were going to shred. (It got away, but that's another fish story.) Because the weather can get nasty, the best time to fish "out on the edge"—as the locals call the canyons—is summer and fall. Shark fishing usually starts in June and slows down for a bit before picking up again around Labor Day.

Directions: By car, follow the Long Island Expressway to exit 70, then go south on NY 111 to its end; follow the Sunrise Highway (NY 27) to Montauk Highway (also NY 27) to Montauk State Park.

FLY-FISHING IN THE CATSKILLS

Location: Roscoe, New York, 122 miles northwest of Manhattan

Fish: Trout

Season: Spring through fall

Heads up: State license required; permits required for reservoirs. For information, call the DEC at (212) 643-2215.

Tackle is available at Beaverkill Angler (607-498-5194, www.beaverkillangler.com) and Catskill Flies Fly Shop & Fishing Adventures in Roscoe (607-498-6146, www.catskillflies.com), among the many informed shops. The Delaware County Chamber of Commerce (800-642-4442, www.delawarecounty.org) provides recommendations on guides. For some local history, stop in at the Catskill Fly Fishing Museum and Center (845-439-4810), located on the Willowemoc River in Livingston Manor.

Description: Let's get something straight about Montana streams and all those rheumy-eyed scenes in *A River Runs Through It:* The Catskills' rivers are the birthplace of American fly-fishing. Not for nothing is the village of Roscoe known as "Trout Town USA." There are 175 miles of trout water here, and any devout fly-fisherman from the Northeast has a yarn or two about the legendary Junction Pool, where the Willowemoc and lower Beaverkill meet.

There are huge browns roaming the Pepacton, Cannonsville, and Schoharie Reservoirs. There are the smaller, hidden-away lakes and creeks. And then there are legendary trout pools in the Willowemoc and lower Beaverkill (the upper Beaverkill, unfortunately, is mostly private). Understanding the nuances of each is like discerning Burgundy's wines; each body of water has a slightly different temperature, range of aquatic life, and chemical makeup. Best to gather as much advice as you can at a fly and tackle shop and head for one of the can't-miss pools. If the crowds get too unwieldy, try the underappreciated upper section of the Delaware's west branch, which is stocked with browns and rainbows.

Directions: Take I-87 north to NY 17; Roscoe is located at the intersection of NY 17 and NY 206.

Where to Connect

Bait and Tackle Shops

- Capitol Fishing Tackle (218 West 23rd Street, Manhattan, 212-929-6132) has been in Chelsea for more than 35 years, which is damn near forever in Manhattan. The staff is liberal with advice, especially when it comes to the aisles of fishing exotica—everything from salmon eggs to Japanese plugs. There are bins of lures, fake worms, and knives, and a forest of slender poles.
- Urban Angler (118 East 25th Street, Manhattan, 212-979-7600, www.urban-angler.com) is the city's upscale fishing mecca. It has its own catalog and travel service, and its Web site updates fishing conditions around the world.
- Rosenberger's Boat Livery (663 City Island Avenue, City Island, 718-885-1842) is the place to keep up with the action in this historic fishing center.
- Jack's Bait & Tackle (551 City Island Avenue, City Island, 718-885-2042)
- Stella Maris Fishing Station (2702 Emmons Avenue, Sheepshead Bay, 718-646-9754) has the weather-beaten Coca-Cola sign and fishy smell you look for in a good bait shop. And they stay atop the Jamaica Bay runs.

- Mike's Tackle Shop (2201 Emmons Avenue, Sheepshead Bay, 718-646-9261)
- Michael's Bait & Tackle (187 Mansion Avenue, Staten Island, 718-984-9733)

Clubs and Organizations

These groups are involved with angling, water-quality improvement, or public access issues—or all of the above.

- New York City Trout Unlimited (917-941-5282, www.nyctu.org)
- Hudson River Foundation (212-924-8290, www.hudsonriver.org)
- Hudson River Fishermen's Association, New Jersey chapter (www.hrfanj.org)
- Coastal Conservation Association of New York (718-945-2255, www.ccany.org)
- Fishing Buddies of America (212-781-3655)

Events

- Hooked on Hudson (www.hrfanj.org) is a festival that includes a shad bake and fishing contest.
- The Northeast Inshore Rally (914-949-8849) is a 2-month catch-and-release event with multiple categories and divisions.
- The Kayak-fishing Tournament (516-889-8300, www.empirekayaks.com) is held in June in Nassau County.
- The Last Chance Catch and Release Surf Fishing Tournament, sponsored by the Coastal Conservation Association of New York, is held annually in November at Fort Tilden. Information: (877) 992-2269.

Books and Resources

- Capossela, Jim. *Good Fishing in the Catskills*. Woodstock, VT: Backcountry Publications, 1992.
- Francis, Austin M. *Catskill Rivers: Birthplace of American Fly Fishing*. New York, NY: Lyons Press, 1996.
- Liftglass, Manny, and Ron Bern. *Gone Fishin': The 100 Best Spots in New York*. East Brunswick, NJ: Rutgers University Press, 1999.
- Mittelbach, Margaret, and Michael Crewdson. *Wild New York*. New York, NY: Three Rivers Press, 1997.
- Sparano, Vin T. *Northeast Guide to Saltwater Fishing & Boating*. Camden, ME: International Marine Publishing, 1996.
- Streeter, Robert W. *New York Fly-Fishing Guide*. Portland, OR: Frank Amato Publications, 2000.
- Waldman, John. *Heartbeats in the Muck: A Dramatic Look at the History, Sea Life and Environment of New York Harbor*. New York, NY: Lyons Press, 1999.
- Waldman, John. *Stripers: An Angler's Anthology*. Camden, ME: Ragged Mountain Press, 1998.
- Two weekly publications, *The Fisherman* and *Nor'east Saltwater* (www.noreast.com), constantly update fishing conditions in the New York Bight and Long Island. Available at most tackle shops.

Scuba Diving

THE FIRST TIME you're descending into New York City's waters, you figure you're about to be immersed in India ink. You think all you'll see is swirling darkness and maybe your fingers if you hold them in front of your face. And then you plunge in, and the conditions happen to be right, and wham. Revelation.

In the protected coves of Far Rockaway, a luminescent spot-fin butterfly fish might flit in front of your face. Seahorses loll past; brightly colored Caribbean jacks and French angelfish dart nearby. So do feather blennies, with their bulging eyes and antlerlike stubs protruding from their heads. Crack open a mussel, and fish are eating out of your hands. And that's only the start.

Venture into the Atlantic and the masses of scuttling crustaceans will have you thinking you fell into the lobster tank at the Grand Central Oyster Bar. And historic shipwrecks—everything from warships to paddle-wheel steamships to German subs—are so abundant that the region has been nicknamed "Wreck Valley." Schools of sea bass, cod, blackfish. Fluke the size of hubcaps. Keep exploring and you'll encounter sharks, dolphins, turtles, pilot whales, giant ocean sunfish.

What you will not encounter are the warm, crystalline blue waters of the Caribbean. Waters this far north are murky with plankton and other tiny organisms. Visibility is usually limited to about 10 feet, and the water is so cold most of the year you'll need a wetsuit at least 6 to 7 millimeters thick—that's a quarter inch of rubber—underneath about 30 pounds of gear and weights, including two tanks for deeper dives. Near the city, fishing hooks and lines can be a threat. Dive charters often leave at 6 A.M. to take advantage of the early-morning calm. "It's not for everyone," says Robert Sievens, operator of Aquatia Scuba, a New Jersey–based scuba instruction and travel company. "There are guys who go down there who say, 'I can't believe this, what a blast!' And there are others who say, 'It's too cold, I can't see anything, it's not for me.'"

Locals say that if you can handle these waters, you can dive just about anywhere in the world. Explore here long enough, and you may never want to go anywhere else.

City Limits

ALMOST PARADISE

Location: Queens

Outfitter: Almost Paradise (120 Beach 9th Street, Far Rockaway, Queens, 718-471-2400) charges one fee for use of the facilities, including showers, wash stations, and changing rooms.

Description: No more than a little spit of beach on the eastern fringe of Queens, this secluded spot has drawn in-the-know divers and snorkelers for decades. The conditions are ideal for scuba training: A pair of jetties sandwiches a 200-foot chunk of beach, creating a sheltered cove in an otherwise swift tidal channel. The inlet also serves as a sanctuary for a striking collection of tropical sea life that rides the Gulf Stream north as eggs; they hatch when the water warms in summer. There are damselfish, seahorses, big-eyed conch, sponges, sea anemones, and soft corals, among many others. They're particularly striking during night dives, in the glow of an underwater flashlight.

The beach remained an informal gathering place until 1993, when Jay Velasquez, a native Colombian who once sold used cars, bought the ramshackle bait shop next door on Beach 9th Street and converted it into a diving center. Three steel contraptions placed 19 feet below the surface give students something to hang on to while practicing skills such as clearing water from their mask and adjusting buoyancy. Schools from as far away as Connecticut and New Jersey certify more than 2,000 students per year here. "Most beach dives, you have a long walk on the rocks before you find twenty feet of water," Velasquez says. "Here, you take five steps and you're in twelve to fifteen feet."

Directions: By subway, take the A train to Mott Avenue. Walk or bike south on Mott, bear right on Beach 13th Street, turn left on Seagirt Boulevard, turn right on Beach 9th Street, and walk to the water.

By car, take the Belt Parkway to the Cross Bay Boulevard; after the Cross Bay Bridge turn left on Rockaway Beach Boulevard; bear right on Seagirt Boulevard.

What Lurks Below

BENEATH THE SURFACE of the salt- and freshwaters surrounding New York is a whole other collection of city dwellers. Native sand tiger sharks grow to 9 feet and 400 pounds, with an impressive set of sharp tricuspid teeth. *Jaws* notwithstanding, they don't find humans appetizing. (For an up-close look, check out the New York Aquarium's 90,000-gallon shark tank.) Other locals include hermit crabs, razor clams, moon snails, and, remarkably, native seahorses that have adapted to the reduced salinity of the Hudson River and are hardy enough to survive the winter.

There are also some surprising guests down there. The eggs of tropical fish wash up on currents from the Caribbean, and those that reach protected areas hatch in summer, when the water warms. The fish live for a couple of months, until the water temperature drops below about 65° F, but for that period the "tropicals" (as divers call them) provide flashes of iridescent color. New York Aquarium curator Paul Sieswerda's favorite is the threadfin jack, a purple-and-gold fish that gets its name from its long, threadlike rays that serve as sensory devices. The rays, which look like flowing hairs, emanate from its fins.

Short Hops

THE BEST OF WRECK VALLEY

There are countless shipwrecks in the waters wrapped around New York, Long Island, and New Jersey. Wrecks have dual value: They're historically significant, and they create habitat for fish and other marine life on the otherwise barren ocean floor. Generally the wrecks closer to the city are more difficult to visit. When the massive New York Harbor empties into the ocean, it creates turbulent conditions and stirs up sediment, cutting visibility. But because of the abundance of sunken ships in Wreck Valley—literally hundreds—there's always something to see. You can reach all the wrecks on charter boats listed in

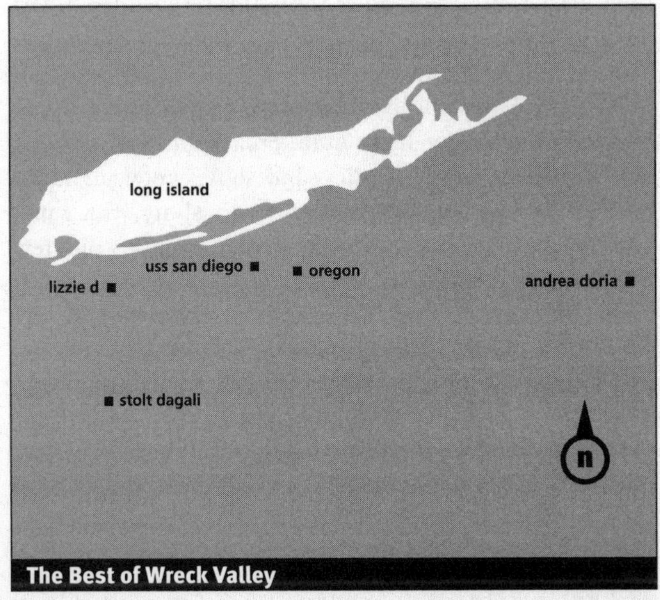

The Best of Wreck Valley

Where to Connect, page 247. For more history and specifics, consult the bible on local wreck diving, *Wreck Valley Volume II: A Record of Shipwrecks off Long Island's South Shore and New Jersey.*

THE BLACK WARRIOR

Location: Queens

Outfitter: See Charters, page 247.

Description: This ship is a New York original: a paddle-wheel steamship built here in 1852 for voyages to Havana and New Orleans. In its short life span, the 225-foot wooden *Warrior* was confiscated by Cuban officials and survived a ferocious storm that tore away its lifeboats and wheelhouse. Then, in 1859, the *Warrior* ran aground in fog on Rockaway Bar. Though the crew was saved, the vessel sank deeper into the sand as the water receded. Four days later, as crews worked to free the *Warrior*, a gale roared through and tore it apart.

The *Black Warrior* lies in about 35 feet of water, a good beginner dive. Though it's quite broken up, you can still see the paddle wheel, boiler, and some wood planking. Because of the wreck's proximity to shore, the sands around it tend to shift during the winter, exposing different parts and occasionally yielding new artifacts. If you're lucky, you may turn up some engraved silverware.

LIZZIE D

Location: Near the Verrazano Narrows, off Brooklyn

Outfitter: See Charters, page 247.

Description: Ostensibly a working tug when it went

down near the Verrazano Narrows in 1922, the 84-foot *Lizzie D*'s real raison d'être wasn't discovered until 50 years later: It freighted hooch during Prohibition. Divers who first located it in 1977 found crates of 100-proof Canadian rye whiskey and Kentucky bourbon, among other then-illicit treasures. Most of the tug's bottles have been removed in the years since, and are displayed in local museums and dive shops and on divers' trophy shelves.

The *Lizzie D*, also known as the *Rum Runner*, lies in 80 feet of water, a solid entry-level wreck dive. Time and water have taken their toll on the hull, stripping much of it away; the ship's ribbed frame and boiler, though, are still intact.

The Urban Diver

TRUST GENE RITTER when he says the water around New York City is vastly cleaner than it was only 20 to 30 years ago. After all, he was one of the few people scuba diving off the beaches around Coney Island in the 1970s. "It was nothing but oil, condoms and dead rats," he recalls. "You dove under and you never got any visibility—usually three inches. If you got three feet you were happy. Six feet, you were in your glory."

Still, Ritter, who grew up in Brighton Beach, was fascinated. A certified diver at age 13, he never took to wreck dives; he wanted to explore places nobody else had found. While other divers headed off to the Caribbean, Ritter explored the murky waters of the city, occasionally immersed in a "bubble of sewage." The floatable items (use your imagination) stay on the surface, but still, he says, "It's like sticking your head in a toilet bowl." (He uses Listerine to kill any bacteria in his mouth.)

But he made some incredible finds. Diving off Coney Island, a wave slammed a hard, metallic object into his head. He grabbed it, and found himself holding a World War I antiaircraft shell. Ritter read up on Brooklyn history and set out after sunken bits of New York. He found evidence of the Steeplechase amusement park, a Coney Island landmark built in 1897. He discovered remains of the Dreamland Pier, another amusement park built in 1904 on a 1,000-foot-long pier that featured a grand ballroom, rides, restaurants, and a 375-foot tower. (Both amusement parks burned—Steeplechase in 1907, Dreamland 4 years later.) In 1995, Ritter located remnants of Fort Lafayette in the churning waters beneath the Verrazano Narrows Bridge. The island fortress, outfitted with 96 mounted guns, was built in 1812 to guard the mouth of the harbor. It was razed in 1960 to make way for the bridge's construction.

Ritter, 41, makes his living as a commercial diver rather than as New York's Jacques Cousteau. To soften accusations that he is looting the city's waters, he formed the Professional Diving Archeology Organization (718-454-1617) to display and discuss the 2,000 or so artifacts he's found. Rather than sell the items, he brings them to local schools for show-and-tell.

STOLT DAGALI

Location: 36 miles out of Debs Inlet, Long Island; 18 miles from Manasquan, New Jersey

Outfitter: See Charters, page 247.

Description: In November 1964 the *Stolt*, a 583-foot Norwegian tanker, was carrying cargo from Philadelphia to Newark, New Jersey, when it slipped into a patch of dense fog. After a few moments, an Israeli luxury liner plowed into its stern, slicing off a 150-foot section. Nineteen crew members perished as the detached stern sank almost immediately in 50° water about 18 miles from Manasquan Inlet, New Jersey. The section lies upright on its starboard side, at about 120 feet, and is an ideal dive site for intermediates. Because of the way the stern was sliced off, advanced divers can swim inside and explore. Just be careful not to stir up sediment, which can cause disorientation. The abundance of mussels and cold-water anemones attached to the *Stolt* make it a magnet for varied predatory marine life, including bluefish, tuna, sea turtles, and the occasional shark.

USS *SAN DIEGO*

Location: Fire Island, New York

Outfitter: See Charters, page 247.

Description: The *San Diego* is one of Long Island's top wrecks—a World War I warship that hit a German surface mine in July 1918 about 13.5 miles from the Fire Island Inlet. The behemoth 503-foot armored cruiser has two dozen cannons and 18 torpedo tubes. It was the flagship of the Pacific fleet in 1914 before being transferred to the Atlantic in 1917. The navy's loss is the diving world's gain.

The *San Diego* lies upside down at about 110 feet below the surface. This is a good dive for intermediates, but only advanced divers should enter the wreck and roam compartments and hallways in the ship's belly—it's easy to get disoriented. There are still bullets and other items down there, but removing artifacts from the *San Diego* is illegal. The wreck was entered into the National Register of Historic Places in 1988, and the Coast Guard aggressively patrols the area.

OREGON

Location: Fire Island, New York

Outfitter: See Charters, page 247.

Description: This one's a beauty: a 518-foot-long steamship built in 1881, the biggest and fastest of its time. On its maiden voyage it crossed the Atlantic in $6^1/2$ days, a record at the time. In March 1886, five miles off Fire Island, an unidentified schooner slammed into the *Oregon*'s port side. It was a clear night, and the cause of the collision remains a mystery, though many suspected crew negligence. The wreck, lying in 125 to 130 feet of water 21 miles southeast of Fire Island Inlet, is crawling with 12- to 15-pound lobsters. Divers have claimed various artifacts, ranging from china to ornate chandeliers. The *Oregon* is an intermediate dive.

Winter Wonders

SOME NORTHERN DIVERS test the limits of their sport by plunging through holes cut into the ice of frozen lakes. Though it seems insane, the water is clearer than in summer because the frigid temperatures kill most aquatic organisms (though there is still an abundance of lobsters to try to catch during winter ocean dives). And, in fact, water temperatures don't vary much year-round for deepwater explorers. During early winter, temperatures hover in the mid-40s at most depths—about the same temperature as at 130 feet in summer.

Outfitter: Mad Dog Expeditions (132 East 82nd Street, 212-744-6763, www.mad-dog.net) offers an ice-diving certification program that includes several dives in New Hampshire.

Meccas

THE SUNKEN FLEET OF 1758

Location: Lake George, New York, 211 miles north of Manhattan

Difficulty: The *Land Tortoise*, located at 105 feet, is an advanced dive. The Sunken Fleet, which lies at 25 to 50 feet, is suitable for intermediates.

Outfitters: Scuba University (518-885-8554) and Lake George Scuba Center (518-798-4486) both run dive charters; Ward's Dockside Marina (518-543-8888) rents out dive boats and equipment. To dive the *Land Tortoise*, open from the second Saturday of June through Labor Day, you must first register at Lake George Beach, located at the south end of the lake on Beach Road. The Sunken Fleet is open on a first-come, first-served basis from Memorial Day through autumn.

Books and maps: The Department of Environmental Conservation (518-897-1200) publishes a comprehensive pamphlet, *A Diver's Guide to Lake George*, that includes maps. Also, check out *Chronicles of Lake George: Journeys in War and Peace*.

Description: Determined to dislodge French troops from Lakes George and Champlain during the French and Indian Wars, the British built a small fleet of warships. Among them were a *radeau* (French for "raft")—a 50-foot-long, seven-sided floating artillery platform—called the *Land Tortoise*. Just before heading south to Albany for the winter in 1758, the Brits loaded the craft with rocks and sunk it to prevent French troops from seizing or destroying it. In spring, when the ice thawed, the British would remove the rocks and refloat it. But the *Tortoise* slipped into deeper-than-expected water and was lost for 232 years. Because the water in Lake George is so cold—temperatures plummet as low as 35° F—the boat is almost perfectly preserved. The Smithsonian Institution has designated the *Land Tortoise* as the oldest intact war vessel in North America. And New York has protected the wreck, and three others, by designating them Submerged Heritage Preserves.

The British also scuttled about 250 bateaux—flat-bottomed vessels designed to ferry troops and supplies across the lake—that same autumn. British forces refloated most of them the next spring, but one set of seven boats lashed together drifted into deeper water. The Sunken Fleet of 1758 is now an attraction for divers.

Directions: The *Land Tortoise* is located midlake, in the South Basin, nearly 2 miles north of Million Dollar Beach. The Sunken Fleet is about a mile north of Million Dollar Beach on the east side of the lake.

ANDREA DORIA

Location: Nantucket, Massachusetts

Difficulty: Dangerous even for experts

Outfitter: Deep Explorers (732-836-0729, www.deepexplorers.com)

Description: The doomed luxury liner is widely known as the Mount Everest of diving. Daniel Berg writes in *Wreck Valley II:* "Those who dare to explore this wreck must endure nitrogen narcosis, staged decompression hangs, strong currents, sharks, and long surface intervals." As on Everest, some have died trying to explore it. It's easy to snag diving gear on ship remains or get lost in its immense interior—especially if you develop nitrogen narcosis, which causes disorientation.

The *Doria* is a staggering 700 feet long—like the Empire State Building turned sideways—and could accommodate more than 1,200 passengers and nearly 600 crew. Shipbuilders believed its watertight chambers made it unsinkable. But a 1956 collision with a Swedish freighter off the coast of Nantucket tore an 80-foot gash in the starboard side, ripping open its watertight compartments. Fifty-one passengers died in the collision, but hundreds of others were saved in one of history's great sea rescues. The *Doria* lies on its starboard side in a daunting 230 feet of water.

Perils of the Deep

DIVING CAN BE hazardous. Several divers have been killed exploring the *Andrea Doria*, but even 100-foot-deep wrecks occasionally claim lives. Divers should never try to go beyond what they're trained to do. "If you stay within the parameters of what you've learned, this is one of the safest sports around," says Di Dieter, owner of Atlantic Divers in Brooklyn and a dive instructor for 32 years. "What happens is people get careless, get sloppy, and get in trouble."

DUTCH SPRINGS

Location: Bethlehem, Pennsylvania

Difficulty: Useful for divers of all aptitudes.

Outfitter: Dutch Springs (610-759-2270, www.dutchsprings.com) charges day fees.

Description: Below the surface of this 47-acre lake lie a Sikorsky H-37 helicopter, an airplane, a fire truck, trolley, and school bus, among other submerged "wrecks." They're part of what makes Dutch Springs a popular dive destination. Equal parts classroom and playground, Dutch Springs —popularly known as "the Quarry"—enables divers to obtain their certification, practice technique at depths up to 100 feet, and acclimate to cold water, all in a highly controlled environment. The wrecks and an artificial reef system attract aquatic life. And because the lake is spring-fed, the water is clean; visibility is around 30 feet. Special annual events include an underwater Easter egg hunt and an underwater pumpkin carving and costume contest.

Directions: By car, take I-78 west to exit 3 and follow US 22 west to PA 191 north. After 1 mile, turn left on

Hanoverville Road. Dutch Springs is 1 mile down on the left.

Where to Connect

Shops

Numerous dive shops in the metropolitan area offer Professional Association of Diving Instructors (PADI) and National Association of Underwater Instructors (NAUI) courses. Once you're certified by one of these two agencies, you'll be able to rent equipment at any dive destination.

- Central SkinDivers (1312 First Avenue, Manhattan, 212-362-7450; 160-09 Jamaica Avenue, Jamaica, NY, 718-739-5772, www.centralskindivers.com) was founded by one of New York's scuba pioneers, "Honest" Archie Orenstein. His son Seth has ensured the business remains among the most respected shops in the city.
- Atlantic Divers (501 Kings Highway, Brooklyn, 718-376-5454) has in Di Dieter one of the most experienced instructors in New York. "If I had a daughter," says Jay Velasquez, owner of the dive center Almost Paradise, "I'd want Di to certify her."
- Village Divers (224 East 10th Street, Manhattan, 212-780-0879, www.villagedivers.com)
- Pan Aqua, 460 West 43rdStreet, Manhattan, 212-736-3483, www.panaqua.com)
- No Limitz Sports (3169 Emmons Avenue, Sheepshead Bay, Brooklyn, 718-743-0054)
- Dave's Scuba (290 Atlantic Avenue, Brooklyn, 718-802-0700)
- Stingray Divers (762 Grand Street, Brooklyn, 718-384-1280, www.stingraydivers.com)

- Captain Mike's Diving Services (530 City Island Avenue, Bronx, 718-885-1588)
- Down Under Sports (88 Guyon Avenue, Staten Island, 718-980-7547, www.downundersports.com)
- Tiedemann's Diving Center (Levittown, NY, 516-756-6560)
- Aquatia Scuba (North Bergen, NJ, 201-662-3483, www.aquatiascuba.com)

Charters

These outfitters serve the major sites in Wreck Valley.

- *Eagle's Nest* (875 Gerry Avenue, Lido Beach, NY, 516-897-9157; www.eaglesnestwreckdiving.com). Captain Howard Klein is one of the top dive captains on Long Island, with a season that runs from April through November.
- *Wahoo* (Captree Boat Basin, Jones Beach, NY, 631-928-3849, www.wahoo2001.com). Captain Steve Bielenda, whose diving experience spans 40 years, runs trips as far out as the *Andrea Doria.*
- *Wreck Valley* (2745 Cheshire Drive, Baldwin, NY, 516-868-2658, www.aquaexplorers.com). Captain Daniel Berg literally wrote the book on Wreck Valley diving.
- *Jeanne II* (3662 Shore Parkway, Brooklyn, 718-332-9574, www.jeanne-ii.com)
- *Diversion II* (281 Timberline Place, Brick, NJ, 732-477-8404, www.njscuba.com)
- *Sea Hunter* Dive Boat (Freeport, NY, 516-546-6205)

Clubs and Organizations

- The New York City Sea Gypsies (www.seagypsies.org) hold monthly meetings and run a diving program featuring visits to area dive sites as well as more distant destinations, such as Rhode Island, North Carolina, the Great Lakes, and the Caribbean.

- The Long Island Groupers (516-756-6560, www.tdconline.com/groupers.shtml) run beach dives, quarry dives, and wreck dives.
- The Explorers Dive Club (732-868-1866, www.explorersdiveclub.org), based in Somerset, NJ, organizes various dives.

Event

- Beneath the Sea (www.beneaththesea.org), at the Meadowlands Exposition Center, Secaucus, New Jersey, is the nation's largest consumer scuba and dive-travel show.

Books and Resources

- Bellico, Russell P. *Chronicles of Lake George: Journeys in War and Peace*. Fleischmanns, NY: Purple Mountain Press, 1995.
- Berg, Daniel. *Wreck Valley Volume II: A Record of Shipwrecks off Long Island's South Shore and New Jersey*. East Rockaway, NY: Aqua Explorers, Inc., 1990.
- Gentile, Gary. *Andrea Doria: Dive to an Era*. Philadelphia, PA: Gary Gentile Productions, 1989.
- ———. *Shipwrecks of New Jersey: North*. Philadelphia, PA: Gary Gentile Productions, 2000.
- *The U.S. Navy Dive Manual* is available online at www.coralspringsscuba.com.

Surfing

THE IDEA OF surfing in New York City is about as unimaginable to some people as the Beach Boys putting out a gangsta rap album. And it's true, Gotham and surf culture is an odder pairing than Felix and Oscar. The city worships money and all that glitters; surfers revere nature and the make-just-enough-cash-to-live-on-the-beach lifestyle. The city moves at a frenetic pace; surfers sleep until noon and move fast only when they're paddling after a wave. But there is room in the naked city even for those baggy shorts. "If you live for surfing," says Tom Sena, owner of Rockaway Beach Surf Shop and the dean of the city surf scene, "you're probably going to live somewhere

else. But it is one of the many vices that's available in New York."

The proof is on Rockaway Beach, home base for a hearty bunch of local surfers who put up with fickle waves and mostly frigid water in hopes of catching the occasional day of dream breakers. Some surfers even come from Manhattan, jumping on the A train when the Weather Channel shows a low-pressure system moving in. For the hard-core guys, this means keeping your wetsuit ready for midwinter forays, even when the water drops to an anesthetizing 35° F.

Yup, it's a long way from Malibu, but there are New Yorkers who've gleaned a lifetime of sustenance from this paltry diet of cold, mercurial, inconsistent waves. Here, after all, you rarely have to worry about someone dropping in on your wave. The moments of glory usually come in September and October, when the water is still warm, crowds are down, and freight-train-sized hurricane swells can last for a week. Of course, there are options beyond Rockaway Beach. Long Island is positioned like a goalie to catch anything moving north from the tropics, making Montauk the surf capital of the Northeast. Short drives bring you to places on the Jersey Shore, and there are more all the way down to Cape May. Some of them are pretty enough, with enough action, to make you forget California, at least for a little while.

The Dean of Surfing

TOM SENA HAS two irreconcilable passions: surfing and Rockaway Beach. At 16 he dreamed of the monstrous waves and endless summers of Hawaii and California. The kid from Queens always had plans to move. He's read *Surfer* magazine all his life; he's missing only four issues from the past 40 years. That was what his life would become. It never happened, and Rockaway Beach is much better for it.

"I've been making surfboards all my life," he says. "I was the first guy to go out in the middle of the winter. I had a full wetsuit, but the rubber was so inflexible and rigid in those days, you could last maybe an hour. But I was constantly mobilizing, trying to keep the sport alive." Sena dropped out of junior seminary school and began building boards at 16, until neighbors complained about the smell of finishing chemicals. He opened his store at 25. Now he's 47, and there's gray creeping into his crew cut. But he's as passionate as ever.

Sena still surfs, but he's an important businessman in the community now. He owns the trademark for several surfboards. His shop is a mainstay in struggling Rockaway, with more than 500 boards in stock at times. A decade ago he bought a building just up Beach 116th Street, an old boardwalk supermarket that had been shuttered for 15 years. He and his friends created The Beach Club, a surfing-theme restaurant complete with antique boards, faux Hawaiian entryway, and three-dimensional murals.

Sena has managed to make a life of the New York surf scene. "I've always tried to sell people boards that work for them. I want it to be something you can learn on and grow into, so you love the sport. People remember that. Now I get people coming in from all over the world. I don't expect to make a great living. This is my life. I just hope they'll come back, and bring their friends."

City Limits

ROCKAWAY BEACH

Location: Queens

Difficulty: Generally fine for beginners

Heads up: The closest wax is Rockaway Beach Surf Shop (177 Beach 116th Street, Brooklyn, 718-474-9345).

Description: There are many great things about New York City, and this is one: You can step on the A train with a surfboard in midtown Manhattan and within an hour exit at Beach 90th Street, a short stroll from the beach and the waves. If the stars are aligned, the tide is about midway between low and high, and a low-pressure system is rolling in, you'll find chest-high breakers at Beach 88th Street, the designated surfing area. When conditions are right, you can also find waves at Bay 1 in Riis Park. There's a sandy bottom and a rock jetty that gathers in waves, but the surf usually breaks on the beach here, so the rides tend to be short. Alternatively, if it's a day of "mushy" waves—barely knee-high—or it's high tide, when things tend to flatten out, you can wander over to Beach 116th Street and commiserate with the crowd at Rockaway Beach Surf Shop.

Directions: By subway, take the A train to Beach 90th Street, walk south on Beach 90th to the boardwalk, then go two blocks east.

By car, take the Belt Parkway to Flatbush Avenue and cross the Marine Parkway Bridge. Take Rockaway Beach Boulevard to Beach 90th Street and look for parking.

Surfin' NYC

When he was a teenager learning to surf on Long Island, Tony Bottero once wiped out so spectacularly he broke his surfboard with his face. He wasn't deterred. The lifeguards, who used to watch waves roll Bottero and dump him into the sand, called him the "wave slave."

It wasn't easy being a wave slave. The summers are short, the water is cold, the waves are fickle. "New York City is the hardest place in the world to surf," says Bottero, who grew up in Manhattan's Upper West Side. "When you learn how to surf, you just keep trying, trying, trying, until boom, it clicks. They kept making fun of me, but I was always out there whether the waves were decent, shitty, whatever. I was always there."

Bottero, 30, embodies the stubborn, surf-at-any-cost culture that persists in the city. He bar-tends all winter so he can surf all summer. He has a tiny patch of hair under his lower lip, an evangelist's boundless energy, and a business card (this is New York City, after all), but he also uses words such as "rad" and "wilbur."

Bottero, who has surfed every hurricane since 1992, says the most dangerous one was Floyd in '99. "It just picked the waves up high and dumped them straight down—that's a 'close-out' wave. Mother Nature is the scariest thing in the world. Never turn your back on a wave, never let down your guard, because you never know when a rogue set is going to come down and kick your ass."

Friends tell Bottero he has a fantasy lifestyle. He surfs and snowboards on his days off in winter. His plans shift with weather forecasts. A friend who sold Bottero his first surfboard is now earning six figures in an office job. Bottero's corporate dealings involve angling for sponsorships (read: free gear) from various surf and snowboard companies. That's all he wants.

So the waves suck today? They could be head-high tomorrow. "A lot of people say to me, 'You're a surfer, why are you in New York?'" Bottero says. "I've been to California, but when you're from somewhere, you always end up going back. I've got it all here. I'll never stop doing this for the rest of my life."

Short Hops

Long Island

LONG BEACH AND LIDO BEACH

Location: Nassau County, Long Island, 25 miles southeast of Manhattan

Difficulty: Intermediate to advanced

Heads up: The closest wax is Long Beach Surf Shop (651 East Park Avenue, Long Beach, 516-897-7873, surf conditions 897-9496) and UnSound Surf Shop (359 East Park Avenue, Long Beach, 516-889-1112, surf conditions 892-7972, www.unsoundsurf.com).

Description: These neighboring Nassau County beaches are among New Yorkers' best quickie options. Lido features monster beach breaks, the best on Long Island, so it's no place for neophytes. Mighty, cavernous, A-frame waves can reach a robust 8 feet—generally a couple of feet higher than Long Beach because a deep channel of water consistently adds volume to the waves. Look for south swells with north winds. Long Beach sees mostly waist- to chest-high conditions, though the occasional fall hurricane will whip up 15-foot faces.

Directions: By train, take the Long Island Rail Road to Long Beach. You can walk east to Lido if you so choose. Both beaches are open to surfers.

By car, take the Belt Parkway to the Sunrise Highway eastbound. Exit at Rockville Center and go east on Merrick Road. Turn right on Long Beach Road and follow the signs. Lido Beach is the next beach to the east.

ROBERT MOSES STATE PARK

Location: Saltaire, Long Island, 56 miles east of Manhattan

Difficulty: Beginner to upper intermediate, depending on conditions

Heads up: The closest wax is Bunger Surf Shop in Babylon (50 East Main Street, 800-698-7873, www.bungersurf.com), an institution; also, Rick's Action Sports and Surf Shop in East Islip (155 Carleton Avenue, 631-581-9424, www.ricksactionsportsandsurfshop.com).

Description: This is one of those places where even if you don't get the best waves, you don't mind settling for average. The lightest summer winds tend to lift up the chop on the park's south face. The shifting sands constantly morph the wave conditions, so finding the best spots sometimes requires a Thoreauvian studiousness. Ask the locals for updates, or watch the weather and study the water for a while. If you do break the code, the payoff is consistent, head-high, beach-breaking swells.

Directions: By car, take the Belt Parkway to the Southern State Parkway. Take exit 40 and cross the Robert Moses Causeway. Follow signs to the park. Ask the parking area attendants to point you to the beaches designated for surfing.

Clean Breaks

ONE UNUSUAL INDICATOR of a cleaner New York City coastline: Tar remover sales have dropped dramatically at Rockaway Beach Surf Shop. In the 1970s, there was so much tar in the water, it formed ball-shaped deposits on surfboards. Surf shop owner Tom Sena says the waters are also free of the syringes, medical waste, and chunks of lumber that surfers used to encounter.

FIRE ISLAND NATIONAL SEASHORE

Location: Sayville, Long Island, 54 miles east of Manhattan

Difficulty: Intermediate

Heads up: The closest wax is Bunger Surf Shop and Rick's Action Sports and Surf Shop (see Robert Moses State Park, page 255).

Description: If you're willing to hoof it out here—the roadless island is accessible only by ferry or private boat (or car at Smith Point if you don't mind walking in)—the reward is consistent waves and smaller crowds. The beaches stretch for more than 10 miles, and the conditions—as with Robert Moses—can be a bit mercurial because of shifting sand. But if the winds are blowing north, the waves are good *somewhere* on the island.

If you win over the locals, they might give you a lift to Democrat Point, a spot reachable only by four-wheel drive. Word has it that if you surf "goofy"—with your right foot forward instead of your left, as is more common—it's the best spot on Long Island, with epic 90-second, 200-yard runs.

Directions: By car, take the Southern State Parkway to

exit 45. Follow NY 85 east into Sayville; follow signs to the ferries. There are designated surfing areas at almost every park beach; ask the lifeguards for specifics.

New Jersey

SANDY HOOK NATIONAL RECREATION AREA

Location: Gateway National Recreation Area, Highlands, New Jersey, 53 driving miles south of Manhattan

Difficulty: Intermediate to advanced

Heads up: The closest wax is Island Style Sun & Surf (1032 Ocean Avenue, Sea Bright, 732-842-0909).

Description: Monmouth Beach to the south of Sandy Hook is more of a household name in the surfing world, but it has developed a reputation as a beach where locals dominate and visitors are not welcome. Sandy Hook isn't known for huge waves, but it does have one of the only point breaks in New Jersey—and you won't find the same crowds or attitude more prevalent to the south. The highlight is a big south swell that offers some amazing rides even when other areas aren't doing much. The Brighton Avenue jetty and Beachcombers also handle south swells nicely.

Directions: By ferry, New York Waterways (800-533-3779) runs ferries to Sandy Hook during the summer. Other times of year, Seastreak (800-262-8743) and New York Fast Ferry (800-693-6933) serve Highlands, just outside Sandy Hook's entrance.

By car, take the Garden State Parkway to exit 117; follow NJ 36 east to the park. There's a vehicle entry fee in summer only.

BELMAR

Location: Belmar, New Jersey, 63 driving miles south of Manhattan

Difficulty: Beginner to advanced

Heads up: The closest wax is Eastern Lines Surf Shop (1603 Ocean Avenue, Belmar, 732-681-6405, www.easternlines.com, surf report 732-681-6407); the shop has everything you'll need.

Description: This is one of those haunted Jersey Shore dives—packed in summer, dead the rest of the year—that inspired Bruce Springsteen (in fact, Belmar's E Street was the inspiration for his band's name). But the waves are always alive, even when the town isn't. The surfers' beach is at Sixteenth Avenue, and the crowds are astounding in summer. Avoid the Eighth Avenue Jetty, which is locals only; instead, try the Belmar Pier when swells are rolling in from the north. Watch out here during hurricane season; the police enforce beach closures.

Directions: By car, take the Garden State Parkway to NJ 138 east; follow signs to the beach. In summer you have to buy a beach "tag."

Talk the Talk

A SAMPLE SURFING glossary, courtesy of Tony Bottero.

Buoy: A surfer who never goes for any waves, just paddles around and floats

Dropping in: Paddling into a wave somebody is already surfing, thus cutting him or her off and potentially causing an accident

Fish: Small board, wide in the nose and tail. Used for small waves and trick riding

Fun shape: A longer, thicker board, easier to learn on and catch small waves

Pack rat: A beginner, usually a kid, who never stops talking in the water

Skeg: A surfboard's fin

Skegging: Slashing someone with the fin of the board

Speed bumps: Boogie boarders and swimmers who get in the way of waves

Thruster: A short board with a three-skeg configuration

Wilbur: A beginner, or someone who is in the water but has no idea what to do with a surfboard

MANASQUAN INLET

Location: Manasquan, New Jersey, 65 driving miles south of Manhattan

Difficulty: Beginner to advanced

Heads up: The closest wax is Inlet Outlet (Main Street, Manasquan, 732-223-5842, www.inletoutlet.com), an outlet-sized outfitter.

Description: The inlet has one of the most popular breaks in the Northeast, as the bumper-to-bumper parking lot will attest on days the waves are rolling in strong. What makes the inlet special year-round is a jetty that corrals the waves into a steep wedge, producing long rides. With a southeast swell, the inlet can handle waves that reach as high as 20 feet. There's a long-established pecking order here on those days, so get a sense of the local protocol before trying to take your turns. If you're inexperienced or an out-of-towner, it's best to try your luck on the days when the conditions are not electrifying.

Directions: By car, take the Garden State Parkway to exit 98. Drive south on NJ 34 and follow signs to the beach. There's a fee in summer.

DITCH PLAINS

Location: Montauk, Long Island, 116 miles east of Manhattan

Difficulty: Beginner to intermediate

Heads up: The closest wax is Air & Speed Boardshop (7 Le Plaza, Montauk, 631-668-0356), which charges $150 for a 3-day surf camp, including 2 to 3 hours of daily instruction. In the Hamptons, Main Beach Surf & Sport (631-537-2716, www.mainbeach.com, surf report 631-537-7873) rents boards and offers instruction. Jeremy Grovesnor (631-537-9327) offers instruction specializing in "beginners and cowards."

Description: Surfers love to keep secrets. And for a long time, this land's-end fishing village, at the remote tip of Long Island, was able to hide its superb surf conditions. No longer. To the dismay of the regulars, the crowds at Ditch Plains have grown to nearly Times Square proportions, and the situation is not likely to change, especially since Air & Speed Boardshop began running a surfing minicamp. "Some people are always going to grumble," says owner Stuart Foley, "but we're only a hundred miles from New York City. It's one of the most populous cities on the planet, and you want to protect the surf break? That's kind of tough."

Even if you have to wait your turn for a wave, Montauk is worth it. Swells headed up the Atlantic hit Montauk first and hardest, creating the biggest and steadiest rips on Long Island. With almost any north or northwest breeze buffeting the water, the waves kick up nicely, and the rock base ensures consistent breaks. And if you tire of waiting, you can always cast for striped bass and blues at nearby Montauk Point State Park (see "Fishing," page 226).

If you're already locked into a share in the Hamptons, the conditions there are fine, too, particularly for beginners—there are gradual waves and no beach break.

Directions: By car, take the Belt Parkway to the Southern Parkway to NY 27 and drive into Montauk.

Mind the Etiquette, Dude

FOR A SPORT with a reputation for being laid-back, surfing has rather strict etiquette. One of the cardinal rules: Don't "drop in" on another surfer's wave—that is, paddle into the wave they're about to ride. Also, don't cut into the lineup to catch waves; paddle beyond other surfers, or defer to those who have waited longer.

Unfortunately, as the sport's popularity has grown, more ill-mannered surfers are violating long-held rules of etiquette, according to the book *Surf Rage*, by Nat Young, a five-time world champion from Australia. For those reasons, some beaches are increasingly territorial. At Monmouth Beach or Belmar in New Jersey, for example, you may not be welcome even if you do wait. Talk to locals about the pecking order if you're new on a beach.

One benefit of surfing in New York: The surfing population is so small, there's little chance of people squabbling over turf. "There are people who think surfing is a contact sport," says Tom Sena. "But there are other people who look at it as an art, an expression. People are pretty low key here. They try not to get in each other's way."

BROADWAY BEACH

Location: Cape May, New Jersey, 163 miles south of Manhattan

Difficulty: Beginner to expert

Heads up: The closest wax is Summer Sun Surf Shop (315 Washington Street, Cape May, 609-884-3422).

Description: The bottom tip of New Jersey has a wide range of options. Broadway Beach has the largest array of swells and draws the biggest crowds, especially when Nor'easters come roaring north. The thing is, there's just enough protection to ride waves here when the rest of the coast has enormous, unmanageable waves. Beginners looking for a steady practice spot should check out the last jetty on 2nd Avenue. To shake the crowds, head a little north to modest, amiable Grant Street Beach.

Directions: By car, follow the Garden State Parkway to its southern terminus and continue into Cape May.

Where to Connect

Shops

- Rockaway Beach Surf Shop (177 Beach 116th Street, Far Rockaway, Queens, 718-474-9345) is one of the bigger shops on the East Coast. From the flip-flops to the Billabong shorts to the *Endless Summer II* poster signed by star Robert "Wingnut" Weaver ("To Rockaway: Stay Stoked!"), owner Tom Sena has it all.
- New York Pipe Dreams (1625 York Avenue, Manhattan, 212-535-7473, www.newyorkpipedreams.com) has a real authenticity for an Upper East Side shop. Reggae music drifts up the steps leading down to the

shop, and there are posters of Sunset Beach in Hawaii, boards and wetsuits on the wall, and ratty furniture.

Organization

- Surfrider (New York City chapter, 146 Frost Street, Brooklyn, www.coastalwaterquality.org/nyc) is an organization dedicated to coastal environmental issues.

Resources

The surf scene has an active Internet presence, with features including surf-cams so you can actually see the waves before heading out. Among the useful sites:

- Newyorksurf.com (www.newyorksurf.com) offers a surfing forum, forecasts, and updates on conditions.
- The Web site www.surfinfo.com has East Coast surf reports.

Sailing

STEVE CARD SEES gusts of wind before he feels them. "See the water over there?" he says, pointing at the far gray reaches of Long Island Sound. "That dark patch means we're about to get some breeze." And sure enough, a powerful blast sends our 21-foot sloop heeling hard to starboard, jerking the rudder in my hand. Card grew up sailing in City Island, where he's now director of the New York Sailing Center & Yacht Club. There are lots of guys like him around the city—sailors who grew up in this sailing town.

Sailing is New York's first adventure sport. Centuries before surfboards, underwater breathing equipment, and recreational kayaks, there was the sail and the mast. The Dutch explored the area in

wooden sailing ships 400 years ago, and New Yorkers established the world's first club for boating enthusiasts, the Knickerbocker Club, 200 years ago. Even in this modern era of high-tech toys, the lure of the sail lives on. The city's powerful currents, winds, and bracingly cold waters continue to challenge sailors, as does its obstacle course of a harbor and shipping channel.

One positive change: Sailing is no longer a bastion of the wealthy. You can now learn to sail in the harbor or City Island in a few days, and rent a sloop to explore Long Island Sound, Jamaica Bay, and the coast of Brooklyn. Get some experience and you can crew boats out to Nantucket, even around the world. Sailing out of the Verrazano Narrows onto the open sea, headed across the Atlantic or down to the howling southern oceans—that's still about as adventurous as this world gets.

The Sandbaggers

IN THE 1860S, fishermen working New York Harbor raced one another back into port after harvesting huge bags of clams and oysters. The contest wasn't just for fun; the first boat to return got the highest prices on the market. But the crews grew so competitive they began to have gentlemen's races on the weekends, replacing the mollusks with sand and taking bets. The "Sandbaggers" races ended more than a century ago with the demise of the clam and oyster beds.

In 1999, the New York Harbor Sailing Foundation and Manhattan Yacht Club revived the tradition, organizing a race of replica 18-foot sailboats. The craft are sleek and notoriously unstable. The boat that held famous author Norman Mailer flipped, dumping him into the harbor. "He told the *Daily News* it was the most fun he'd had in fifteen years," says Mike

Hartenbaugh of the Manhattan Yacht Club. "It wasn't much fun for us. The police and Coast Guard get nervous if you capsize in the harbor, and this was a man of letters. Marla Maples was on another boat that flipped right after she got off. No one noticed the boat flipped because they were paying so much attention to her."

No race was held in 2000 because the boats were being modified to keep them from tipping so easily, but the Sandbaggers are expected to continue racing annually.

City Limits

NEW YORK HARBOR

Outfitters: Floating the Apple (212-564-5412, www.floatingtheapple.org) has boathouses in Manhattan, Brooklyn, the Bronx, and New Jersey. You can ride along for free, but expect to be recruited for various projects. It's possible to get a boat through the New York City Community Sailing Association (212-222-1405, http://ourworld.compuserve.com/homepages/rer/sailny.htm) if you're qualified (see The Basics, page 278).

Description: There are some 3 million New Yorkers within walking distance of the waterfront, but almost no one uses it because they can't get to it. The harbor is a massive, untapped resource. Gradually, though, that's changing. Floating the Apple, an organization dedicated to expanding waterfront access, conducts sailing and rowing trips along the Brooklyn waterfront, up to Roosevelt Island, across to Staten Island or Liberty State Park in New Jersey, and up the Hudson. You don't need experience to go along, just a willingness to pitch in. The rewards are bountiful. Depending on the season, you'll encounter sea turtles and seals, stop at tucked-away beaches, watch horseshoe crabs plant their eggs. "It dazzles," executive director Mike Davis says. "It's always a different experience, depending on what the tide is doing, which way the wind is blowing, or what the weather brings in."

Don't miss the outings along Red Hook and the Brooklyn waterfront. If you're a Brooklynite, it's a chance to see the fronts of all the buildings you always see from the rear. If you live in Manhattan, the close-ups of the buildings visible from the water are fascinating: the antebellum arches of pier buildings, a towering grain elevator, and a sugar refinery that looks like a large-scale version of the Tin Man from the *Wizard of Oz*.

The Pioneer

MIKE HARTENBAUGH SITS at the helm of a speedboat in New York Harbor, having just fired off a tiny cannon to start the night's racing. Out here, he looks about as happy as a man can be. Jimmy Buffett songs drift from onboard speakers. The sun drops behind New Jersey, igniting the Manhattan skyline. "This is a special place," Hartenbaugh murmurs. "You're much more in touch with the environment and weather out here."

This is how he imagined it when he set out to start a sailing club in 1987, at the tender age of 23. At the time there was virtually no recreational sailing in the harbor. "People said, 'You're crazy. There's no way you can sail here—it's too crowded, too polluted, and there are no facilities,'" Hartenbaugh recalls. "We were the first ones trying to convince people you could do this."

Hartenbaugh had a distinctly egalitarian idea for the Manhattan Yacht Club he created. Instead of an exclusive club where you had to own a yacht to join, the club would own the boats, and the boats would be available to anyone who joined. "It's not for prestige, but for fun," he says. "We want to make sure people love sailing so much they stay in the sport." The first years were tough. The club had no waterfront access. Hartenbaugh had to squeeze the club's dozen or so boats between several tall ships. But he knew he had a workable concept, and he loved sailing; his oldest son, William, is nicknamed "Skipper."

Hartenbaugh's vision paid off. Manhattan Sailing School, a branch of the yacht club, is entering its eighth year and is the largest school in the harbor; it enrolled 500 students in 2000. The races regularly draw 20 or more crews—up to 120 people. And there are plans to add weekend races and expand the business to Hoboken.

CITY ISLAND AND WESTERN LONG ISLAND SOUND

Outfitter: New York Sailing Center & Yacht Club (560 Minneford Avenue, City Island, 718-885-0335, www.startsailing.com) rents 21-footers. Charts are available at JJ Burke Hardware & Discount Marine Supplies (526 City Island Avenue, 718-885-1559).

Description: In the old days of shipping, pilots were stationed at City Island specifically to help barges navigate Hell Gate and the treacherous East River channels to reach New York Harbor. As a recreational sailor, you'll be headed the other way, to the open waters of Long Island Sound. From City Island, get your bearings in quiet Eastchester Bay, which is pinched between the island and the mainland Bronx, before riding the gusts out and away in the busy Sound. A common day-sailing route: Head east between Orchard Beach and Hart Island to Execution Rocks Lighthouse in the Sound. Legend holds that the British chained Revolutionary War prisoners to the lighthouse rocks to drown in the rising tide, but the story is probably apocryphal. More likely the lighthouse owes its ominous appellation to the numerous shipwrecks the rocks caused before the lighthouse was built in 1849. Hart Island, meanwhile, has its own eerie past, as well as present. Now a mass burial ground for the city's unclaimed dead, this 101-acre outpost was used to isolate yellow fever patients in 1870, before becoming a sort of prison for a rotating cast of characters, including drug addicts, violent youths, and German prisoners during World War II.

Mindful of Execution Rocks, I painstakingly noted each gull-covered rock, but without Steve Card's expertise I also would have needed charts; not all of the obstacles are exposed. The storied lakelike harbors of the western Sound —Manhasset Bay, Little Neck Bay, and Oyster Bay—are pleasant destinations, with waterside restaurants. And it only gets better the farther you go. The Sound has mild currents, steady breezes, and compelling destinations such as Greenport and Sag Harbor, which is why it's among the top multiday cruising grounds in the country.

Directions: By subway, take the 6 train to Pelham Bay Park. You can walk or take the BM29 bus to City Island Road or (in summer only) the #12 bus to Orchard Beach. Or bring a bike and use the greenway path.

By car, cross the Triboro Bridge and go east on I-95 to the Pelham Bay/Orchard Beach exit; follow signs to City Island.

On Your Mark

SUMMER EVENINGS ARE busy on New York Harbor. Pale blue police boats, the Hoboken ferry, and sea kayakers crisscross the water. There seems to be hardly room for a lone swimmer to do the backstroke, much less for a cluster of sailboats. For sailors, though, racing is about precision as well as speed, so the traffic is part of the fun. The sport draws after-work sailors to the harbor and City Island, as well as to ports all over Long Island and New Jersey.

The New York City Community Sailing Association (see The Basics, page 278) races year-round, sponsoring the only frostbite series in the city. The races are on smaller boats with no spinnakers; being on deck working them means risking a dump in the icy water. Manhattan Yacht Club (see *The Pioneer*, page 268) races its fleet of J24s from spring through late October.

Certified sailors can hitch onto a boat that needs extra crew in either series. The boats can accommodate four to six. Most races start between Ellis Island and the Liberty State Park ferry terminal; boats head down the harbor to the Statue of Liberty and Governor's Island, though the direction could be reversed depending on wind, weather, and the amount of daylight left.

Races on Eastchester Bay in City Island draw some of the top amateur sailors from up and down the Sound. City Island Yacht Club (718-885-2487, www.cityislandnyc.org) welcomes freelancers for boats short of crew.

JAMAICA BAY

Location: Queens and Brooklyn

Outfitter: There are no rental places in the area, but Miramar Yacht Club in Sheepshead Bay (3050 Emmons Avenue, 718-769-3548, www.miramaryc.com) has a fleet of boats and open memberships.

Description: For birds and bridges, the beautiful and the bizarre, you can't do much better than Jamaica Bay. Once you pass under the Marine Parkway Gil Hodges Memorial Bridge and head east on Runway Channel—named for the seaplanes and amphibious craft that used to take off from nearby Floyd Bennett Field—you're in a New York far removed. If you stay south, Beach Channel leads up past JFK International Airport all the way to Head-of-Bay, technically in Nassau County.

The 7-mile-long, 3.5-mile-wide bay of hassocks and marshes features views of up to eleven bridges, including six that open for boats. (One is a "swing" bridge used by the A subway train.) There are houses on stilts on Broad Channel, the only inhabited island in the bay. You'll pass sewage treatment plants and places with names such as Dead Horse Bay and Barren Island, but it's not nearly as gloomy as it sounds. The bay has sprung to life in recent years, and it's now common to see oystercatchers, herons, ibis, peregrine falcons, and snow geese, among other waterfowl. There are century-old pine trees at the edge of Bayswater Point State Park, across from Grassy Point and the intrusive airport runway built across the Grassy Bay.

Jamaica Bay can be a tricky destination; there are strong tides and currents, and the wind sometimes can alter the effect of both. Parts of the bay are shallow, so be sure to stick to the channel. Don't sail in without a motor and a full tank of gas; you may need them to help you get back out. Another good choice: Sail in the opposite direction, along the New York Bight toward New Jersey.

Directions: By train, take the Q train to Sheepshead Bay; turn right out of the train station and turn left at the waterfront on Emmons Avenue.

By car, take the Belt Parkway east to exit 9B for Sheepshead Bay. Head west on Emmons Avenue, where Miramar Yacht Club and other bay-oriented activities are centered.

The World's Toughest Sailors

IT WAS LATE October and Alec Decker had spent 2 full days freezing, exhausted, and frightfully seasick. He was having the time of his life.

Decker, of Brooklyn, was enduring an ocean-sailing initiation off the coast near Boston, learning how to crew a 72-foot yacht. Ever the taskmaster, nature was pounding the boat with 9-foot waves and keening 40-knot winds. Decker felt as though he was inside a beating drum. "I was weak, but I was able to sit upstairs and sort of look around and realize what enormous fun this would be if I wasn't completely miserable," he says, laughing.

Why go through all that? In spring 2002, Decker will join scores of other amateur sailors in San Francisco for the New World Challenge, a round-the-world race that pits a dozen identical yachts against the planet's prevailing westerly winds and currents. The crew is made up of "volunteers"—sailing amateurs from across the country—who pay $44,850 for a berth on a vessel and training. For 30,000 miles, over 10 months, the crews will bash heads with some of the world's fiercest seas. Organizers call the event "the world's toughest yacht race."

Decker, a Princeton graduate who has been a mutual fund analyst and a CFO for an Internet start-up, spent his childhood summers on his family's small sailboat on Long Island Sound. One night several years ago he picked up *Close to the Wind*, a book by Pete Goss about the New World Challenge. Decker read it in one sitting, then sent a late-night e-mail to the Challenge Business, which runs the event. He sent his deposit the day after receiving the application. He'll celebrate his thirty-first birthday on the first full day of the race.

The trip includes the raucous roaring forties and a treacherous rounding of Cape Horn. Decker will need every bit of his training. "The thought comes to mind: What the heck am I doing here?" Decker says of his experience. "I decided it was because I want to be here. You have to be ready for some hardships and suck it up. I'm just going to repeat the mantra: 'I'm having a really good time.'"

Short Hops

HAVERSTRAW BAY

Location: Croton-on-Hudson, New York, 40 miles north of Manhattan

Outfitter: Croton Sailing School (Croton-on-Hudson, 800-859-7245, www.crotonsailing.com) offers basic beginner and cruising courses; sailing club membership privileges include the use of the sailboats.

Description: An hour north of the city, under the shadow of the Palisades, the glacier-carved Hudson River widens and flattens until it stretches more than 3.5 miles across. Much of the powerful current disperses, leaving the residents of Croton-on-Hudson with a lakelike body of water on the eastern shore called Haverstraw Bay. There's plenty of room to learn to sail and take day trips in scenic confines without the crowds of western Long Island Sound. Some days the osprey and cormorants cruising the shallows will be your only company. It wasn't always so peaceful here. During the Revolutionary War, colonists fired a cannon from the southern end of the bay, Teller's Point, to deter a British ship heading to meet Benedict Arnold.

For more history, sail downstream to the Philipsburg Manor Upper Mill on the Tarrytown shore. In the late 1600s this gristmill used river water to grind out 5,000 pounds of grain daily. After plying the Hudson, grab something to eat and a beer at Elmer Suds, a pub-restaurant just off Grand Street, Croton's main drag.

Directions: By train, take Metro-North to Croton-Harmon; if you're taking lessons, the school will pick you up. Otherwise, it's a 2-minute cab ride or a short walk to the water.

By car, take the Saw Mill River Parkway north to the Taconic State Parkway; take exit 129 and follow the signs for the Croton Sailing School.

GREENWOOD LAKE

Location: Greenwood Lake, New York, 54 miles northwest of Manhattan

Outfitter: South Shore Marina (Hewitt, New Jersey, 973-728-1681, www.southshoremarina.com) rents sailboats, pontoon boats, canoes, and kayaks.

Description: Split between New York and New Jersey, Greenwood is a 9- by 1-mile finger of a lake. About 7 miles of the lake is navigable by sailboat. Though the lake is a tad overdeveloped, it's in a beautiful area, wedged between Sterling Forest State Park on the east and the Appalachian Trail on the west. Great blue herons and egrets hang out here most of the year. If you've got a fishing pole, dangle some line for the bass and muskies, particularly in the weedier south end.

Directions: By car, take I-87 north over the Tappan Zee Bridge to exit 15A. Follow NY 17 north to NY 17A; follow signs to Greenwood Lake.

Coveting the Cup

New York City has a strong connection to the America's Cup, the world's oldest sporting trophy and most prestigious sailing competition. In 1851 the New York Yacht Club claimed the first cup, and the U.S. entry in several competitions was built on City Island in the Bronx. The city has lost some of its America's Cup prestige lately; a team sponsored by the New York Yacht Club hasn't claimed a title since 1980. But, as the saying goes in baseball, wait 'til next year: Three-time cup winner Dennis Conner will take the helm for New York in 2003.

Meccas

NEWPORT, RHODE ISLAND

Location: 175 miles northeast of Manhattan

Outfitter: Bareboat Sailing Charters (800-661-4013, www.bareboatsailing.com) is one of several full-service outfitters.

Heads up: The Bank of Newport Sailing Festival, held in May, includes a day of free sailing with Sail Newport volunteers.

Description: With its consistent breezes, expansive maritime history, and extraordinary patchwork of nearby islands, Newport is the sailing capital of the Northeast.

This famed seaport is within a day's cruise of Nantucket, Block Island, Martha's Vineyard, and Fishers Island, among other prime Northeast destinations. Racing of aficionados won't get to see the America's Cup here anytime soon—defending champion New Zealand hosts the race in

2003—but there are numerous national and international sailboat competitions, including the Newport Regatta, which draws about 250 boats and 1,500 competitors from more than a dozen states and Canada.

Newport, of course, is where Thurston Howell should have been sailing, instead of being on that tiny ship with Gilligan. The city is dauntingly exclusive—walk around and check out the mansions along the shore and the enormous yachts in port—but there are places to rent and launch boats. To get started, contact Sail Newport (401-846-1983, www.sailnewport.org), a clearinghouse for everything from weather reports to boat launches.

Directions: By car, take I-95 north to RI 138 east. Follow US 1/RI 138 north, then continue on RT 138 when it branches off to the right. Drive over the Jamestown and Newport Bridges into Newport.

CAYUGA LAKE

Location: Ithaca, New York, 225 miles northwest of Manhattan

Outfitter: Ithaca Yacht Club (607-272-4113, www.iyc.baka.com)

Description: This is listed here for this compelling, whimsical reason: You can sail from this inland lake all the way to Key West. There's a continuous water passage to Lake Ontario, and from there you can pick up the St. Lawrence Seaway to the Atlantic. The thing is, once you get here you'll be in no hurry to leave. Cayuga is the longest of the Finger Lakes, a set of glacial claw marks gouged out of central New York. Immortalized in the Cornell theme song, it sits in a gorgeous, narrow valley of shale cliffs, lighthouses, and mercurial winds. There are races here in summer. Another idea: Find out which way the wind is blowing—sometimes it's in multiple directions, so keep an open mind—and just follow it. The lake stretches out for 40 miles, so don't worry about running out of room. And when you do, there are some pretty good vineyards in these parts, as well as largemouth bass to drop a hook in front of.

A little farther north you can set sail on Lake Ontario, essentially a 200-mile-long inland sea, complete with its own Great Lakes climate.

Directions: By bus, take Greyhound (800-231-2222) or Short Line (800-631-8405) to Ithaca.

By car, take I-87 north to NY 17 west to NY 96 north to NY 96B north to Ithaca.

Where to Connect

The Basics

If you don't know how to sail and haven't quite mastered the sport's distinct lingo (a "sheet" is actually a rope), New York is an intriguing place to get an education. You can learn the difference between a halyard and a spinnaker, among other fundamentals, in 2- to 4-day courses at schools affiliated with the American Sailing Association (ASA) or the U.S. Sailing Association. Certification by either organization will allow you to rent boats anywhere in the country.

A number of New York sailing schools—undaunted by the currents and commercial traffic—have popped up around New York Harbor in recent years. By far the most inexpensive option is the New York City Community Sailing Association, a nonprofit outfit created in 1994 that charges only a few hundred dollars for a 16-hour course.

Once you become an experienced sailor—capable of rigging sails, sailing a triangular course, and guiding the boat to a mooring without power under normal conditions—and you promise not to venture out in conditions that exceed your ability, you have access to boats for a reasonable membership fee.

The other public option is the Manhattan Yacht Club, which offers two levels of membership that amount to a fraction of what it would cost to own and maintain a boat.

Schools and Boat Rentals

New York Harbor/Hudson River

- New York City Community Sailing Association (212-222-1405, http://ourworld.compuserve.com/homepages/rer/sailny.htm) offers courses and access to boats for qualified sailors.
- Manhattan Yacht Club (393 South End Avenue, Manhattan, 212-786-3323, www.myc.org) is open to anyone qualified to sail; membership allows you to crew or captain boats, depending on your skill level.
- Manhattan Sailing School (393 South End Avenue, Manhattan, 800-859-7245, www.sailmanhattan.com) is the instructional wing of the Manhattan Yacht Club.
- North Cove Sailing School (303 South End Avenue, Manhattan, 800-532-5552, offers basics and courses in keelboat sailing and coastal cruising.
- Chelsea Sailing School (Pier 59, Chelsea Piers, 212-627-7245, www.chelseasailing.com)
- ASA Newport Sailing School (500 Washington Boulevard, Newport Center, NJ, 201-626-3210) offers basic to advanced instruction.
- Offshore Sailing School (Exchange Place, Jersey City, 800-221-4326)

- Croton Sailing School (Croton-on-Hudson, 800-859-7245, www.crotonsailing.com) is located on the Hudson's Haverstraw Bay. Instruction, sailing club, and rentals.
- Great Hudson Sailing Center (West Haverstraw and Kingston, 845-429-1557, www.greathudsonsailing.com) has lessons and rentals.

City Island, Westchester County, and Western Long Island

- New York Sailing Center & Yacht Club (560 Minneford Avenue, City Island, 718-885-0335, www.startsailing.com) offers basic to advanced instruction, rentals, and boat storage.
- New York Sailing School (22 Pelham Road, New Rochelle, 914-235-6052, www.nyss.com) offers courses, private instruction, and several types of rentals.
- Oyster Bay Sailing School and Charters (800-323-2207)

Events

- The Around Long Island Regatta (516-671-7348, www.alir.org) is a prestigious race from Sheepshead Bay in Brooklyn to Sea Cliff, Long Island.
- The New York National Boat Show (212-984-7005, www.boatshows.com/newyork01) is held each January at the Jacob Javits Center in Manhattan.

Books and Resources

- Adams, Arthur G. *The Hudson River Guidebook*. Bronx, NY: Fordham University Press, 1996.
- Duncan, Robert C., Roger S. Duncan, W. Wallace Fenn, and Paul W. Fenn. *The Cruising Guide to the*

New England Coast. 12th ed. New York, NY: W. W. Norton & Co., 2001.

- Marian, Thomas W. *A Cruising Guide to the Northeast's Inland Waterways: The Hudson River, New York State Canals, Lake Ontario, St. Lawrence Seaway, Lake Champlain.* Camden, ME: International Marine Publishing, 1995.
- New York City WPA Writers Project. *A Maritime History of New York.* New York, NY: Doubleday, 1941.
- Seitz, Sharon, and Stuart Miller. *The Other Islands of New York City.* 2d ed. Woodstock, VT: Countryman Press, 2001.
- Waldman, John. *Heartbeats in the Muck: A Dramatic Look at the History, Sea Life and Environment of New York Harbor.* New York, NY: Lyons Press, 1999.
- Boating on the Hudson Online (www.boatingonthehudson.com) has tide tables and classifieds.

Windsurfing

WIDE-OPEN PLACES such as Colorado and Oregon get all the attention in the windsurfing world, but where it's good in the Northeast, this little niche sport is very, very good. For New Yorkers, unfortunately, this means traveling an hour or two. The sport requires open water with little traffic and mild currents—not exactly in abundance around these parts. But the sailing rigs are getting better all the time, and a week in Napeague Bay on Long Island or Lakes Bay in New Jersey ought to be just enough for you to get hooked.

Windsurfing appeals to anyone from the quiet, meditative type to the extreme athlete who likes to take on hurricane conditions. And there are

advantages to addictions to less-popular sports. At a time where adventure sports are growing exponentially, you probably won't have to worry about your favorite bay being overrun by fellow windsurfers. And as for the sailors you do meet: Windsurfers tend to be a friendly, clubby, type-A bunch—think surfers with MBAs.

Another advantage: With the recent increase in windsurfing equipment prices came a stark improvement in technology. There is still a learning curve in windsurfing, but the rigs are lighter and easier to use; with a few lessons, the falling-on-your-face period is shorter than ever. Before long you'll be tacking and jibing off Sandy Hook, waiting for blustery thermals to help you haul ass across the open water. Though many sailors like to just breeze across shallow bays, others sail through hurricanes or use surf to launch into midair flips. Then it becomes a year-round obsession, and you'll find yourself out on your rig on Budd Lake, with your board fitted with blades, flying across the ice at 60 mph.

City Limits

PLUMB BEACH

Location: Brooklyn

Description: Situated on a calm inlet within Sheepshead Bay, this modest, rough-around-the-edges beach is an option for windsurfers who can't escape the city for the weekend. As it stands now, this National Park Service property is far more popular among folks looking for crabs and clams than it is with sailors. But there's plenty of parking and pretty good sailing when the wind is coming from any direction but the north. Unfortunately, New York Pipe

Dreams, the last windsurfing outfitter in New York, dropped its windsurfing stock.

Directions: By car, take the Belt Parkway to exit 9B and look for parking on Emmons Street. At Knapp Street, walk on the greenway a short distance to the beach.

The Big Blow

SURFERS ARE KNOWN for their affection for hurricane conditions, but they're not the only adventurers heading for the beach while everyone else is boarding up windows and stockpiling food. When the hurricane isn't hitting dead-on, it kicks up the sort of winds that windsurfers dream about. "We always pray for a hurricane, but we haven't been that lucky the last couple of years," says Jack Barrett, a windsurfing instructor at West Point Military Academy. He ranks Hurricane Bertha in 1996 as the best of the past decade.

For ideal hurricane windsurfing, the conditions have to be powerful but reasonable—up to 40-mph winds. Anything stronger would overwhelm the rig. What does it feel like? "It's a cross between 'Oh my God, what am I doing, I'm going to die,' and 'Wow, only the fin is touching the water, and I'm moving as fast as the wind,'" Barrett says. "And that's like no drug known to man."

Short Hops

SANDY HOOK NATIONAL RECREATION AREA

Location: Gateway National Recreation Area, Highlands, New Jersey, 53 driving miles south of Manhattan

Outfitter: The closest is Windsurfing Bay Head (732-899-9394, www.bayheadtrading.com)

Description: Peninsulas such as Sandy Hook are invaluable to windsurfers for two reasons: They create harbors, and they provide access to breezes that come strong and undiminished from any number of directions. Lot C is the epicenter of Sandy Hook windsurfing activity; prime time is afternoons when the wind is blowing from the south or southeast, or when northwesterly gusts kick up swells that are ideal for jumping. (On weekend days when the weather is good, come early—the lot sometimes fills up and closes by 11 A.M.) The best winds blow in May and, not surprisingly, the hurricane-prone months of September and October. Boat traffic is a consideration here, so stay alert. Beginners should stick close to shore; there are hefty swells and strong currents on the open bay.

Directions: New York Waterways (800-533-3779) runs ferries to Sandy Hook during the summer.

By car, take the Garden State Parkway to exit 117; follow NJ 36 east to the park. Lot C is the second parking lot after the entrance station. There is a vehicle entrance fee in summer only.

CALF PASTURE BEACH

Location: Norwalk, Connecticut, 46 miles northeast of Manhattan

Outfitter: Norwalk Sailing School (203-852-1857, www.norwalksailingschool.org) offers lessons and rents windsurfing equipment. If you join the windsurfing club here for a modest fee, you get a nonresident parking pass that allows you to use the beach during the summer (parking regulations are not enforced the rest of the year).

Description: The beach is located on Calf Pasture Point, a peninsula that pokes far enough out into the open water of Long Island Sound to provide access to various breezes. In particular look for southerlies to blow throughout long summer afternoons. Unlike most windsurfers, sailors at Calf Pasture actually set out with a destination in mind: the Norwalk Islands, a chain of a dozen uninhabited islets that shelter thriving bird rookeries. The 1- to 3-mile trip is easy, because the shallow harbor limits boat traffic to the shipping lane and the islands cut down the chop.

Directions: By train, take Metro-North to East Norwalk. Walk to East Avenue and take the bus marked "beach," or walk 0.75 mile to the beach.

By car, take I-95 to exit 16 and follow blue signs to the beach.

Autobahn on Ice

IMAGINE HURTLING ACROSS a frozen lake, clinging to a sail rigged on ice skates, at 60 mph. Crazy? Of course—that's what makes it fun, says Bruce Caslowitz, owner of the Norwalk Sailing School and an aficionado of windsurfing on ice, also know as freeskating or ice sailing. "You've got to scare yourself a little bit every now and then," Caslowitz says with a chuckle. "That's what it's all about." Caslowitz uses his windsurfing sail, but instead of a surfing-type board, he rides a skateboard with skating blades instead of wheels. If the ice is smooth, skaters can hit 60 mph on 20-mph breezes.

A helmet, elbow pads, knee pads, and a life jacket are, needless to say, strongly advised. Popular freeskating lakes include Budd Lake in New Jersey, Candlewood Lake in Danbury, Connecticut, and Bantam Lake in Litchfield, Connecticut. Island Surf and Sail (609-494-5553, www.islandsurf-sail.com) in Brant Beach, New Jersey, manufactures and distributes freeskates.

HECKSCHER STATE PARK

Location: East Islip, Long Island, 52 miles east of Manhattan

Outfitters: Main Beach Surf & Sport (631-537-2716, www.mainbeach.com) and Windsurfing Hamptons (631-283-9463, www.w-surf.com) are the closest shops.

Description: There's decent sailing in Great South Bay from this huge state park, and thermals blowing in from Fire Island Inlet, out of the southwest, tend to hit their peak in the afternoons. Southeast breezes also provide a steady ride. Something to keep in mind here: The mild ocean current can be a factor if the winds are light. If the thermals aren't strong enough to carry you back to your launching point, don't fight it; it's much easier to walk back. Consider pitching a tent here (see "Camping," page 354) and making a weekend of it.

Directions: By car, take the Belt Parkway to the Southern State Parkway; follow the Heckscher Spur into the park. Circle the loop road and look for the parking area with the windsurfing rigs.

Meccas

NAPEAGUE BAY

Location: East Hampton, Long Island, 105 miles east of Manhattan

Outfitters: Freelance instructor Jeremy Grovesnor (631-537-9327) teaches on the bay. Main Beach Surf & Sport (631-537-2716, www.mainbeach.com) and Windsurfing Hamptons (631-283-9463, www.w-surf.com) rent equipment at Napeague.

Description: God probably isn't a windsurfer, but divine intervention seems the only way to explain the windsurfing perfection of Napeague. Easily Long Island's premier windsurfing location, it has steady summer sea breezes without the vagaries of the open sea. It gets better. Napeague, part of the larger Gardiners Bay, is shallow enough that you can stand in most places, and it has a firm, sandy bottom. There's plenty of open terrain, so Napeague is built for speed. And if you're looking to learn, mild July and August mornings are sublime. The best breezes blow in from the Atlantic, carrying over the narrow South Fork, but sailable winds will come from other directions as well. If you stick to the northern half of the bay, you'll encounter fewer weeds and boats. The one drawback: Because of its shallowness, there are few waves until the wind tops 20 knots.

Directions: By car, take the Montauk Highway (NY 27) to East Hampton and continue through town. One mile past the railroad crossing, bear left at the fork onto Cranberry Hole Road, and follow it to the parking area at the end. A parking permit is required year-round for non–East Hampton residents; purchase a permit at East Hampton Town Hall (631-324-4142).

LAKES BAY

Location: West Atlantic City, New Jersey, 126 miles south of Manhattan

Outfitter: Extreme Windsurfing in West Atlantic City (609-641-4445, www.extremewindsurfing.com) offers rentals and instruction.

Description: If you're picturing a mud puddle ringed by casinos, guess again. The tidal Lakes Bay, behind Absecon Island, is sandwiched almost completely by a bird sanctuary, so you won't hear any slot machines jangling. What's remarkable about this spot is its consistency: From April until Labor Day, the winds blow a steady 15 to 20 mph, and they're only slightly less reliable through November. In fact, you can sail here year-round if your constitution is sturdy enough (only 2 months of the year, July and August, are really bathing-suit weather). The water is shallow and the conditions are forgiving, making it a particularly prime location for beginners. The bottom isn't weedy, but there are some sharp shells and rocks in the sand, so bring protective footwear.

Directions: By car, take the Garden State Parkway to exit 37; turn right off the exit ramp and go 0.5 mile to the traffic circle. Follow US 40 east for nearly 4 miles, to the Hampton Inn. Extreme Windsurfing and the bay's only water access are at the back of the hotel.

CAPE COD

Location: Hyannis, Massachusetts, 259 miles northeast of Manhattan

Outfitter: For the full local lowdown, the Cape Cod Windsurfing Association (508-778-7105, www.capecodwindsurfing.org) is an excellent resource.

Description: Call it a mini-Civil War. The locals here duke it out with the folks in Cape Hatteras, North Carolina, over bragging rights to the best windsurfing on the East Coast. Cape Hatteras may be more dramatic, but Cape Cod has more variety and a higher average wind speed. And though they don't like you to know it, even Cape Hatteras sailors come north in fall. September is when the big winds start blowing, and the local racing series—as well as the U.S. Windsurfing Nationals competition—revs up. Also, many launch-site restrictions are lifted after Labor Day.

November and December are popular, too, because the water hovers in the 70° F range until almost the first of the year.

Where to go? The options abound, because the Cape has the advantage of both the enormous bay and the open ocean. Kalmus Beach in Hyannis is one of the most popular spots, but it draws crowds. Pemlico Bay, with its steady 15-mph-plus winds, is a winner. For advanced sailors, there's some dramatic open-ocean sailing on the outer Cape, in Truro and Provincetown, among other sites.

Directions: To get to the Cape by car, take I-95 north to I-195 east to US 6 east.

Where to Connect

Shop

New York Pipe Dreams (1625 York Avenue, Manhattan, 212-535-7473, www.newyorkpipedreams.com) no longer sells equipment but can offer advice and hook you up with instructors on Long Island.

Resource

The Web site iWindsurf.com (www.iwindsurf.zulusports.com) has detailed wind reports by region.

Swimming

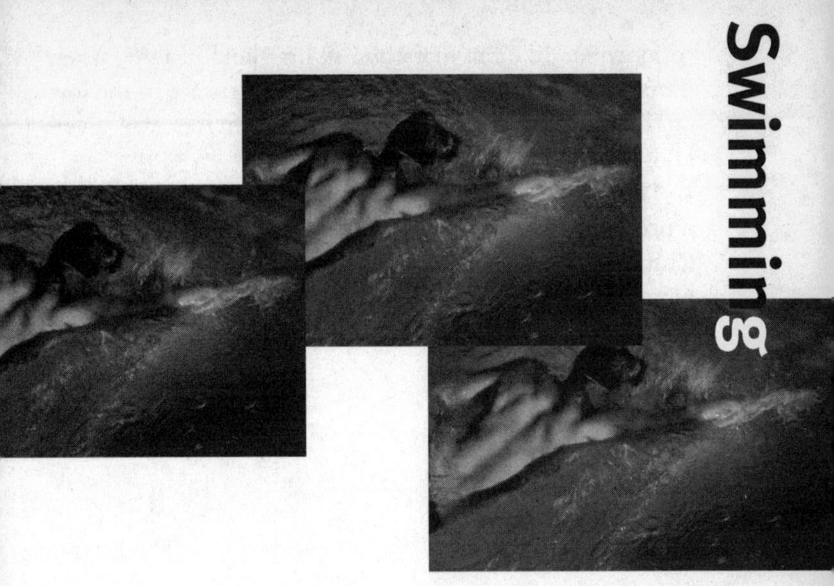

MOST NEW YORKERS do the crawl and sidestroke in swimming pools, except for a few months in summer when thousands wade in at Rockaway and Orchard Beaches. But an adventurous few venture from those tame environments into the swirling currents of the city's harbor and rivers. An organization called the Manhattan Island Foundation has initiated a series of competitive swims in the city to promote the improvements in local water quality. The big event is the epic Manhattan Island Marathon Swim, but shorter events are now drawing hundreds of competitive swimmers. These remain pretty rugged swims. Water temperatures rise to comfortable levels for only several months a year, so in events like the marathon swim—held in June, when temperatures in the Hudson and East Rivers are in the low 60s—only hardy, well-conditioned athletes are even allowed in the water.

Then again, some extreme types liken water in the 60° F range to a sauna. We speak of the Coney Island Polar Bear Club, an exceptionally sturdy group of winter swimmers who gather at the legendary beach to "celebrate" water temperatures in the 30s. Icebergs optional.

City Limits

Five Swim Races

Unless you've developed gills or fins, chances are you're not up for the marathon swim. But if you've put in your share of pool time and want to test your crawl stroke against your peers, there's good news: Manhattan Island Foundation, the organizer and primary sponsor of the marathon, also sponsors five shorter races. They're held in the Hudson River between June and September. Contact the foundation (888-NYC-SWIM, www.nycswim.org) for dates, applications, and other information.

COVE TO COVE SWIM

Location: Manhattan

Length: 0.5 mile

Description: This is the shortest of these events, from the South Cove of the World Financial Center to the North Cove.

Marathon Man

HENRY ECKSTEIN'S ALARM goes off at 4:15 every weekday morning. He leaves his midtown apartment before five and is waiting at the edge of the Asphalt Green pool when the lifeguard blows the opening whistle at 5:30. He swims 4 to 5 miles.

Starting in May, his training gets even more rigorous. On weekends at dawn, Eckstein, 53, steps into the excruciating 51° F waters of either Long Island Sound or the Jersey shore. He swims for up to 2 hours without a wetsuit. The following weekend, when the water is about 54° F, he swims for 4 hours, and so on, until it's midsummer and he is acclimated to spending half the day swimming in 60° F water. The payoff: Eckstein can last 7 to 9 hours crawling through the Hudson and East Rivers in the Manhattan Island Marathon Swim.

In 2000, Eckstein used the marathon to train for the biggest event of his life: a swim across the English Channel. "In both cases, it was very spiritual," says Eckstein, who has a stocky body and a broad, calm face topped by a thicket of black curls. "Manhattan looks tremendous from the water, and you're in these big rivers, and you feel very small down there, and cold. You're so much at the mercy of the elements. In 2000 I swam it like a race, and it was pretty painful to keep that up. Anything I saw—a bridge or a building or something familiar—became such an exciting event."

Finishing was incredibly difficult because of challenging conditions. Battling the wind and choppy water, he completed the swim in just over 9 hours. And when it was over? "I felt," Eckstein says, "like I owned the island."

PARK TO PARK ONE MILER

Location: Manhattan

Length: 1 mile

Description: The inaugural Park to Park One Miler was held in 2000. Swimmers race from the World Financial Center's South Cove to the Hudson River passenger terminal pier.

RACE FOR THE RIVER SWIM

Location: Manhattan

Length: 2.4 miles

Description: Competitors swim upstream from the World Financial Center's North Cove to Pier 62 at Chelsea Piers.

GREAT HUDSON RIVER SWIM

Location: Manhattan

Length: 2.8 miles

Description: Competitors swim north to south, from the 79th Street Boathouse to Pier 62 at Chelsea Piers.

LITTLE RED LIGHTHOUSE SWIM

Location: Manhattan

Length: 7.8 miles

Description: Introduced in 1998, this swim has already had an interesting history. Hurricane Floyd washed out the '99 event. Competitors swim from the George Washington Bridge to Pier 62 at Chelsea Piers.

Coney Island Polar Bears

The Atlantic Ocean and the air temperature both hover at 32° F—the point at which, says Tom McGann of the Coney Island Polar Bear Club, "men become women real fast." McGann has swum in those conditions nearly every winter weekend for 12 years. He is standing on the beach wearing sunglasses, a crew cut, a black cotton T-shirt, and blue swim trunks. His face, arms, and legs have the blotchy pink complexion of a slightly underripe tomato.

To McGann, today's conditions are pretty mild. "We never cancel, ever," he says. "Our philosophy is, every day is a good beach day." The sky hangs over him like a slab of gray marble; splotches of graying snow dot the beach. Indeed, the weather is more temperate than on New Year's Day, when the club tends to draw its biggest crowd. On that day, when it was barely 20° F and a fresh foot of snow covered the beach, 125 polar bears swam—or at least ran into the water and hooted in pain before exiting.

The 14 or so swimmers on the beach today do some perfunctory calisthenics, then charge the water with a war whoop. They splash about, forming a circle and hollering, screaming, and giggling in their pain and pleasure. The newcomers shuffle quickly back out, leaving a core group of four or five people bobbing quietly in the ocean. One swimmer does the backstroke. Another practices some Bruce Lee moves. Within 6 or 7 minutes, they're all back on shore.

Why do it? For many, it's a New Year's lark or a dare—a one-time-only thing. But others actually seem to like the way it feels—and have developed a strong tolerance for cold. Group president Ken Krisses is among them. Several years ago, he developed symptoms of hypothermia when he stayed in 36° F water for a half hour. But his body seems to have gradually acclimated with repeated exposure. Today, he swims quietly for a while, then stands on the beach, talking, for about 10 minutes without a single shiver. A teenage girl in a black parka approaches Krisses with a horrified expression. "Why were you in the water?" she asks.

"It's good for you," Krisses says. "We enjoy it."

She walks away shaking her head. "Most people are incredulous," Krisses says. "But we really do like it, and the colder the better." He grins and adds, "We almost canceled today because it was too warm."

Heads up: The Coney Island Polar Bear Club (www.winterbathers.com) meets every Sunday at 1 P.M. between Thanksgiving and Easter at the boardwalk and Stillwell Avenue.

Directions: By subway, take the W, F, or Q train to the Stillwell Avenue/Coney Island stop. Walk south on Stillwell Avenue to the boardwalk.

The Manhattan Island Marathon Swim

THIS IS EASILY the toughest sporting event in the city. The world's longest annual swim marathon circles Manhattan, covering 28.5 miles. Swimmers deal with current-propelled flotsam, unpredictable winds that can turn the rivers against them, ferry traffic, and water temperatures hovering around 63° F.

Few swimmers are willing or able to handle the fierce rigors of this event. The field in 2000—at the time the biggest in the event's history—consisted of 35 participants (long-distance swimming experience is necessary to qualify). By comparison, the New York Marathon draws about 29,000 runners. The swiftest swimmers usually circle the island in 7 hours, though mercurial conditions sometimes toy with finishing times. In

June 2000, the skies and waters were calm when the swimmers left Gangway Six, on the Hudson River side of Battery Park. They swam around the bottom tip of the island and headed up the East River with the incoming tide. By the time they reached the notorious currents of Hell Gate and crossed the Harlem River to the Hudson, a fierce northerly wind was blowing up through the Verrazano Narrows. The gusts buffeted the river, creating a nasty chop and headwind. The result: Australian John van Wisse won the race with a time of 7 hours, 53 minutes—more than 80 minutes slower than the previous year's winner.

Though it's strange to think of the race as a stepping-stone rather than a summit, some competitors use the marathon race as a training event for the Mt. Everest of swimming: the English Channel.

Where to Connect

Clubs and Organizations

- The Manhattan Island Foundation (888-NYC-SWIM, www.nycswim.org) organizes swimming races in the city, donates money to learn-to-swim programs for New York City children, and supports the rehabilitation of city pools and the ongoing cleanup and protection of its rivers.
- The Red Tide of New York (212-439-4676, www.geocities.com/Yosemite/Rapids/2737/redtide) is open to swimmers of all skill levels interested in both fitness and competition.
- Team New York Aquatics (212-691-3440, www.tnya.org) is a gay organization that offers weekly practices, meets, and water polo games. It's open to people of all orientation.

Pools

There are scores of pools around the city. Here are a few open to the public, either through annual memberships or day fees. For a longer list, see the Manhattan Island Foundation's Web site: www.nycswim.org.

- Asphalt Green (1750 York Avenue, Manhattan, 212-369-8890) is popular among distance swimmers.
- Vanderbilt YMCA (224 East 47th Street, Manhattan, 212-756-9600) has a pool open 24 hours a day during the week.
- Chelsea Piers Sports Center (Pier 60 at 23rd Street, Manhattan, 212-336-6000)
- Sheraton Manhattan Fitness Center (790 Seventh Avenue, Manhattan, 212-581-3300)
- YWCA (610 Lexington Avenue, Manhattan, 212-755-4500)

Horseback Riding

MENTION HORSEBACK RIDING and New York City in the same sentence and most people chortle. Our "dusty trails" are greasy, gridlocked streets; the tumbleweed and cacti are in-line skaters and bikers. And the cowboys all seem to be cabbies—or you'd think so, the way they drive. These days, a saddled horse looks like the ultimate anachronism—as passé as peep shows in Times Square.

But horses were the chief mode of transportation in New York City only a century ago; a bridle trail once ran from Prospect Park all the way to Coney Island. In the 1950s, horses were still common in the outer reaches of Queens and Brooklyn. As Lynne Holzhauser, a second-generation Queens

stable operator puts it: "We were the country then, like Montauk is now."

Those days aren't yet committed to history's dusty tomes. Horses have been here for centuries, and like most native New Yorkers, they're unflappable. Several parks have surviving stable and bridle trails where you can escape the urban bump and grind. You won't confuse even the leafiest New York setting with *Big Valley* reruns, but without leaving the five boroughs, you can ride through dense forest, along gurgling creeks, and on beaches. And you don't have to be the Lone Ranger to pull it off; the rides discussed here are suitable for novices. (New York is so anathema to home-on-the-range types, nearly all walk-up customers are beginners.) If you get hooked, academies from Central Park to Jamaica Bay cover the fundamentals and finer points of both western and English riding styles.

The Urban Stable

TWO STABLE FIRES in 2000 increased concern about horses' safety in the city. In the worst incident, a fire at Brooklyn's Bergen Beach Stables killed 21 horses. A 17 year old was later charged with causing the blaze by igniting hay while smoking marijuana after the stable closed at night.

Kensington Stables in Brooklyn is located in a 100-year-old building without sprinklers. But with the narrow profit margin in running a stable in the city these days, a sprinkler system is a prohibitive expense. Kensington owner and manager Walker Blankinship's solution: EquiPosse, a nonprofit organization designed to help preserve "the human-horse relationship in the urban environment." The first order of business is to raise enough money for sprinklers for Kensington's two barns. To donate or help, call 718-788-2979 or email equiposse@kensingtonstables.com.

City Limits

PROSPECT PARK

Location: Brooklyn

Outfitter: A 1-hour trail ride at Kensington Stables (51 Caton Place, Brooklyn, 718-972-4588, www.kensingtonstables.com) covers about 3 miles.

Description: When you first hit the bridle trail here, it feels as though you're sharing it with half of New York City's most populous borough. You weave between picnickers on Prospect Lake and legions of cyclists and in-line skaters on South Lake Drive. After Wollman skating rink, you pass under Nethermead Arches, and a rocky stream leads you into Midwood. Dense and arboreal, it's the park's Sherwood Forest, and the quiet, winding trails purge your senses of the city's relentless honk and hustle. The bridle trail, one of the 133-year-old park's original features, then loops around by Friends Cemetery and the edge of the vast Long Meadow lawn before returning on West Lake Drive.

Unless you're willing to spend some serious time on foot, a trail ride is the best way to experience the varied landscapes of the 526-acre park—arguably the crowning achievement of Frederick Law Olmsted and Calvert Vaux, the architects who also designed Central Park. If you have even rudimentary riding ability, the guide will probably goad you into trotting over several sections. (I barely knew how to hold the reins, yet somehow I spent a third of the ride loping through the woods.) Avoid summer weekends, when picnic blankets and volleyball nets spill over onto the bridle path. Off-season can be the most rewarding; in autumn, the maples explode in vibrant reds.

Directions: By subway, take the F train to Fort Hamilton Parkway; exit onto Greenwood Avenue and walk toward the park. Turn right on Sherman Street and take the pedestrian walkway over the highway. Turn left down East 8th Street; the stable is on the next corner.

Home on the Range?

LYNNE HOLZHAUSER IS a real New York City horsewoman. That sounds oxymoronic, but she values horses as much as any Montana equestrian. Her parents opened Parkside Stables in Queens 56 years ago; she took over in 1982. "I worked for them from the time I was a little kid, and just stayed on," says Holzhauser, who has short-cropped reddish hair and sharp blue eyes. "We were on horseback before we could walk. My father's grandfather took products to market with a team of horses. When people started using trucks, the workhorses had no job, so the family opened riding stables.

"When my father was a kid, there were 17 stables here, and they all did business. When I was young, kids in the neighborhood rode horses; now kids from the neighborhood are in the mall."

The stable is open every day. "I've been with the horses since I got out of high school," she says. "I don't know if I could be away from them."

Lynne's Riding School is the kind of place where former students return to visit. She talks about one reluctant woman she coaxed onto a horse. Holzhauser walked her around the indoor ring at her stable for 30 minutes. The woman was crying when she got off. "I've wanted to do that for twenty-five years," she told Holzhauser.

As we talk, Holzhauser gets word that one of her students, a 7-year-old girl, broke her wrist. Her mother called to say the girl was more distraught about missing her riding lessons than school. Holzhauser smiles. Her enthusiasm for horses is contagious, but business is a struggle. She holds pony parties for kids' birthdays to keep the stable going. Holzhauser isn't crazy about the parties. It's time spent not riding, or teaching riding. But if she has to be Martha Stewart in a Stetson for groups of first-graders, so be it. "This is what I love," she says, "and I'm holding out."

FOREST PARK

Location: Queens

Outfitters: Lynne's Riding School (88-03 70th Road, Queens, 718-261-7679), or try neighboring Dixie Dew Stables (88-11 70th Road, 718-263-3500). One-hour trail rides cover about 3 miles.

Description: There are only 165 acres of forest left in Forest Park, which is hard to believe given the bewildering Hansel-and-Gretel network of trails winding through thick forests of maple, oak, beech, and yellow poplar.

The park, 3.5 miles long by 1 mile wide, stretches over 535 acres. The ride begins on a dirt path in a narrow stretch of woods sandwiched between Union Turnpike and the Jackie Robinson Parkway. Within minutes it veers off into a quiet, winding, wooded trails—4 to 5 miles of them in this section, and even on summer days only a few people pass by. The horses amble up and down a series of undulating hills shoved into place during the last ice age. There are also a few straightaways, where the horses accelerate.

The stables have a strong neighborhood connection. Charlie, my guide from Lynne's Riding School, is a Queens native who tells funny stories about being a cabbie; the famed journalist Jimmy Breslin was one of his regular fares. He's enjoying a slower pace these days. "You can ride for an hour and a half in here and never see the same scenery twice," Charlie says. Late afternoon is a good time for birding; look for rare species such as the summer tanager, red-headed woodpecker, and olive-sided flycatcher.

Directions: By subway, take the E, F, R, or V train to Forest Hills (71st Avenue), then take the Q-23 bus to Metropolitan Avenue. Turn left on 70th Road; D&D and Lynne's are at the end of the block. Alternatively, you can walk 15 minutes from the subway. Go 12 blocks south on 71st Avenue. Turn right on Metropolitan Avenue, then left on 70th Road.

Call in the Hounds

HERE'S AN IDEA next time you can't escape to the countryside on Christmas: a "hunt" in Central Park. Riders bedecked in silk top hats, black boots, and ivory breeches gather to gallop on their steeds as if they were thundering through the British moors. It feels like the real thing—minus the hounds, which don't meet animal-control regulations, and, of course, minus the foxes. The ride winds up at Tavern on the Green for stirrup cups of mulled wine, and the horses eat carrots off silver platters.

CENTRAL PARK

Location: Manhattan

Outfitter: Trail rides at Claremont Riding Academy (175 West 89th Street, 212-724-5100) last 1 hour; instruction is also available.

Heads up: Because there is no guide, riders should have at least a modest background in English-style riding.

Description: If you're a celebrity-obsessed type who likes those degrees-of-separation games, here's a good one: The Claremont Riding Academy saddle you're riding on may have once cradled the rear end of Matthew Broderick,

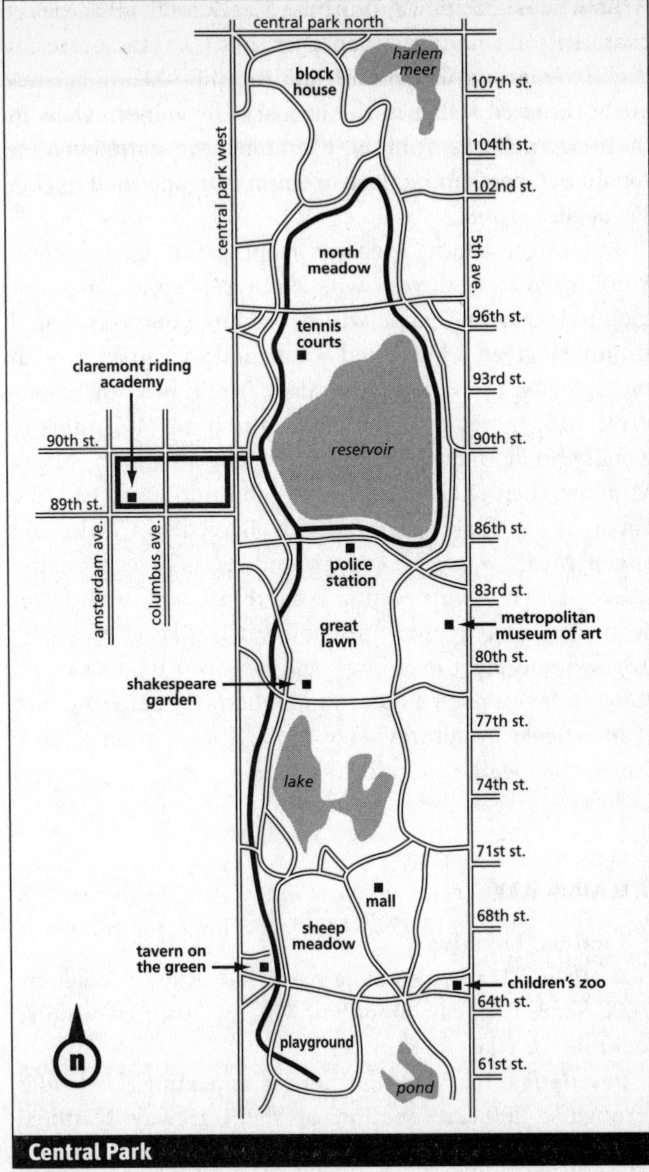

Central Park

Arnold Schwarzenegger, or Andie MacDowell, all academy customers at one time or another. Actually, the horses at the 109-year-old Claremont facility, the oldest continuously operated stable in the country, are minor celebs in their own right. Some of these mounts have starred in Metropolitan Opera productions of *Carmen* or appeared in *GQ*, *Vogue*, or *Cosmo*.

But forget about celebrity scoping for the moment. You'll need to keep your wits about you on a Claremont mount because no guide will be leading your way; you'll simply be given a horse and a map and told to cross with the lights on the way into the park. You'll head east along West 90th Street into the park, which has 4.5 miles of woodsy bridle trails. Head north and loop around the North Meadow, then circle the reservoir and ride south past the Great Lawn, Shakespeare Garden, Belvedere Castle, and Sheep Meadow to the playground near Tavern on the Green. The northern section is more pastoral, with fewer people and more room to trot and canter. Expect passersby to gawk and fawn over you—and hey, you might as well enjoy it. If you're on a horse in Manhattan, *you're* the star.

Directions: By subway, take the 1, 2, or C train to 86th Street, then walk three blocks north.

JAMAICA BAY

Location: Brooklyn

Outfitter: Trail rides at Jamaica Bay Riding Academy (7000 Shore Parkway, Brooklyn, 718-531-8949, www.horsebackride.com) last 45 minutes.

Description: The concept here is appealing: trail rides through a 300-acre section of the Gateway National Wildlife Refuge, including 3 miles of Jamaica Bay beaches. Riders saunter past ponds generously sprinkled with geese and ducks, across several wide expanses of sand, and through the wooded trails of the Bergen Beach neighborhood. Some aspects of the experience are disappointing, however. Even though it's far from the clamor of the city, trail riders go out in groups (unless you pay double the fee), which cuts down on the bird-watching possibilities. The riding academy here features an Olympic-sized indoor arena and an equally spacious outdoor riding ring. For advanced riders, there's an area with more than 50 cross-country fences.

Directions: By subway, take the Q train to Sheepshead Bay. The academy is about 3 miles from the station. Take a cab (follow signs leading to the academy on the eastbound Belt Parkway) or bring a bike and ride on the greenway path. Go to Emmons Avenue on the waterfront and turn left (east). Pick up the path at Knapp Street and follow signs to the academy.

By car, take the Belt Parkway; the academy exit is on the eastbound side between the Flatbush Avenue and Rockaway Park exits. (Signs on the westbound side indicate how to circle back.)

Short Hops

EAGLE ROCK RESERVATION

Location: West Orange, New Jersey, 19 miles west of Manhattan

Outfitter: Montclair Riding Academy (12-22 Woodlawn Avenue, West Orange, 973-731-4182, www.montclairriding.com) charges by the hour for rides. Riders must be at least 18 years old.

Description: Featuring 408 acres of relatively unmolested red oak forest tucked inconspicuously into the West Orange landscape, this swatch of the Watchung Mountains is an antidote for a soul wearied by the Gaps and Kmarts of the 'burbs.

Named for bald eagles that once nested in rocky cliffs along the park's eastern edge, Eagle Rock has plenty of wide-open space where you can canter, but lots of stuff to keep your attention, too. Shallow streams and fallen trees crisscross the trails, and horses scamper up rock-strewn slopes. There's a healthy deer population here. Afterward your ride, hike up to Lookout Point, where you'll be surprised to learn that you're close enough to New York to take in views of the skyline from the George Washington Bridge to the Verrazano Narrows.

Directions: By bus, take New Jersey Transit bus 108 from Port Authority to Newark Penn Station (973-762-5100 for the schedule). Switch to the 71 West Caldwell bus and ride to Eagle Rock Avenue in Orange. Walk down the Prospect Avenue hill 0.25 mile to Woodlawn Avenue. Turn left; the stables are on the left.

By car, take the Holland Tunnel to the New Jersey Turnpike north. Take I-280 west to exit 8B. Turn left at the fourth light. The barn is on the left.

THE SHAWANGUNKS

Location: Ellenville, New York, 102 miles northwest of Manhattan

Outfitter: The Saddle Club (845-647-7556) is located on the grounds of the Nevele Grand Hotel, US 209, Ellenville. Rides can range from 1 hour to a half day; reservations are required for trips of 2 hours or more.

Description: The Gunks boast some of the best climbing in the East (see "Climbing," page 155), but the crags aren't just for the rock rats to enjoy. On horseback, you clop along an old railroad bed trail into the foothills of the Catskills. From there, with 1,000 acres to choose from, you'll find all the streams, sylvan woods, and undulating hills you can handle. Check out the logging canals built to float logs alongside the railroad.

More experienced and adventurous riders can arrange a guided trip up the side trails, some of which ascend high into the hills. Those winged shadows passing over you? Not birds of prey, but hang gliders taking off from their perches high above (see "Hang Gliding," page 321). This is an ideal ride in winter, when horses outfitted with studded shoes travel along snow-covered paths. There's also downhill and cross-country skiing nearby (see "Cross-country Skiing," page 333).

Directions: By bus, take the ShortLine from Port Authority to Ellenville; the Grand Hotel is a short walk.

By car, take I-87 to exit 16. Drive west on NY 17 to exit 113, then follow US 209 north to Ellenville.

Meccas

THE ADIRONDACKS

Location: Eagle Bay, New York, 277 miles north of Manhattan

Outfitter: Rides at Adirondack Saddle Tours (877-795-7488, www.geocities.com/adkhorse) range from 3 to 5 1/2 hours, covering between 8 and 12 miles.

Description: The Lake George area was known in the 1940s and 1950s as the "dude ranch capital of the East." But the best of the trails are to the north and west, in the sublime Pigeon Lake Wilderness Area. Here, "the Adirondacks sell themselves," says John Evans, owner of Adirondack Saddle Tours. The forests teem with bear, deer, and wild turkey. The lonely lakes glitter. The craggy peaks soar. The ride takes in Moss Lake, Cascade Lake, and 40-foot Cascade Falls. Evans shows beginners how to canter across open meadows.

The area is also ideal for fishing and hiking; a 2.5-mile trail circles Moss Lake, and there's an osprey nest on one of the lake's islands. Great blue heron loom on tree branches over the water; loons cruise the currents, torpedoing the water in search of dinner.

Directions: By car, take I-87 north to I-90 west. In Utica, take NY 12 north, then pick up NY 28 north. Ten miles north of Old Forge, turn left on Uncas Road; the outfitter is 0.25 mile down on the right.

GRAND CANYON OF PENNSYLVANIA

Location: Wellsboro, Pennsylvania, 233 miles west of Manhattan

Outfitters: Tioga Trail Rides of Wellsboro, PA (570-724-6592, www.pavisnet.com/trr), has 2-day trips that include 4 to 6 hours of riding, or 10 to 12 miles, each day. (Shorter trips are available from 1 hour to 1 day.) A highlight at Mountain Trail Horse Center (877-376-5561, www.mountaintrailhorse.com) is a 4-day trip in September to watch elk. You can't miss the bugling of male elks during mating season.

Description: Shrink the scale of the big hole in Arizona; blanket it with eastern forest; sprinkle generously with red fox, coyotes, wild turkeys, and a few black bears; and you've got the Pennsylvania version of the Grand Canyon. The canyon was created eons ago when a glacier dammed a small valley cut by Pine Creek, reversing the flow of water and carving a 50-mile-long, 1,000-foot-deep gorge. The canyon, a half-day's drive from New York, has been declared a Natural Landmark by the National Park Service.

The rides with either of two local outfitters will fulfill your inner cowpoke. You'll climb mountain trails, gallop through open fields, splash through streams, wander along old logging roads, clop down into hollows and valleys. Both outfitters offer overnight trips where you will, yes, ride off into the sunset before gathering around a campfire for the night.

This is also a great stream- and pond-fishing destination in April and May. And save a little time to ply Pine Creek's timeless currents in a canoe from Pine Creek Outfitters (717-724-3061).

Directions: By car, take the Holland Tunnel to the New Jersey Turnpike north. Take I-280 west to I-80 west to I-180 north. In Williamsport, take US 15 north. Take US 6 west to Wellsboro.

Where to Connect

Riding Academies

- Claremont Riding Academy (175 West 89th Street, Manhattan, 212-724-5100)
- Chelsea Equestrian Center (63 North River Pier, Manhattan, 212-367-9090)
- Kensington Stables (51 Caton Place, Brooklyn, 718-972-4588, www.kensingtonstables.com)
- Bronx Equestrian Center (9 Shore Road, the Bronx, 718-885-0551)
- New York City Riding Academy (Randalls Island, 212-860-2986)

- Lynne's Riding School (88-03 70th Road, Queens, 718-261-7679)
- Dixie Dew Stables (88-11 70th Road, Queens, 718-263-3500)
- Seguine Equestrian Center (440 Seguine Avenue, Staten Island, 718-317-1121)

Tack Shop

- Miller Harness Company (117 East 24th Street, Manhattan, 212-673-1400, www.millerharness.com) is one of the world's leading distributors and manufacturers of equestrian apparel and equipment, with its own catalog. The store, which opened in 1912, is worth a visit.

Resources

- O'Dell, Anne M. *Ride New York: 35 Horse and Multiple-Use Trails in the Empire State*. Woodstock, GA: Crazy Horse Ranch, 1997.
- *Horse Trails in New York State* is a booklet published by the state Department of Environmental Conservation; call (518) 897-1200 for a free copy.

Caving

THE CAVERS IN New York City don't seem at all put off by the fact that there are no caves here. They find their way into caves all over the Northeast and the world. Occasionally, out of curiosity, they even worm their way into the labyrinthine tunnels and holes beneath the city. "There's an alien quality about it that I enjoy," says member Tom Oakes.

The cavers, who have formed a group called Met Grotto, can take you to caves. This is important to know, because without them you will never find the caves—unless you go to "show caves" such as Howe Caverns near Albany, developed sites with paved paths and lights to accommodate tourists.

The cavers visit "wild" caves around the Northeast—caves with no infrastructure other than a locked gate. They are accessible only to those who join Met Grotto, or any other group affiliated with the National Speleological Society. Most sites are kept locked and their identities hidden, both to protect the caves from thrill seekers and to protect the thrill seekers from the caves. There are also property-liability issues to consider. Unlike western caves, most of which are on government land, many of the caves in New York and surrounding states are on private property. "Farmers are not thrilled about having caves on their property," says Chris Nicola, a past president and trip leader for Met Grotto. "Nobody wants strangers tramping all over their vegetable garden in the middle of the night." To remain in good stead with property owners, cavers often put up the locked gates, carefully control access to them, and draw up liability waivers.

The Northeast is not particularly renowned for its caves, because they tend to be shallow and not very deep. One of the largest is New York's McFails Cave, which is only about 90 feet deep but almost 7 miles long. There are, fortunately, plenty of other caves to choose from—and they're multifaceted, with vertical and horizontal passages and conditions that range from low, watery crawls to open caverns.

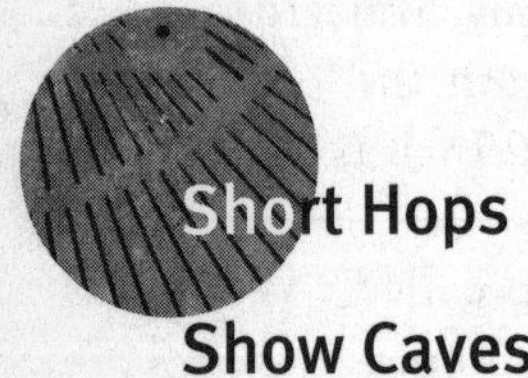

Short Hops

Show Caves

There are three New York tourist caves.

HOWE CAVERNS

Location: Howes Cave, New York, 193 driving miles northwest of Manhattan

Description: Carved by an underground river over the course of 6 million years, Howe Caverns (518-296-8900, www.howecaverns.com) are 156 feet deep. Eighty-minute guided tours conclude with a boat ride on the quarter-mile-long Lake of Venus; other highlights include the Titan's Temple, a winding passageway, and an altar where more than 430 weddings have taken place. Located in the town of Howes Cave, about 40 miles west of Albany.

Directions: By car, take I-87 north to exit 25A. Take I-88 west to exit 22 and follow signs to the caverns.

SECRET CAVERNS

Location: Central Bridge, New York, 190 driving miles northwest of Manhattan

Description: A tour of Secret Caverns (www.secretcaverns.com) leads 103 steps down to ancient calcite formations, prehistoric fossils, and a 100-foot underground waterfall—all created by a glacial waterfall at the end of the last ice age. There are plenty of the obligatory stalactites and stalagmites.

Directions: By car, take I-87 north to exit 25A. Take I-88 west to exit 22 and follow the signs.

NATURAL STONE BRIDGES AND CAVES

Location: Pottersville, New York, 248 miles north of Manhattan

Description: This complex (518-494-2283, www.stone

bridgeandcaves.com) features Trout Brook, an underground river that pours through a series of caves and chambers. The tour ends when the stream emerges in a gorge, then disappears into a place called Noisy Cave.

Directions: By car, take I-87 north to exit 26 and follow signs to US 9 north. Drive on US 9 to Stone Bridge Road, turn left, and follow signs to the cave.

The Cave Man of New York

IN 1977, CHRIS Nicola and five friends—all open-water scuba divers—decided on a whim to explore an underwater cave in Florida. They entered a place called Devil's Ear, a 110-foot-deep tube about 3 feet in diameter. Each went in, one after the other—always a mistake, because the divers in front can't turn around if there's a problem. Nicola, the first one in, experienced a malfunction in his regulator. Squelching panic, and still able to breathe for the moment, he swam on. Eventually the group arrived at a sign with a skull and crossbones warning untrained cave divers to turn around. "We all got the hell out of there," he says. Nicola, a stocky man with a sandy beard, chuckles at the memory of his youthful recklessness.

Nicola gave up diving when he moved to New York in the 1980s. But he couldn't do without extreme sports. Facing his fortieth birthday, and sensing the onset of a midlife crisis, he started pursuing distance running. He had four marathons—and was pushing himself hard—when he suffered a heart attack during a triathalon. Feeling weak and unsure what was wrong, he finished the event before landing in the hospital. "I was devastated," he recalls. It turned out the condition was caused by a cold medication he was taking, but he was still despondent; he feared his adventurous life was over.

Nicola was recovering in the hospital when his girlfriend

brought him an article on dry caving. A week later, he was crawling through a 100-foot-long, 2-foot-diameter tunnel in Wards-Gregory Cave in Clarksville, New York. "I came out newborn," he says. "I realized my life wasn't over. It was only beginning in a sense."

Nicola has been a fixture at Met Grotto ever since, serving as president and organizing and leading trips to exotic locales such as Russia and Ukraine. Far from squelching his love of adventure, he's put skills associated with caving to other extreme uses—such as rappelling 800 feet off West Virginia's New River Bridge.

Underground New York

NEW YORK CITY has no caves, but it has the next best thing: a series of underground water mains and tunnels. Officially they're off-limits, but unofficially the tunnels are accessible to anyone bold and resourceful enough to find them. When members of Met Grotto explored a forgotten, century-old water main under Manhattan, they found huge populations of startled bats and stalactite formations created by water seeping through mortar.

Where to Connect

Met Grotto (http://grotto.peikes.com/index2.html) is the local chapter of the National Speleological Society. Met Grotto was formed in 1949, making it one of the oldest NSS-chartered clubs in the country. In summer, members set up shop upstate in Albany and Schoharie Counties, where they have the use of a cabin and campground alongside the 3,000-foot-long Schoharie Cave. They lead bimonthly trips to central Pennsylvania and quarterly trips to West Virginia. Once every 2 years they travel to "TAG" territory—the caving hot spot near where Tennessee, Alabama, and Georgia meet. There are also caving journeys to far-off places such as Russia, the Ukraine, and Mexico. The group meets monthly at the Thai Café in Manhattan, where it discusses future trips and club members' exploits. There's a nominal fee for membership.

Hang Gliding

THE RULES OF gravity haven't changed a bit, but flying gets easier all the time. User-friendly, high-tech hang gliders and paragliders now can have you airborne on your first day of lessons. The sports merely require patience, good weather, a bit of technique, and a conquerable fear of heights. Once you have the fundamentals in place, and you're cruising over the Long Island shores or the New Jersey farmlands, altitude will feel like an old friend. As for skydiving, all you have to do is jump (in tandem with an instructor the first time around), and find right-side-up as you rocket at 130 mph toward a green patchwork of earth below.

You've got quite an assortment of flying con-

traptions to choose from these days. Queens-based outfitter Airsports USA offers motorized versions of hang gliding and paragliding—rigs that Igor Sikorsky might have revolutionized if Mary Poppins had been his chief engineer.

Metro New York lacks an abundance of mountains from which to launch flights. And there's a limited supply of thermals, the streams of rising hot air that pilots use to gain altitude. Area hang gliders and paragliders get around that by having an ultralight plane tow them into the air to heights of up to 2,500 feet.

Maybe in the future, hang gliders will be allowed to launch from the Brooklyn Bridge. For now, you'll have to settle for a number of area launch sites within an hour or two of the city. The most prominent local site to connect with your inner Superman is Ellenville, New York, in the Shawangunks.

The Basics

If you can run, you can fly, they say in the hang-gliding business. And once you're airborne, it's more about relaxation than strength or stamina. There's just the soft nudge of the wind and the occasional flap of a nylon wing.

A brief primer: Hang gliding, the best known of the "flying" sports, involves being attached to a winged rig in which you launch either by jumping from a high point or being towed into the sky. In good conditions, pilots can stay up for hours and reach altitudes of 4,000-plus feet.

Paragliding is a hybrid of hang gliding and skydiving. Skydivers in the French Alps invented the sport in the 1970s when they grew tired of waiting for lifts back to the sky and began running with their canopies to lift off. Like a hang glider, paragliders can hang in the air for hours at thousands of feet—but instead of wings, they use a 30-foot parachute that hangs overhead like a crescent moon. A paraglider—which can be stuffed into a backpack—is smaller and easier to handle than a hang glider.

City Limits

AIRSPORTS USA

Location: Astoria, Queens

Outfitter: Prices at Airsports USA (29-31 Newtown Avenue, Astoria, Queens, 718-777-7000, www.flyforfun.net) vary, but introductory courses generally begin at about $200.

Description: Airsports USA has more flight options than the United desk at La Guardia. The company, founded by several New York hang-gliding aficionados back in 1991, offers hang gliding and paragliding as well as their more exotic motorized counterparts. They also sell and manufacture some of the equipment, and teach you how to use it. Ground classes are taught in Astoria, but you don't actually fly in the city; instruction is in New Jersey, upstate New York, or Long Island, depending on the sport and the weather.

The sports' motorized versions are quirky and expensive, but intriguing. Power hang gliding, also known as "trike" flying because the rig has a three-wheeled carriage, uses a hang glider powered by a motorized fan. With power paragliding—also called Parawing (after one of Airsports USA's products) or paramotoring—a fan is used to keep the chute filled. The devices are portable (the fan is foldable), safe, and easy to use, instructor Steven Makinos says.

Directions: By subway, take the N train to 30th Avenue.

Walk one block uphill, turn left on Newtown Avenue, and walk two blocks.

Grounded

PART-TIME BROADWAY actor Alex Santoriello opened Parasail New York to widespread praise among adventurous New Yorkers in 1997. His 10-minute rides 300 feet above New York Harbor—powered by his 31-foot custom boat, *Airgasm*—were huge with adrenaline-loving Wall Streeters. Unfortunately, the city shut down the business the following year, citing a law that prohibits takeoffs and landings anywhere other than in designated areas.

Short Hops

ELLENVILLE MOUNTAIN

Location: Ellenville, New York, 102 miles northwest of Manhattan

Outfitters: East Coast Paragliding (150 Canal Street, 845-647-3377, www.ecp.flightschool.net) and Mountain Wings (same address and phone, www.serioussports.com/mtnwings) offer introductory programs. Mountain Wings has a 6-day program designed to bestow a novice license. The paragliding school's Take Off Program enables you to use the equipment and take unlimited classes until you obtain your Novice P2 paragliding rating, which you'll need to fly at most places insured by the U.S. Hang Gliding Association.

Description: The locals call Ellenville Mountain the hang-gliding capital of the Northeast, and they've got some gaudy numbers to back up their claim. A pilot who launched there flew for 98 miles, remaining airborne for 11 1/2 hours, both records at the time. East Coast Paragliding Flight School and Mountain Wings, which teach hang gliding, both operate on the site. Students learn at the base of the mountain, with the experienced pilots launching overhead serving as their inspiration. Among the advantages to this location: The gently sloping bunny hills face different directions, so you can fly regardless of the wind direction.

Directions: By bus, take the ShortLine (800-651-8405) to Ellenville; the bus drops you 1 block from the school.

By car, take I-87 north to exit 16. Follow NY 17 west to exit 113. Follow US 209 north to Ellenville.

Air and Space

SOARING IS LIKE high-altitude meditation. You're essentially in an airplane with no engine, riding drafts and thermals; there's no engine noise and no wind in your ears. Once a single-engine Cessna tows you aloft and releases you, there's nothing but quiet and the distant earth below. An introductory lesson at Wurtsboro (845-888-2791), in the Shawangunks, includes a 20-minute piloted ride over the mountains. If you go through the whole course, you can return and rent a glider.

GMI PARAGLIDING

Location: Allentown, New Jersey, 58 miles southwest of Manhattan

Outfitter: GMI (516-676-7599, www.supair-usa.com) runs a 5-day instructional program.

Description: GMI Paragliding School outside of Newark has been around for more than a decade, making it one of the granddaddies of the local scene. Training for paragliding and power paragliding takes place on an enormous New Jersey farm, but owner Philippe Renaudin will have you dreaming of more exotic turf with videos of his organized trips to the Alps. On one of his annual European excursions involves "paraskis"—a sport in which skiers lift off the mountain using a paraglider while halfway through a ski run. The goal is to touch down inside a circular target somewhere below.

Directions: Request directions from the outfitter.

TEK FLIGHTS

Location: Winsted, Connecticut, 120 miles northeast of Manhattan

Outfitter: TEK Flights (860-379-1668, www.tekflight.com) offers both single lessons and the Spectrum course.

Description: Tek is something of a Luddite in the flying community: It remains a hang-gliding-only facility. A 400-foot mountain near the school provides pilots with upward mobility. Students can pay one price for the Spectrum course, in which they get up to 30 lessons to learn to successfully fly off the mountain.

Directions: By car, take I-87 east to the Cross County Parkway east to the Hutchinson River Parkway, which becomes the Merritt Parkway in Connecticut. Take CT 8 north to Winsted; from there, Tek provides directions (provided only for students because of property-liability issues).

Skydiving

It's a simple sport, but what a rush—this notion of free-falling for almost a minute, plummeting 9,000 to 13,500 feet. The first time around, the instructor will yank the cord or tap you on the shoulder when it's time to deploy. You don't have to sit in a classroom for long beforehand; some preliminary sessions last only 20 to 30 minutes. Then it's up in the plane, and the moment of truth. All it takes is 5 to 7 minutes of gravity to change you from a "whuffo" (skydiver-speak for a nondiver, as in someone who asks, "Whuffo you jump out of them airplanes?") to a hero among your earthbound friends. Tandem jumps generally cost about $200, with a discount if you pay in cash.

Free Falling

NEVER LIKED CLIMBING trees or dangling from ropes. I tend to feel unsteady at the edge of a cliff or roof. So I was amazed at how relaxed I felt leading up to my first skydiving experience . . . until the airplane's bay door flew open, and a photographer for the Ranch Parachute Club in Gardiner, near the Shawangunks, vanished into the crisp air. Gone. And fast. A school of piranhas started gnawing at my stomach. The four other newbies packed into the bay—including my future brother-in-law, Dave Carvajal, looked as tense as I felt.

I reminded myself that Geoff, my tandem partner, had dropped out of an airplane about three thousand times before. In good weather, he does half a dozen tandem jumps a day. "Like a goddamned yo-yo," he'd boomed back on the ground, all crew cut, British accent, and timely bravado, as he packed our parachute.

As the airplane rose and banked, I scanned the Gunks, some of the reservoirs that form New York City's drinking supply, and the Hudson River. Then, at 13,500 feet, Geoff nudged me, and we began to shuffle forward toward the door. We're both tall and run the risk of knocking ourselves out on the door frame as we exit the plane, so we kneel rather than stand at the abyss. This is good, I figure, because my legs won't have the chance to turn into jelly at the critical moment.

As instructed, I look toward the back of the plane and arch my back on command. And then we're flying. The rush of wind is immense—so fierce that I tried to howl and couldn't manage a sound. The wind pulled the flesh away from my cheekbones as we dropped a thousand feet every five seconds. I checked the altimeter on my hand as instructed, but somewhere in the middle of the nearly minute-long freefall, I was so enraptured by the whole experience that I forgot to pull the chute. Good thing for Geoff.

We landed softly, sitting. I laughed and rolled on the grass, my fear of heights conquered at least for a day.

Drop Zones

New Jersey

SKYDIVE SUSSEX

Location: Sussex, New Jersey, 54 miles west of Manhattan

Outfitter: Skydive Sussex (973-702-7000, www.skydivesussex.com)

Description: On a clear day you can see Manhattan during your descent

Directions: By car, take I-80 west to exit 53. Follow NJ 23

north to Sussex. Turn left on CR 639. The outfitter is 1 mile down on the left.

SKYDIVE JERSEY SHORE

Location: Farmingdale, New Jersey, 61 miles south of Manhattan

Outfitter: Skydive Jersey Shore (877-444-5867, www.skydivenshore)

Description: Jumps with ocean views

Directions: By car, take the Garden State Parkway to exit 98. Make the second right.

Follow signs to Allaire Airport.

SKY'S THE LIMIT SKYDIVING CENTER

Location: Newton, New Jersey, 60 miles west of Manhattan

Outfitter: Sky's the Limit Skydiving Center (973-940-6998, www.skysthelimit.net)

Description: Among the closer drop zones to New York City. Reservations strongly recommended.

Directions: By car, take I-80 west to exit 25. Take US 206 north about 9 miles to Stickles Pond Road and turn right. The airport is about 0.5 mile down, at 248 Stickles Pond Road.

Upstate and Long Island

RANCH PARACHUTE CLUB

Location: Gardiner, New York, 91 miles northwest of Manhattan

Outfitter: Ranch Parachute Club (845-255-4033, www.ranchskydive.com)

Description: Jumps with views spanning the Shawangunks and Catskills

Directions: By car, take I-87 north to exit 17 (Nerburgh-Stewart Airport). After the tollbooth, take the first right onto NY 300 north. Continue straight onto NY 32 north. Turn left onto US 44/NY 55 west and continue to Gardiner. Where 44/55 makes a sharp right bend, turn left on Sand Hill Road. The ranch is 0.25 mile down on the left.

SKYDIVE LONG ISLAND

Location: Calverton, Long Island, 71 miles east of Manhattan

Outfitter: Skydive Long Island (631-208-3900, www.skydivelongisland.com)

Description: North Fork beauty from the sky

Directions: By car, take I-495 (Long Island Expressway) to exit 69. Turn left on Wading River Road. Drive almost 3 miles and turn right on Grumman Boulevard. The entrance to Calverton Airport (Calverton Enterprise Park, 4062 Grumman Boulevard) is about 1 mile down.

Connecticut

CONNECTICUT PARACHUTISTS

Location: Ellington, Connecticut, 131 miles northeast of Manhattan

Outfitter: Connecticut Parachutists (860-871-0021, www.skydivect.com)

Description: Run by one of the oldest sport parachuting clubs in the United States.

Directions: By car, take I-95 (Cross-Bronx Expressway) north into Connecticut; in New Haven, take I-91 north to exit 45 (Warehouse Point). Take CT 140 east. Turn left onto CT 83 north. After 1.3 miles, look for a dirt road on the left; follow it around the runway to the drop zone.

Where to Connect

Getting Started

It no longer takes a week to get a handle on hang gliding. New generations of gliders are made from seamless aircraft tubing or carbon fiber, making them more birdlike. And the U.S. Hang Gliding Association (USHGA) has instituted a highly successful training program. The result: Hang gliding is easy to learn and safer than many action sports.

Most instructors provide an initial classroom session, simulator training, and instructions for setting up the glider and handling it before your takeoff. Not everyone is comfortable floating at 1,000 feet, so many schools have an introductory package. The training gets you up in the air on day 1; if you continue, your training will include visits to increasingly large hills.

Most outfitters will rent hang gliders only to USHGA members who have a minimum pilot rating, which typically takes two to five lesson days to obtain. The season generally runs from spring to early winter.

Shop

- Airsports USA (29-31 Newtown Avenue, Astoria, Queens, 718-777-7000, www.flyforfun.net) is the undisputed king of wings in New York City. The place has a wondrous assortment of flying contrivances.

Cross Country Skiing

WHEN IT SNOWS in New York, especially when the city gets a really good dump of a foot or more of fresh powder, all of Manhattan turns into a Frank Capra movie set. Perfect strangers actually make eye contact and say things like, "Isn't this beautiful?" After a snowstorm around New Year's Eve 2000, the *New York Times* reported on a sudden outbreak of goodwill: people smiling in the streets, shoveling snow off sidewalks with evident pleasure, and banding together to help stranded cabs regain their traction.

The parks, usually quiet in winter, fill with jovial, parka-clad crowds. They seem to hunger for something adventurous; there's lots of space, and the ground stays white long after the streets turn to gray slop. In Central Park, I see people wandering around, blinking, throwing snowballs, looking giddy. This is about the time when a line forms at the *one* place in the city that rents cross-country skis. Let's see, that's about 120 pairs of skis for 8 million people. You do the math.

I blame the city for this. The cross-country skiing possibilities are plentiful, yet when I inquired at park offices I may as well have been asking them to interpret ancient Sanskrit. At Van Cortlandt Park in the Bronx, for example, several staffers weren't sure whether Nordic skiing was even allowed (it is); others had no idea where skiers could or should ski (the correct answer: anywhere there's snow). At Prospect Park, the same thing. This was in the middle of winter, with snow on the ground.

The city should do more. Groom trails. The fact that it doesn't snow as much as it used to is no excuse. Westchester County, which gets only a bit more snow than the city, has a well-laid-out series of trails, and maps, in its parks. The city could invest in some snowmaking equipment, turn it into a concession and make the money back. Rent out skis.

The present alternative is to buy your own skis—they don't cost nearly as much as their slicker downhill cousins—and be a pioneer in places such as Van Cortlandt and Forest Park in Queens. Or if you just don't want to do the hard work of blazing your own trails—and who can blame you—there are plenty of trails out in the 'burbs and hinterlands that are already groomed and blazed. Some of them—we're thinking specifically of the Adirondacks—are also pretty spectacular.

City Limits

CENTRAL PARK

Location: Manhattan

Terrain: Mostly flat fields and gently rolling hills

Rentals: As of this writing, Scandinavian Ski and Sports Shop (40 West 57th Street, 212-757-8524) is the only place in the city to rent cross-country skis. When it snows, the shop limits rentals to a half day and a day because of the huge surge in demand.

Maps: Available at the Arsenal on 64th Street and Fifth Avenue, second floor, or at the Dairy, located midpark at 65th Street

Description: The good news about Central Park is that when 6 or more inches of snow fall, the whole park is fair game, including paved trails and sidewalks. The bad news? You'll need to look pretty hard for open spaces. Start at the Sheep Meadow (around 66th Street, midpark) and head north, staying on the western fringe of the meadow. Go past Central Park Lake and check out the Great Lawn for possibilities; if there are tracks and it's not overrun, that's a good spot. Otherwise, keep going to the North Meadow, with a loop around the reservoir on the way. This is your best chance to ski in solitude.

Seeing Stars

S THE NIGHT sky visible from New York City? The midnight-sun atmosphere in Times Square has led many New Yorkers to assume the answer is no. The city does create extensive light pollution, but from Central Park many stars are still visible, especially through a high-powered telescope. The Central Park

Conservancy introduces urban dwellers to the heavens with a series of free lectures on topics ranging from mythology to the motion of the sun. The talks are followed by stargazing parties from Belvedere Castle in Central Park.

The astronomy program generally takes place in winter, when the sky is clearest. For more information, call the Conservancy at (212) 772-0210, or see www.centralparknyc.org.

VAN CORTLANDT PARK

Location: Bronx

Terrain: Flat in the park's open expanses, hillier on wooded trails.

Rentals: Go to Scandinavian Ski and Sports Shop (see Central Park, above) then jump on the subway at 59th Street.

Description: Covering 1,146 acres, Van Cortlandt offers plenty of space, and it won't attract the large swarms of people that Central Park does when there's snow. The potential downside is you may end up blazing your own way. But you'll have miles of wooded trails in the northern quadrant of the park to choose from. Or try the Putnam Railroad trail, a walking and biking path that borders Van Cortlandt Lake and bisects the park. Another possibility in the Bronx: Use the bike greenway trails through Pelham Bay Park to City Island and Orchard Beach.

Directions: By subway, take the 1 train to Van Cortlandt Park.

LA TOURETTE PARK GOLF COURSE

Location: Staten Island

Terrain: Rolling hills

Rentals: Scandinavian Ski and Sports Shop (see Central Park, page 335)

Description: Remember the good old days, when Mom and Dad took all the neighborhood kids out onto the cross-country ski trails on the public golf course? Me neither, and it seems kind of an odd concept. (If they'd let you take the carts out in 15 inches of snow, *then* I'd have been instantly sold.) But, in fact, there is some solid potential here. The undulating hills over La Tourette's 125 acres—which merge with 455 more acres of woodland trails in the Staten Island Greenbelt—offer plenty of cool challenges for Nordic skiing. If you don't have skis, bring a sled or a toboggan. Someday maybe we'll be able to take one to Fresh Kills Landfill, which is on the verge of becoming the second-highest peak on the Atlantic seaboard.

Directions: By public transportation, take the Staten Island Ferry; then take bus S74 to Richmond Hill Road in Richmondtown and walk up Snake Hill.

By car, take the Staten Island Expressway (I-278) to the exit for Manor Hill Road/Bradley southbound; go left on Bradley. Bear right on Brielle. At the park, bear right on Rockland. Turn left on Richmond Hill Road.

Short Hops

WARD POUND RIDGE RESERVATION

Location: Cross River, New York, 48 miles north of Manhattan

Terrain: Varied, with some modest hills. Skiing is also permitted on open slopes.

Rentals: Jagger's Camp & Trail Outfitters (359 Adams Street, 914-241-4448) in nearby Bedford Hills

Maps: Available at the entrance to the park (914-763-3993) and the Trailside Museum

Description: Here are cross-country ski trails the way God meant them to be. No matter how soon you go to Westchester's premier Nordic skiing park after a fresh dump of snow, the packed trails always seem groomed and ready. Ward Pound Ridge has well-laid-out, color-coded trails that cover 9 miles in three loops. The woods are attractive and filled with deer; both the animals and their tracks are likely to be visible. Check out the intersection of the red and yellow trails; the view out over the valley will stop you in your tracks.

Directions: By train, take Metro-North to Katonah, then Katonah Taxi (914-232-5772) 4 miles to the park.

By car, take the Hutchinson River Parkway to I-684 to Katonah. Take NY 35 east to NY 121; go south about 100 yards to the park entrance.

FAHNESTOCK WINTER PARK

Location: Cold Spring, New York, 54 miles north of Manhattan

Terrain: The trails are marked for skill levels ranging from beginner to expert, so pick up a map at the winter park office.

Rentals: The winter park office (845-225-3998) by Canopus Lake rents both standard and skate-style skis. There's a fee for a trail pass.

Maps: Available at the park

Description: The Fahnestock property—all 6,700 acres of it—lurches upward from the Hudson River Valley in a series of ridges. At this elevation, after a snowy winter, the trails usually remain viable well into March. Machine-groomed for both classic cross-country and skate-style ski-

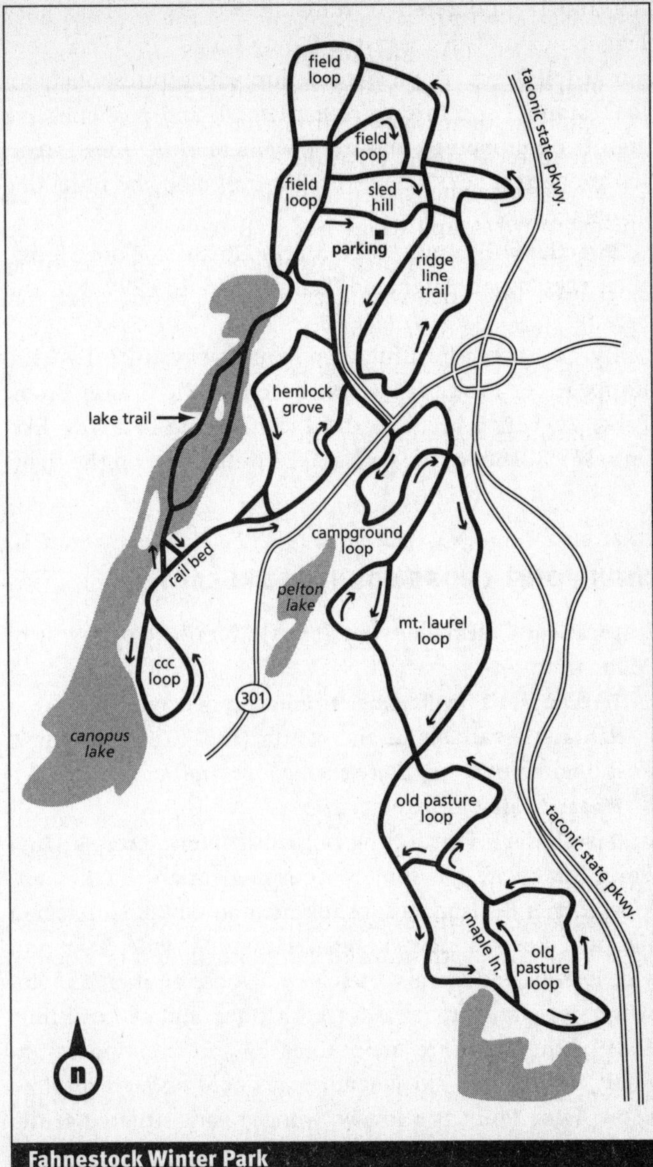

Fahnestock Winter Park

ing, the 15 kilometers of trails are worthy of these lofty heights. One of the best, the windy Ridge Line Trail, tops out at 1,180 feet. You'll swoosh through pastures, old hemlock stands, and forests of hardwood, and past massive granite outcroppings, and stone walls marking long-forgotten property lines. There's even a trail atop the mile-long Canopus Lake.

Directions: By train, take Metro-North to Cold Spring, then take a cab (Highland Transit, 845-265-8294) to the park.

By car, take the Bruckner Expressway (I-278) to the Bronx River Parkway, which becomes the Sprain Brook Parkway, which becomes the Taconic State Parkway. Exit onto NY 301 west; the park is 0.25 mile down on the right.

HIGH POINT CROSS COUNTRY SKI CENTER

Location: Colesville, New Jersey, 72 miles northwest of Manhattan

Terrain: Trail levels range from beginner to expert

Rentals: Available at the center (732-702-1222, www.kcskihighpoint.com); there's a fee for a trail pass.

Maps: Available at the center

Description: This skiing hotbed in New Jersey's High Point State Park has some serious credentials: Its director, Hans Petter Karlson, is a former member of the Norwegian national cross-country ski team. He and his wife, Kim, provide lessons and rentals, then let you loose on their 15 kilometers of trails groomed for both track and skate skiing. Half of the trails are maintained by snowmaking equipment, so you can ski whenever it's cold enough to blow snow. High Point is a lovely, wooded park situated at the highest point in Jersey (called, not surprisingly, High Point, which reaches 1,803 feet), near the state's far northwest corner. There are another 4 kilometers of trails for snowshoeing, and a lodge by Lake Marcia where you can defrost with some hot chocolate and lunch.

Directions: By car, take US 80 west to NJ 15 north to NJ 94 north. Near Hamburg, take NJ 23 north to the park in Sussex.

BRIARCLIFF PEEKSKILL TRAILWAY

Location: Ossining, New York, 35 miles north of Manhattan

Terrain: Challenging in places, with some steep hills

Rentals: Jagger's Camp & Trail Outfitters in Bedford Hills (see Ward Pound Ridge Reservation, page 337).

Maps: Available from the Westchester County Department of Parks, Recreation & Conservation (914-242-7275)

Description: In addition to skiing, snowshoeing is a good option on this slim finger of a trail, which isn't likely to be groomed and emerges onto the shoulder of a road for a brief stretch. One of the appealing things about this path is its span; you can start in Ossining on an old wooded road and finish 12 miles later at Blue Mountain Reservation in Peekskill. The trail property was originally designated in 1929 for a parkway, but road construction halted in Ossining. Among the trail's highlights: You'll pass Teatown Lake, climb through a forest, and follow Bailey Brook north to Croton Gorge Park, where water rolls off the Croton Dam Spillway into the reservoir. The trail wends through woods and wetlands on the way to Spitzenberg Mountain's 560-foot summit. Catch your breath and relax; it's all downhill from there. If you have any energy left, Blue Mountain has plenty of good loop trails. *Note:* You'll need to bring two cars because cabs in this area are unable to accommodate skis.

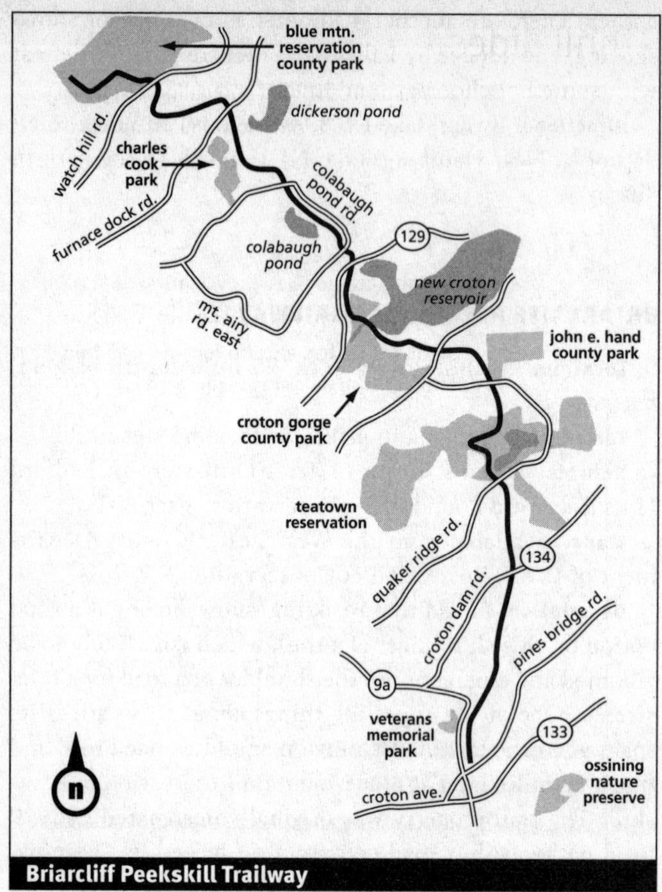

Directions: By car, take the Bruckner Expressway (I-278) to the Bronx River Parkway, which becomes the Sprain Brook Parkway, which becomes the Taconic State Parkway. Exit at NY 133 and drive west. Turn right on NY 9A to the Ryder Road intersection, where the trail begins. To leave your second car in Blue Mountain, take NY 9A north to US 9 north and exit at Welcher Avenue in Peekskill. Turn right and follow Welcher into the park.

Thrill Rides

hen you need a shot of adrenaline and a blast of wind in your face, only downhill skiing will do. Here is a sampling of mountains within two hours of New York City.

The Catskills

- **Hunter Mountain** (518-263-4223, www.huntermtn.com, 800-367-7669 for conditions), which along with Windham is the biggest Catskill resort, has a 1,600-foot vertical drop. Scattered about the mountain are 53 trails, a terrain park and half-pipe, and a tubing park.
- **Belleayre Mountain** (845-254-5600, www.belleayre.com, 800-943-6904 for conditions) has 35 trails descending a 1,404-foot summit. Bonus: A Trailways bus goes straight to the lodge daily from the Port Authority.
- **Ski Windham** (800-754-9463, www.skiwindham.com, 800-729-4766 for conditions) has an expert park, a snowboard park, a tubing park, and 34 trails that run as long as 2.25 miles down the 1,600-foot peak.

Connecticut

- **Powder Ridge** (877-754-7434, www.powderridgect.com) is another quick jaunt, about 2 hours from Manhattan. The variety of offerings includes a terrain park with a half-pipe and an extreme spine.

New Jersey

- **Mountain Creek** (973-827-2000, www.mountaincreek.com) has 43 trails covering 15 miles and descending 1,040 feet. The terrain park has 8,500 feet of obstacles. It's in Vernon, only 47 miles from Manhattan.

A bit farther afield:

Vermont

- The Green Mountains of western Vermont—including **Stowe,**

Smugglers North, and **Sugarbush**—provide some of the top skiing in the Northeast. Ski Vermont (802-223-2439, www.skivermont.com) has a wealth of information.

PENNSYLVANIA

- **Blue Mountain** (610-826-7700, www.skibluemt.com, 877-754-2583 for conditions) touts the highest, steepest trails in Pennsylvania—a dubious honor, perhaps, but still . . . The mountain tops out at 1,082 feet.

CONNETQUOT RIVER STATE PARK

Location: Oakdale, Long Island, 56 miles east of Manhattan

Terrain: Mostly flat tire roads and horse trails

Rentals: Eastern Mountain Sports in Carle Place (221 Glen Cove Road, 516-747-7360) is the nearest shop.

Maps: Available on site

Description: This is your best choice for skiing if you're confined to Long Island for the winter. There are numerous trails crisscrossing this gorgeous 3,475-acre preserve, and you can follow the banks of a 6-mile-long stream. This is a prize patch of virgin forest, extremely popular in warmer weather among anglers and birders, so it's carefully protected. You need a permit to visit (P.O. Box 505, Oakdale, NY 11769; 631-581-1005); the permit is free and is good all year.

Directions: By car, take exit 44 off the Southern State Parkway onto NY 27 (Sunrise Highway); because the park is on the north side, you have to go 0.3 mile past the park entrance and make a U-turn. The year-round vehicle entrance fee is $5.

Alive and Kicking

SKATE SKIING IS for those who crave a little zip with their cross-country journey. Skate skiers step out of the ski tracks with their dominant leg and kick diagonally for propulsion while gliding on the other ski. They wind up moving substantially faster. Bill Koch, the only American ever to win a medal in Nordic skiing, popularized the technique in the 1980s.

Meccas

THE JACKRABBIT TRAIL

Location: Lake Placid, New York, 290 miles north of Manhattan

Terrain: All types from remote wilderness to groomed trails

Rentals: Ski areas include Mount Van Hoevenberg (800-462-6236) and Cascade Cross Country Center (518-523-9605), www.cascadeski.com. The New York State Cross-Country Ski Areas Association (518-283-5509) provides an overall listing of Adirondack ski areas. For information on the Jackrabbit Trail, call (518) 523-1365. For Garnet Hill info, call (518) 251-2444, or visit www.garnethill.com.

Description: The Adirondacks have it all. There are nearly 500 miles of designated cross-country skiing trails laid across the wilderness of the nation's largest state park, some in swanky resorts and others in lonesome, beautiful backcountry. The Lake Placid area is a focal point, mostly because of the Jackrabbit Trail, a 34-mile backcountry path that links the area's top ski lodges. The trail, named after

Herman "Jackrabbit" Johannsen, a Norwegian who helped build the sport in the Adirondacks in the 1920s, runs from Paul Smiths to Keene. Among the stops is the Mount Van Hoevenberg Olympic Sports Complex, which features 31 miles of groomed trails and some exhilarating side trips, among them the toboggan chute on Mirror Lake and the bobsled and luge runs in the 1980 Olympic facilities. The Cascade Cross Country Center, meanwhile, runs overnight and full-moon ski tours.

Garnet Hill Lodge, located to the south in the Lake George area, was rated one of the nation's ten best cross-country ski resorts by *Snow Country* magazine. Garnet Hill offers 34 miles of groomed trails, some of which are lighted.

Directions: By car, take I-87 north to exit 30. Follow NY 73 north and west to Lake Placid.

LITCHFIELD COUNTY

Location: Litchfield Hills, Connecticut, 110 miles northeast of Manhattan

Terrain: Mostly fine for beginners and intermediates

Rentals: The Wilderness Shop (85 Route 202, Litchfield, 860-567-5905)

Maps: Available at the respective parks. For more information, call White Memorial (860-567-0857), Steep Rock (860-868-9131), Pine Mountain (860-653-4279), or Woodbury Ski Area (203-263-2283, www.woodburyskiarea.com).

Description: The land rises and falls like sea swells here, and the undulating hills combine with plentiful trails and small-town sensibilities to make Connecticut's northwest corner a solid destination. The White Memorial Foundation in Litchfield is one of my favorites. It's a 4,000-acre sanctuary with 35 miles of trails weaving through pine forests, streams, and bogs. Steep Rock Preserve in Washington has both spindly mountain-goat trails and wide, flat ones on either side of the Shepaug River. Pine Mountain Cross-Country Ski Touring Center in East Hartland is perched atop the second-highest point in Connecticut, so it tends to remain snowy longer than most of the state. It has 15 miles of machine-packed, groomed trails; if you want to blaze your own way, detour into the backcountry of adjoining People's State Forest.

If there's no natural snow, head to the Woodbury Ski Area, one of the few places around that grooms trails with machine-made stuff. The ski area, which has 20 kilometers of groomed trails, offers moonlight tours and races.

Directions: By car, take I-95 north to CT 8 north to exit 42. Follow CT 118 west into Litchfield, then take US 202 west to White Memorial. To get to Washington, continue on US 202 and turn left on CT 47.

PINERIDGE CROSS-COUNTRY SKI AREA

Location: East Poestenkill, New York, 167 miles north of Manhattan

Terrain: Groomed trails in the foothills of the Taconic and Berkshire Mountains that are suitable for all levels

Rentals: Available at the center (518-283-3652, www.xcski.org/pineridge), which charges a trail fee. Snowshoe rentals are also available.

Description: This ski area offers a full range of services in a gorgeous, manageable setting. There are more than 20 miles of groomed runs—including several lighted trails—weaving through forests of evergreens and hardwoods and along Poestenkill Creek. If you're up for a workout, hump up to 1,746 feet for a wintry view of the Taconic Mountains and Mount Greylock. You can also rent snowshoes for an additional 6 miles of ungroomed trails, so you can see where those fox and deer tracks lead.

Directions: By car, take I-87 north to I-787 north to I-90 east. Take exit 8 and follow NY 43 east through West Sand Lake, then turn left on NY 351. In Poestenkill, turn right on Plank Road (CR 40); drive 6 miles and follow signs.

Where to Connect

Ski Shops

- Princeton Ski Shop (21 East 22nd Street, Manhattan, 212-228-4537) sells skis and apparel and is one of the bigger shops in the city.
- Scandinavian Ski and Sports Shop (40 West 57th Street, Manhattan, 212-757-8524) rents and sells alpine and Nordic skis and runs trips to Hunter Mountain and other area sites.
- New York Pipe Dreams (1623 York Avenue, Manhattan, 212-535-7173, www.newyorkpipedreams.com) runs ski trips and sells snowboards.
- Paragon Sports (867 Broadway, Manhattan, 212-255-8036) carries skis and accessories.
- Emilio's Ski Shop (112-32 Queens Boulevard, Forest Hills, Queens, 718-544-0404)
- Panda Ski & Sport (9213 Fifth Avenue, Brooklyn, 718-238-4919)
- Pedigree Ski Shop (White Plains, NY, 914-948-2995, www.pedigreeskishop.com)

Clubs

- Outdoor Bound (212-505-1020) organizes cross-country ski trips to upstate New York.

- Miramar Ski Club (71 West 23rd Street, Manhattan, 212-978-9191) is a nonprofit outfit that runs weekly trips to its lodge in Waitsfield Village, VT, where skiers can access various ski areas and cross-country trails.
- The Swiss Ski Club of New York (6 East 87th Street, Manhattan, 212-978-7541, www.swissskiclub.com) is a nonprofit group that owns property in Vermont and organizes ski trips to various destinations.
- Snow Flyers (212-439-4799, www.snowflyers.com) runs group ski trips and events.

Books and Maps

- Farra, Johanna, and Ron Farra. *Winter Trails New York: The Best Cross-Country Ski & Snowshoe Trails.* Guilford, CT: Globe Pequot Press, 2000.
- Freeman, Rich, and Sue Freeman. *Snow Trails: Cross-country Ski and Snowshoe in Central and Western New York.* Fishers, NY: Footprint Press, 2000.
- *The New York State Winter Travel and Tourism Guide*, a free booklet published by the state tourism office (800-456-8369), provides a complete list of cross-country ski areas.

Camping

I F YOU GREW up out in the country, chances are you spent a few nights eating melted marshmallows and studying constellations until, lulled by chirping cicadas, you retired to your canvas boudoir. Chances are that those experiences seem like a zillion miles away from New York City. But there's no need to pawn your camp stove and sleeping bag just because you moved to Gotham. Even without a car, there are many intriguing camping options nearby that don't involve pitching a tent on Central Park's Great Lawn (not a good idea). You can, for example, shove your gear in a backpack and head for the Appalachian Trail. There's a campground right on the banks of the Hudson River within a stone's

throw of a train station. There are spots on the shore of Long Island within reach of the Long Island Rail Road. There's even wilderness camping in New Jersey.

I can hear those crickets chirpin' already.

Within 15 Miles

LIBERTY HARBOR RV PARK

Location: Jersey City, New Jersey

Sites: 60 tent and trailer sites

Heads up: The fishing for striped bass and bluefish is pretty good in season at nearby Liberty State Park.

Information/reservations: (800) 646-2066

Description: Camping in Jersey City, just across the dark waters of New York Harbor from the Big Lady and Manhattan? Hard to believe, but true. The park is only four blocks from the PATH station. There's a 2-mile-long promenade, a historic train terminal, and a 36-acre remnant of the salt marshes that used to dominate the estuary before New York Harbor became seaport to the world. The campground is open year-round, but make reservations well in advance in summer.

Directions: By train, take PATH to the Grove Street station, then walk four blocks north.

By ferry, take New York Waterways (800-533-3779) to the park.

By car, take exit 14C off the New Jersey Turnpike, turn left off the ramp, turn left at the first light, and turn left onto Grand Street. Marin Boulevard is about eight blocks down on the right.

Within 30 Miles

Westchester County, New York

CROTON POINT PARK

Location: Croton-on-Hudson, New York

Sites: 180 tent and trailer sites

Heads up: Play options range from a nature center to hiking trails to a pool.

Information/reservations: (914) 271-3293

Description: A great place to commune with the big river. Croton Point is situated on a rocky peninsula that pokes out between the Hudson River and Croton Bay. There's a beach and a huge meadow created atop an old landfill that attracts monarch butterflies and all kinds of birds, including kestrels and bluebirds. At the tip, Tellers Point, there's a beach with nice views of the 3-mile-wide river and the Tappan Zee Bridge.

Directions: By train, take Metro-North to Croton-Harmon. The park is right next to the station.

By car, take the Saw Mill River Parkway to exit 25. Take NY 9A north for 10 miles to the Croton Point Avenue exit. Turn left and cross a narrow bridge over the railroad tracks and into the park.

New Jersey

CHEESEQUAKE STATE PARK

Location: Matawan, New Jersey

Sites: 53 tent and trailer sites, 2 group camping areas

Heads up: Swimming, canoeing, hiking, and mountain biking are among activities at Cheesequake.

Information/reservations: (732) 566-2161

Description: Cheesequake is a slice of green space shoehorned into the Jersey 'burbs. The 1,284-acre park has some compelling features: A white cedar swamp and pine barrens typical of regions farther south are mixed with the sorts of hardwood forest you see in the north. There are also saltwater and freshwater marshes, mountain biking trails, and a modest 53 campsites.

Directions: By car, take the Garden State Parkway to exit 120. Drive through a park-and-ride parking area and turn right on Matawan Avenue. Turn right at the first light onto Cliffwood Avenue. Turn right at the next light onto Gordon Avenue. The park is less than a mile down the road.

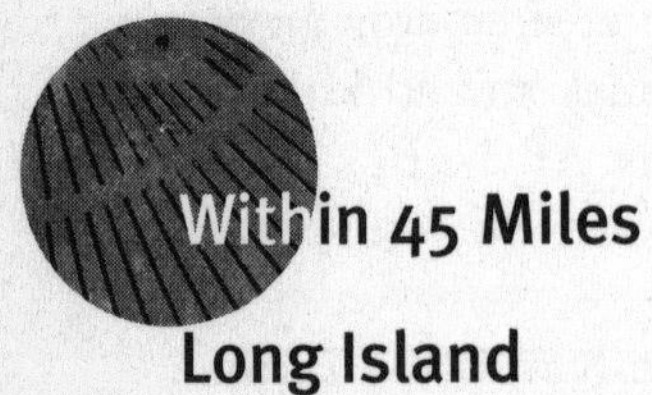

Within 45 Miles

Long Island

HECKSCHER STATE PARK

Location: East Islip, Long Island

Sites: 69 tent and trailer sites

Heads up: Bring your mountain bike; there are deer trails throughout the sizeable forest.

Information: (631) 581-2100. Reservations: (800) 456-2267.

Description: This big, sprawling park on the south coast has plenty of room to stretch out—so much so that the sites seem a little closer together than they should be. But that just means there's more room to play. Windsurfers flock here when the conditions are right (see "Windsurfing," page 288), but you can simply wander off to the many secluded beaches on Great South Bay.

Other area camping: Blydenburgh County Park, Smithtown, (631) 854-3712

Directions: By car, take the Belt Parkway to the Southern State Parkway; follow the Heckscher Spur into the park.

FIRE ISLAND CABIN

Location: Atlantique, Long Island

Heads up: The Audubon Society offers birding walks in spring.

Information/reservations: (212) 606-2293. All weekends must be reserved in advance. For midweek stays, call the cabin directly at (631) 583-5366. There's a 2-night minimum on weekends. The cabin is available to AMC members, and nonmembers with a $15 guest card.

Description: The Appalachian Mountain Club runs a sweet little cabin on the bay just a short stroll from the beach. There's not a whole lot of privacy here—the cabin sleeps up to 24 in two bunk rooms (bring your own sheets or sleeping bag)—but that's not the point. Small sailboats and canoes are available for buzzing about Great South Bay; AMC members even offer courses on both on weekends. Or just hang out in a hammock. This is the beach, after all. Guests pitch in on weekend meals under the guidance of volunteer hosts; you're on your own during the week, but the kitchen is available.

Directions: Ask for directions when you make reservations.

Westchester County, New York

WARD POUND RIDGE RESERVATION

Location: Cross River, New York

Sites: 23 Adirondack-style lean-tos, 10 tent sites

Heads up: Trails run along the Cross and Stone Hill Rivers and lead to majestic overlooks.

Information/reservations: (914) 864-7317

Description: The county's oldest park covers nearly 6 miles of vast gullies and ridges that rise to about 800 feet. There's also the Leatherman's Cave, named for a 19th-century character who repeatedly hiked the same long loop around the countryside, never speaking to anyone and sleeping in caves and shelters (this being one of them). The lean-to shelters and tent-only sites at Ward Pound Ridge evoke the park's early years.

Directions: By train, take Metro-North to Katonah, then take a cab 4 miles to the park.

By car, take the Hutchinson River Parkway to I-684 to Katonah. Take NY 35 east to NY 121; go south about 100 yards to the park entrance.

MOUNTAIN LAKES PARK

Location: North Salem, New York

Sites: 240 tent sites and 7 lean-to sites

Heads up: Hiking and fishing are popular pastimes here.

Information/reservations: (914) 669-5793 or (914) 864-7317

Description: The park was named for the four lakes it includes in its nearly 1,100 scenic acres. Like Manhattan, the land was purchased from the Indians. Unlike Manhattan, it's still more or less in its natural state, which means it's ideal for a swim in summer or ice skating in winter. The 1,000-acre camping area features several ponds and the headwaters of Crook Brook.

Directions: By car, take I-684 to exit 6 (Katonah/Cross River), then follow NY 35 east. Turn left on NY 121, and drive to Grant's Corners. Turn right on Hawley Road. The park is 2 miles down on the left.

BLUE MOUNTAIN RESERVATION

Location: Peekskill, New York

Information/reservations: (914) 737-2194

Description: This is one of the best mountain biking parks around (see "Mountain Biking," page 121), but the 15-plus miles of trails also allow hikers to access the peaks of the two mountains (Blue and Spitzenberg), which overlook the Hudson River Valley and Harriman State Park. There's no camping, but the Blue Mountain Trail Lodge provides dorm-type accommodations and a dining area for groups up to 30.

Directions: By train, take Metro-North to Cortlant and take a cab (914-737-3753) to the park.

By car, take I-87 north to I-287; exit onto US 9 north. In Peekskill, exit at Welcher Avenue; turn right and follow it into the park.

Rockland County, New York

HARRIMAN STATE PARK

Location: Suffern, New York

Sites: 146 tent and trailer sites

Heads up: The Appalachian Trail runs through this state park.

Information: 845-947-2792. Reservations: 800-456-2267.

Description: With more than 200 sites to choose from, you should be able to find a place to pitch your tent here even on crowded summer weekends. The Beaver Pond Campground is among the best. The park caters to both hard-core hikers and softer-adventure seekers. For the latter group, there are cabins at Lake Sebago. The former group can camp on the trail; shelters are available for one-night stays on a first-come, first-served basis.

Directions: By car, take the upper level of the George Washington Bridge to the Palisades Interstate Parkway north to exit 14. Turn left onto Willow Grove Road. Beaver Pond Campground is 2 miles down on the right, just east of Lake Welch. For the Sebago cabins, take exit 16 off the Palisades Parkway and take Lake Welch Drive to 7 Lakes Drive. Turn right, then left at the next traffic light to go the opposite way. Turn into Sebago Beach on the right and drive one mile to the cabins.

Within 60 Miles

Long Island

FIRE ISLAND NATIONAL SEASHORE

Location: Watch Hill, Long Island

Sites: 26 sites on the sand

Heads up: Try fishing Great South Bay.

Information: The park service holds a lottery each April to allocate campsites for the season. Submit an application (available at www.nps.gov/fiis) between January 1 and March 21. If sites are available during camping season, reservations are taken at 631-597-6633 on Thursdays and Fridays between 9 A.M. and noon. If any sites are left, they're made available on a first-come, first-served basis. Between Watch Hill and Smith Point, backcountry camping is allowed in some areas with a permit. Call 631-289-4810 for more information.

Description: Walk the beach, visit saltwater and freshwater marshes, play in the waves, and wander the forests and thickets until you retire to your tent in the dunes along this 30-mile-long barrier island. Backcountry camping is permitted in selected areas (see "Hiking," page 47, for more information).

Other area camping: Cathedral Pines County Park in Middle Island (631-854-5502; reservations not available) and Southaven County Park in Brookhaven (631-854-1418).

Directions: By train, take the Long Island Rail Road to Patchogue. From the station, take a right on Division Street, and a left on West Street; the Watch Hill Ferry terminal (631-475-1665) is on the right.

Putnam County, New York

FAHNESTOCK STATE PARK

Location: Cold Spring, New York

Sites: There are 81 sites, 30 of which can accommodate trailers.

Heads up: Choose from 60 miles of nature trails and 14 miles of mountain-biking trails.

Information: (914) 265-3773. Reservations: (800) 456-2267.

Description: Fahnestock is a big, sprawling park high on a ridge. There are sturdy forestlands sprinkled with lakes and crisscrossed by trails, including a section of the Appalachian Trail. Canopus Lake has boat rentals in summer and is ideal for a posthike swim.

Directions: By train, take Metro-North to Cold Spring, then get a cab (265-8294) to the park.

By car, take the Taconic State Parkway to NY 301 west in Cold Spring; the park is 0.25 mile down on the right.

New Jersey

ROUND VALLEY

Location: Lebanon, New Jersey

Sites: 106 wilderness sites accessible by boat, canoe, or foot

Heads up: Swimming, fishing, and mountain biking are popular here. Scuba diving is allowed with a free permit.

Information/reservations: (908) 236-6355

Description: This place is a treat. The 106 wilderness campsites are 3 miles from the nearest parking lot and can be reached only by foot, boat, or mountain bike. That means no RVs, no car stereos, no disruptions. There's a gorgeous lake with great fishing, drinking water, and hiking trails. What more could you ask for?

Directions: By car, take the New Jersey Turnpike to I-78 west. Take exit 20A to US 22 west and follow the signs.

DELAWARE WATER GAP AREA

Location: New Jersey

Sites: 22 tent and trailer sites, two group sites, eight shelters near the top of Jenny Jump Mountain that accommodate four people each.

Heads up: A local astronomy club offers programs at the on-site Greenwood Observatory on Saturdays from April through October.

Information/reservations: (908) 459-4366

Description: The northwestern part of the state is home to arguably New Jersey's most beautiful real estate. There's High Point Monument, which at 1,803 feet is as far above sea level as you can get in Jersey, with comely views of three states. There's the Delaware Water Gap National Recreation Area, with its dramatic Kittatinny Mountain vistas and access to the Delaware River's many charms (see "White Water," page 200). And there's the Appalachian Trail's ridges and forests (see "Hiking," page 49). There are also several lakes and ponds and a plethora of camping options.

One of the best is Jenny Jump State Forest, a 2,400-acre, glacier-gouged site with impressive vistas from the top of the mountain. Rock outcroppings and boulders line the slender path to the summit. If you like winter outdoor experiences, there are eight shelters with wood-burning stoves near the peak.

Directions: By car, to get to Jenny Jump, take I-80 west to exit 12. In Hope, turn north on SR 519. Take the third right onto Shiloh Road; turn right after 1 mile onto State Park Road.

Other area options:

1 High Point State Park, Sussex, NJ (973-875-4800)
2 Stokes State Forest, Branchville, NJ (973-948-3820)
3 Mohican Outdoor Center (cabins), Blairstown, NJ (908-362-5670, www.mohicanoutdoorcenter.com)
4 Worthington State Forest, Columbia, NJ (908-841-9575)
5 Dingman's Campground, Dingman's Ferry, PA (717-828-2266)

BULL'S ISLAND RECREATION AREA

Location: Stockton, New Jersey

Sites: 69 tent and trailer sites

Heads up: Explore a lowland floodplain forest of sycamore and silver maple along a canal towpath.

Information/reservations: (609) 397-2949

Description: Ah, island life. Okay, it's not the tropics, but still, the waters of the Delaware River surround you. There's a 24-acre natural area thick with sycamore and silver maple, and shad fishing in season.

Directions: By car, take I-287 to US 202 in Somerville; follow US 202 south to the exit for NJ 29 north. The entrance is 6 miles up on the left.

Within 75 Miles

Connecticut

LAKE WARAMAUG STATE PARK

Location: New Preston, Connecticut

Sites: 78 tent and trailer sites

Heads up: Lake Waramaug hosts the Women's National Rowing Regetta annually.

Information/reservations: (860) 868-0220

Description: There are 78 shore sites here, but book early. This campground, on the immensely popular 3-mile-long lake, fills up fast. Native Americans named the lake Waramaug, which means "good fishing place"; the largemouth bass ensure the name lives up to the billing.

Directions: By car, take the Hutchinson River Parkway to I-684 north. Take I-84 east to US 7 north. Get off in New

Milford at US 202 east; in New Preston, turn left on CT 45. Bear left on West Shore Road and drive several miles to the park.

More Than 75 Miles Away

Long Island

THE HAMPTONS

Location: Long Island

Sites: 30 tent sites and 40 trailer sites

Heads up: Take a sunset trail ride with Sears Bellows Stable.

Information/reservations: Call 631-852-8290 or 631-244-7275. A Suffolk County Parks tourist reservation key is required for all three campgrounds; they're available for a fee at the parks' administration office.

Description: Can't afford a summer time-share in the high-rolling Hamptons? There are several other options that may actually get you closer to the natural world that makes the South Fork so appealing. The best of three county parks is Sears Bellows, which has a campground tucked in among eastern Long Island's pine barrens. There's a beach and rowboats available for rental on freshwater Bellows Pond, and numerous trails to explore.

Other area options:

- Shinnecock East, Southampton (631-852-8899)
- Cedar Point, East Hampton (631-852-7620)

Directions: To Sears Bellows by car, take the Belt Parkway to the Southern State Parkway to the Sunshine Highway (NY 27) and take exit 65 north. Follow NY 24 to Bellows Pond Road and turn left; the park entrance is on the right.

HITHER HILLS STATE PARK

Location: Montauk, Long Island

Sites: 165 tent and trailer sites

Heads up: There's a 40-acre freshwater pond in addition to 2.5 miles of ocean beach.

Information: (631) 668-2554. Reservations: (800) 456-2267.

Description: This is another spot that's a winner because you can camp on the beach, just behind the dunes. The park draws crowds of RVs, but it's still ideal for itinerant surfers, anglers, and bikers.

Also in Montauk: Theodore Roosevelt County Park (631-852-7878)

On the North Fork: Eastern Long Island Campgrounds (631-477-0022) in Greenport is near the landing for the Connecticut-bound ferry.

Directions: By car, take the Belt Parkway to the Southern State Parkway to the Sunrise Highway (NY 27). Turn right on Old Montauk Highway (NY 27A) and follow the signs.

Where to Connect

Camping Gear

- Eastern Mountain Sports (20 West 61st Street, 212-397-4860; and 611 Broadway, 212-505-9860) stocks extensive camping supplies.
- Paragon Sports (867 Broadway, 212-255-8036) carries camping, hiking, and mountaineering gear.
- Tent and Trails (21 Park Place, 212-227-1760) carries all camping essentials.
- Sports Authority (401 Seventh Avenue, 212-563-7195,

and several other Manhattan locations). In Queens, the store is located at 51-30 Northern Boulevard, Woodside, 718-205-4075.

- Modell's (200 Broadway, 212-964-4007)
- Camping R Us Corp. (375 Johnson Avenue, Brooklyn, 877-664-8444)
- Recreational Equipment (New Rochelle, 800-426-4840)
- Campmor (Paramus, NJ, 800-226-7667, www.campmor.com)

Books and Resources

- Appalachian Long Distance Hikers Association. *The Appalachian Trail Thru-Hikers' Companion*. Harpers Ferry, WV: Appalachian Trail Conference, published annually.
- *Woodall's New York, New England & Eastern Canada Campground Guide 2002 Camping Guide.* Lake Forest, Ill: Woodall Publishing Company, 2002.
- The Web site www.licamping.com has a wealth of information about Long Island camping.
- The Web site www.co.westchester.ny.us/parks covers camping in Westchester County.

Index

K

L

M

S

Y